GHOSTS IN THE DARKNESS

Book V in the Series

Mysteries of the Appalachian Wilderness

Ghosts, Creatures & Vanishings in America's Old Mountains

By Timothy D

First Edition — 2025
Ghosts in the Darkness Series — Book V

ISBN:978-1-0699180-9-3

design & layout by Timothy D
Photography, maps, and illustrations by the author unless otherwise noted.

Author's Note

The Appalachian Mountains have a way of swallowing stories.
Some disappear into the fog. Some slip between the ridgelines. Some linger in the hollers, whispered from one generation to the next but never spoken loudly, as if the mountains themselves might hear.

These are the oldest mountains on the continent—weathered, quiet, and patient.
Older than the Rockies. Older than the forests covering them.
Old enough that **whatever lives in their depths has had a very long time to hide.**

Here, hunters hear footsteps pacing them through the timber.
Lights drift silently along the slopes.
Hikers vanish without a single track.
And entire abandoned settlements sit rotting beneath the canopy, waiting.

In these pages, we'll walk into those places where daylight dies early.
Where the trees lean close.
Where the strange isn't an anomaly—it's a tradition.

Welcome to the Appalachian Wilderness.
Walk softly. The mountains are listening.

Chapter One — The Old Mountains

There's a moment, somewhere around the edge of the Cumberland Plateau, where the land begins to change without announcing itself. You're driving along a stretch of highway you've been on for hours—flat or gently rolling farmland—and then, almost without transition, the ground starts to lift. The trees thicken. The horizon tightens. The air takes on a dampness you can't quite place. The Appalachians don't appear all at once the way the Rockies do; they gather around you slowly, like a crowd forming out of silence.

The first time I drove through them, I didn't fully understand what I was looking at. I'd seen plenty of documentaries, read plenty of historical accounts, heard more than enough stories from hikers and researchers. But none of that prepares you for the moment you realize the mountains around you are not young and arrogant—they're ancient and patient, and they've been here long enough to know every secret you haven't learned yet.

The light changes first. It filters differently through trees that have grown tightly along the hillsides, their branches leaning over the road the way people lean in to hear a whispered conversation. Then the colors shift. Greens darken. Shadows thicken. The land folds and folds again, the ridges layered so deeply that even the sky seems to hesitate before shining over them.

I remember my hands tightening on the steering wheel. Not from fear. More like recognition. A feeling that I'd crossed into a place where the rules change—not the physical ones, but the ones that govern how people move, how stories settle, how silence behaves.

The Weight of Age

If you stand on an overlook anywhere in these mountains, it doesn't take long before you begin to sense the age in them—the kind of age that doesn't just predate people, but civilizations. The Appalachians were old before the first humans reached this part of the continent. Old before mammoths. Old before most of the continents were shaped the way we know them today.

You don't need a geology degree to feel that. All it takes is a quiet moment.

The ridges soften not because they're gentle, but because they've been worn down for hundreds of millions of years. Their sharp edges have been smoothed by time, like a knife blade kept in a pocket with loose coins. The slopes are rounded, but the valleys between them are deep, coiling, and often hidden beneath canopies that stay thick from spring until late fall.

Those valleys—those hollers—hold more than water and fog. They hold memory.

Some mountains radiate power because of height. The Appalachians radiate power because of endurance. They feel... settled. Established. Like something that has seen everything that has come and gone in their shadows and will still be here when everything else is forgotten.

Whenever I travel through regions like this, I can't help but think that if mystery has a home, it lives in old places. And these mountains are about as old as it gets.

Fog Like a Living Thing

Fog in the Appalachians does not behave like fog anywhere else I've seen. In Northern Ontario, I'm used to morning mist burning off by mid-day, rising off lakes in ghostly columns that scatter into the sky. Here, the fog stays low. It clings to the earth like something reluctant to leave. It hugs the hollers, spills onto the roads, rises up the slopes in thin veils, and then settles again.

People here say fog has moods. Some mornings it sits still, thick and silent, blocking everything more than twenty feet away. Other mornings it moves—slowly, deliberately, sliding through the trees like it knows where it's going.

One West Virginia hunter once told me, "Fog moves like an animal in these parts." He wasn't saying it for effect; he said it the way a person might mention a detail about their backyard—matter-of-fact, familiar, almost casual.

I've seen enough strange weather patterns in wild places not to dismiss that sort of comment outright. Fog can do strange things when it's guided by the shape of the land, the pull of temperature, rivers breathing out mist, and valleys funneling cold air. But something about the fog here feels personal.

Driving those roads in early morning, you sometimes get the unsettling impression that the fog knows you're there before you know it's there.

Roads That Wander Like Stories

If you want to understand the Appalachians, don't look at the highways. Look at the side roads. The narrow ones that drop suddenly to one lane without warning, twisting through hills that don't care whether the road makes sense or not.

Some of these roads feel like they've been there forever, long before pavement, long before cars. They curve around old farmhouses, burrow through thickets, pass under canopies so dense the branches almost touch overhead. When you drive them, it feels less like you're choosing a direction and more like the road is deciding where you're allowed to go.

There's a particular stretch I remember—somewhere between Virginia and Tennessee. A foggy morning, soft rain, headlights barely piercing the grey. The trees leaned in over the road so heavily that the world felt like a tunnel. Every curve revealed another, then another, as if the mountains refused to let me see more than a few car lengths ahead. It wasn't frightening. It was… controlling. Guiding. Like the land wanted to make sure I stayed focused.

I passed old houses tucked tightly into hollers, some with smoke trailing from chimneys, others with porches collapsing under years of rain. A few had plastic over the windows, a detail that somehow made the isolation feel deeper. Each one seemed to have its own small story—none of them happy, none of them quite forgotten. That's the thing about these mountains: nothing truly disappears. It just gets buried under time.

Cemeteries appear out of nowhere on these back roads. Small ones, sometimes hidden behind thickets. Leaning stones with names that haven't been spoken aloud in generations. Rusted gates. Moss eating its way into carved letters. If you're sensitive to atmosphere, those cemeteries don't feel dead. They feel aware. As if the people buried there know the land better than you ever will.

Silence That Grabs Your Attention

Forests make noise. That's one of the basic rules of wilderness. Birds, insects, wind, water. Even the quietest woods aren't truly silent.

But in the Appalachians, silence can drop in an instant—as if someone hit a switch.

I experienced it first in the Smokies. I'd pulled off at a scenic area, got out of the car, walked maybe thirty steps into the woods, and stopped to listen. There were birds, distant traffic, leaves rustling. All normal. Then everything stopped. Every last bit of it. The silence fell so suddenly that it felt like the forest itself had inhaled and forgotten to exhale.

That's a moment you don't forget.

Even experienced locals pay attention when the woods go quiet. Hunters take that sort of silence seriously; they say it means something with a presence is nearby. Not necessarily a predator—just something that changes the mood of the land.

In places as old as these mountains, I don't think silence is random. I think it's a sign.

Stories That Drift in Through Open Doors

You can learn a lot about a place just by sitting in a diner long enough. One of the first things I do when I'm passing through a new wilderness region is stop for coffee, sit by a window, and listen to the kinds of conversations people have when they aren't really paying attention to who else is in the room.

In the Appalachians, those conversations tend to revolve around weather, family, work, hunting, fishing—and the strange things people see in the woods when they've lived there long enough.

You'll hear someone mention a "tall fella" pacing the treeline while they were checking trail cameras. Another guy will talk about hearing someone walking behind him on a logging road, even though he was alone. A woman might describe a scream that didn't sound like a bobcat, didn't sound like a person, and didn't sound like anything she'd ever heard in her life.

Nobody tells these stories the way city people tell spooky stories. There's no dramatic buildup, no embellishment. Just the facts. Plain, direct. When you hear stories told that way, they stick with you.

There was an older couple about two booths over from me one morning —this was in North Carolina—talking about noises outside their home at night. Something heavy moving through the yard. A sound like knocking on the side of the house. Their dog refusing to go outside for hours afterward. They didn't say the word Bigfoot. They didn't have to. The tone in their voices told the whole story.

People here don't jump to conclusions, but they also don't dismiss what their senses tell them.

A Landscape That Hides What It Wants

The Appalachians can swallow a person faster than almost any wilderness I've seen. Not because the terrain is overwhelmingly large— though in some regions it absolutely feels that way—but because the land folds in on itself. Trails switchback along slopes, then vanish into thickets of rhododendron, then emerge onto ridges that split into multiple animal paths. Streams hide their crossings under fallen leaves. Fog blinds you in an instant.

Even experienced hikers can lose their bearings.

There are stories of people disappearing here that go back centuries. Settlers who walked out to check fences and never came home. Hunters who left their camps in the morning and weren't there by nightfall.

Children who stepped off a trail and into the trees and were never seen again.

Not all disappearances are mysterious. Wilderness can be unforgiving. But some cases… the circumstances around them are hard to shake.

You find accounts where trackers couldn't pick up a trail. Dogs wouldn't follow a scent. Boots were found without footprints leading to them. Weather was clear. The person was experienced. Then they were gone.

The mountains don't owe explanations. Sometimes they don't give any.

The Things People Don't Like to Talk About

Even though the Appalachians have a long history of strange sightings, locals often speak about them cautiously. Not out of fear of ridicule, but out of respect for the land. You'll hear things like:

"Don't go up that ridge after dark."
"I wouldn't camp near that creek."
"That's old ground up there — leave it be."
"You won't catch me in that holler alone."

You ask why, and the answers are vague.
Sometimes it's an old story.
Sometimes it's a gut feeling.
Sometimes it's something they saw once and don't want to see again.

There's a humility in those warnings that you don't find everywhere. It's the same tone people use around Temagami or Algonquin when they're talking about places that feel different — charged, watchful. The Appalachians have dozens of those places.

Light That Doesn't Behave Properly

I've spent enough time in the bush to know the difference between headlights on a distant road, a plane passing overhead, and the glow of someone's lantern on a trail. In these mountains, though, I've seen lights that don't fit any of those categories.

Small ones, mostly—moving between trees, rising up from the ground, drifting in ways that don't match wind or terrain. Sometimes they pulse. Sometimes they blink out like someone flipped a switch.

Ball lightning is rare but real. Reflected headlamps can play tricks through fog. Fireflies can form strange patterns. But when you talk to rangers, hunters, and people who've lived in the same holler for forty years, and they all describe the same kind of drifting orb-like lights... you pay attention.

Lights like that have been seen across Appalachia for generations. Brown Mountain in North Carolina is famous for them, but they're not limited to one location.

Whatever those lights are, they don't behave like anything mechanical or modern. They feel older, stranger, and deeply tied to the land itself.

The Sense of Being Watched

Every wilderness has moments where you feel like you're not alone. But in the Appalachians, that feeling has a weight to it. It settles between your shoulders. It prickles at your instincts. It stays with you longer than it should.

I've felt eyes on me in forests before—Ontario is full of places where moose, wolves, and bears watch from the treeline. But this was different. Less like an animal tracking you... more like the land itself watching.

It's the kind of feeling that makes your senses sharpen. Your breath goes a little quieter. You walk a little slower. You start scanning the slope ahead of you because you're not entirely convinced you're the only one on that trail.

And the strange part is, the locals I've spoken with describe the same thing. It's not panic. Not paranoia. Just awareness. A sense that something else has been living here much longer than anyone realizes.

Old Mountains, Older Stories

By the time you reach the heart of the Appalachians—true ridge country, where the forest crowds the road and the valleys drop out beneath you— you begin to understand why stories stick here.

Old places hold old memories. They soak into the soil, the trees, the water. Everything in these mountains feels layered with something— history, tragedy, mystery, fear.

People have been telling stories about this land since long before Europeans arrived. Cherokee oral histories speak of shadow figures in the woods, strange cries at night, forbidden mountains, lights that float above ridges, creatures that watch from the trees. Those stories aren't told for entertainment; they're warnings, passed down because someone, somewhere, experienced something that left a mark.

And the more time you spend here, the more you begin to realize those stories weren't exaggerations. The woods really do go silent. The fog really does move strangely. People really do vanish. And something large, quiet, and aware really does walk the timber.

You don't need to believe every story. But it's impossible to ignore all of them.

A Threshold into Darkness

Every region has its gateway—the point where you cross from a familiar world into something that feels wilder, more ancient. For me, the first drive through the Appalachians was that threshold. Not a dramatic one. Just a long, unfolding realization that I wasn't passing through ordinary land.

Somewhere between a fog-choked valley and a ridge where the trees seemed to absorb the headlights, I felt it.

A shift.
A presence.
A sense that the mountains were paying attention.

People talk about the wilderness like it's passive, like it's just there. But I've been in enough remote places to know better. Wilderness can be indifferent, welcoming, or hostile. It can invite you in or push you out. And the Appalachians... they don't push. They *observe*.

They wait.
They listen.
And every so often, they let you see something you can't explain.

Chapter One isn't about the creatures or the vanishings yet.
It's about the land.
Because in the Appalachians, the land is the first mystery.

If you spend enough time in the hollers and on the ridges, walking the trails at dusk or driving those narrow side roads when night settles early, you start to understand something:

The old mountains aren't empty.
They're alive.
And they're watching.

In the chapters ahead, we'll walk deeper into that living darkness — into the places where the fog thickens, the stories gather, and the forest doesn't always behave the way a forest should.

The Appalachians have waited a long time to tell these stories.
It's time to listen.

Chapter Two — The Hollow Roads & Fog Valleys

There's a different kind of silence that settles in the hollers. Not the
stillness you get in open wilderness—where sound spreads out like
breath over water—but a close, pocketed quiet, the kind that seems to
fold back against the hills and stay there. If the ridges are the spine of the
Appalachians, the hollers are the lungs. They hold things. Fog. Sound.
Stories. Secrets. And sometimes they don't give any of it back.

Before I ever stepped foot on a trail here, I'd heard the word *holler* my
whole life. People say it casually—like it's just another way of saying
"valley." But driving into your first real mountain hollow changes that.
You realize "valley" is too flat a word. A holler is something else entirely.

A holler is a feeling. A holler is a mood.

And if you're not careful, a holler will swallow you whole.

Where Roads Go to Forget the Outside World

When you turn off the main asphalt and onto one of those narrow
mountain roads—one lane, no shoulder, trees growing so close they
scrape the mirrors—you know almost immediately you're leaving
something behind.

Some of these roads feel like they were carved into the mountainside
with a stubborn mule and a dull shovel. They dip and twist as if dodging
invisible obstacles, designing themselves around the land's oldest moods.
You see driveways that are barely more than ruts, disappearing into
thickets. Mailboxes leaning forward like old men who've given up trying
to stand straight. Homes tucked so far back that you wonder how the
residents ever get out after the first snowfall.

But it's not the isolation that gets you.
It's the sense of repetition—road after road, turn after turn, each one
feeling vaguely familiar yet entirely new.

There's a stretch in eastern Kentucky I drove one foggy morning. The
kind of morning where the mist isn't just sitting on the ground—it's

flowing. It moves across the road in slow, quiet bands, like the forests are exhaling. The pavement was cracked from years of winters and freeze-thaw cycles. A creek on my right bubbled along, half-hidden behind scraggly brush. Houses dotted the slopes—some lived-in, some abandoned, some somewhere in between.

Every time I thought I was coming out of the holler, the road bent and dove deeper. That's when I started to feel like I wasn't navigating by map anymore. The holler was choosing my direction.

I passed a porch with an old rocking chair moving slightly in the breeze —or maybe it wasn't the breeze. Further on, a dog barked once and then abruptly stopped. A crow perched on a road sign stared down like it was inspecting me. It didn't feel eerie, exactly. More like… expected. As if this road had seen a thousand mornings like this one and would see a thousand more after I was gone.

That's the thing about hollers: once you're in, time stops keeping track of you.

A Geography Built for Quiet Disappearances

The topography of the Appalachians creates these long, narrow valleys— often dead ends, sometimes barely wide enough for a single lane of traffic, a creekbed, and the skeleton of an old barn. The mountains rise steeply on both sides, creasing the land like folded paper. Trees grow thick and close, roots gripping slopes that crumble at the edges.

When you're deep in a holler, the ridgelines feel impossibly high, even when they're not. The sun is slower to reach the valley floor. Shadows linger longer. Even the temperature feels different—a notch cooler, as if these pockets of land hold onto night long after daylight should have washed in.

It creates a sense of being held. Contained. Almost watched.

I've heard locals say a holler can hide anything.
People. Animals. Entire chapters of history.

And if you really think about how these valleys twist and turn, you understand why.

A scream could echo strangely. A flashlight beam could vanish into fog. A person could wander just a few yards off the road and suddenly find themselves on a slope so steep they can't climb back out. It wouldn't take much to get lost. It wouldn't take long to disappear.

Which is why you hear stories of hunters finding lone boots. Or hikers being found miles from where search teams expected. Or families reporting sounds outside at night—heavy footsteps, pacing, breathing—things that never quite make it into official reports but live on in porch-talk and whispered warnings.

A holler is the kind of place where you don't even need darkness to feel uneasy.
Daylight just makes the shadows easier to count.

Fog That Behaves Like it Has a Mind of Its Own

Fog in the Appalachians doesn't act like a weather pattern—it acts like a character.

I remember one morning near the Tennessee–North Carolina border. I'd pulled off at a trailhead, opened my door, and stepped onto gravel that was still damp from the night. The fog was settled low across the creek, drifting in slow waves. A few birds were chirping, but muted, as if even their voices didn't want to echo too loudly.

I stood there for a moment, watching as the fog crawled across the parking area, sliding around my feet and then slipping back into the trees. It wasn't thick enough to block vision entirely, but it moved with a deliberateness that felt strange—almost purposeful.

When fog sits still, you can predict it. When fog moves like water, you can understand it. But when fog moves like an animal—crawling, withdrawing, pausing, drifting sideways in a direction that doesn't match the terrain—you start to feel like the mountains are breathing.

And fog in the hollers... it breathes a lot.

You hear this from hunters who sit in tree stands for hours. They'll talk about fog rising and falling without any wind at all. Or strange shapes forming inside it. Or a moment when something large moved through the mist — quietly, steadily — and disappeared before they could make sense of it.

Fog becomes a veil. A filter. A boundary between what you should see and what you *actually* can.

And there are mornings, I've been told, where the fog feels like it doesn't want you to see at all.

The Sound of Something You Can't Place

The hollers have a unique effect on sound. Noise doesn't just echo — it ricochets.

You might hear a branch snap, think it's close, and then realize it's coming from somewhere behind you. Someone could be walking a ridge two hundred yards away, and it'll sound like they're moving just out of sight. Water trickling down a slope can sound like footsteps if you're not paying attention.

But the real strange thing isn't how sound travels — it's when sound stops.

Every woodsman knows that animals stop making noise when a predator is near. Birds fall silent. Insects go still. The background hum dies. It's a natural warning system. But in the hollers, the silence feels heavier. Thicker. Almost intentional.

There was a trail I walked one afternoon — narrow, damp, winding along a slope. It was late in the day, the sun starting to drop behind the ridge. The forest was alive with noise: crickets, rustling leaves, movement in the underbrush. Then everything stopped. All at once.

It was like someone turned off the world.

I froze. Not because I felt in danger—but because I've learned to respect the silence in wild places. Silence means something's watching. Something's moving. Something's close.

After a moment, I noticed something else—my heartbeat sounded louder than the forest.

And just when that stillness began to settle into the back of my neck, I heard it: a soft, deliberate *tap-tap* from the slope above me. Not a woodland noise. Something knocking. Not loudly—just enough to register as intentional.

Two taps.
A pause.
Two more.

Cold ran up my arms.
Wood knock? Possibly. There are primates that use tree knocking. But in the Appalachians, locals have a different interpretation.

"Something's saying it knows you're there," an old man in Boone once told me. "Sometimes it taps. Sometimes it whistles. Sometimes it walks just where you can't see it."

He said it so calmly that the memory of those taps has never left me.

Places Where the Road Shouldn't Be This Quiet

There are stretches of hollow road where you realize you haven't passed another car in half an hour. Maybe longer. The pavement feels abandoned, even if it isn't. You'll see a mailbox, maybe two, but no houses. Just forest. A cabin set way back under the trees. A trailer with its porch light still on even though the sun is up. A shed half-swallowed by vines.

You can get trapped in your own thoughts on these roads. Not in a negative way—more like the landscape forces you to slow down, whether you want to or not. You start to notice things you wouldn't in a busier place: a shape in the trees, a rusted gate, a pile of stones that looks like it used to be something important.

Some roads feel normal during the day but take on a different personality at dusk. They darken early, shadows gathering long before sunset. The air cools. Fog creeps back in. And the mountains seem to lean closer, as if listening.

In those moments, you understand why so many Appalachian legends start on the side of a road. Someone driving home late. Someone seeing something crossing the pavement. Someone spotting a figure standing between the trees.

These stories aren't born from imagination—they're born from environment.

Roads that twist like thoughts. Darkness that arrives before you expect it. And just enough quiet to make you second-guess every shape in your headlights.

When Locals Say "Don't Go Down That Way"

One of the quickest ways to identify a place with a history is to ask locals which roads they avoid. They won't always tell you directly. Sometimes they'll shrug it off, or give a vague answer, or redirect the conversation. But if you listen carefully, you notice patterns.

"That road floods easy."
"That holler's real slick after rain."
"Too many bobcats down that way."
"Things disappear in that stretch."
"I wouldn't go up there alone."

People who live in the Appalachians aren't superstitious in the cartoonish sense. They're practical. Observant. Attuned to the land in a way outsiders seldom are. So when they give warnings, it's not out of irrational fear—it's experience.

A man in Virginia once told me, "Some hollers just ain't right. Not evil. Just... wrong."
He didn't elaborate, and I didn't push.

Because sometimes the absence of detail speaks louder than any story.

Where Darkness Reaches First

Something I noticed early on is how differently dusk behaves here. In flat land, daylight fades evenly. In mountains, light disappears ridge by ridge.

In the hollers, darkness arrives two or three hours early.
Not full night, just a dimming—like the world is turning down the volume.

Rhododendron thickets become black walls. The creek loses its shimmer. The shadows between the trees deepen into shapes. And the fog, that ever-present fog, comes back like a tide returning.

It doesn't take long before the valley feels too narrow, the road too empty, the silence too attentive.

That's when your instincts wake up.
Not fear—instinct.

A quiet, internal voice that tells you this is a place where anything could step out of the timber. A person. A bear. A shadow. Something that has watched a thousand travelers pass before you.

And maybe, if the stories are true, something that doesn't want to be seen.

The Holler as a Living Entity

The longer I've traveled through the Appalachians, the more I understand the holler not as a location, but as an organism. A holler breathes. A holler remembers. A holler communicates through fog, silence, wind, sound.

And a holler definitely watches.

Some places in the world make you feel like you're on their land. The Appalachians make you feel like you're in their care—or their custody. The land decides which.

I've spent countless hours in wilderness across North America, and I've learned that certain environments cultivate certain types of mystery. Swamps create one atmosphere. Boreal forests create another. But mountain hollers… they create something else entirely.

A holler is a **container** for the strange.
A funnel for stories.
A cradle for the unexplained.

Creatures can move quietly through hollers without leaving tracks.
Lights can drift without being seen from a distance.
Voices can echo in ways that don't match any human source.
And people can vanish in a 200-yard stretch of land without a trace.

That's not paranormal.
That's geography being used by something else.

The Other Side of the Fog

As I drove out of one particularly narrow valley in Tennessee, the fog finally began to lift. The sun broke over the ridge with hesitant light. The forest warmed by a few degrees. Sound returned—birds, insects, the rush of water. Everything snapped back to normal as if someone had released a held breath.

But I felt changed. Not dramatically—just subtly, like something inside me had shifted.
That's the effect hollers have on people. They get under your skin. They settle behind your ribs. They whisper to your instincts in a way you don't forget.

Every wilderness region has its own presence.
Its own personality.
Its own warnings.

The Appalachian hollers tell you something in a voice that's easy to miss but impossible to misinterpret:

Watch your step.
Watch your breath.

Watch the fog.
And don't assume you're alone.

Because in these narrow valleys—between the dark ridges and the cold mornings—something walks the timber. Something moves through the mist. Something keeps its distance but never leaves.

And the holler, patient as time, keeps its secrets.

Chapter Three — Witnesses of the Wild

There's something different about the people who live in and around the Appalachian Mountains. You feel it the moment you speak to them—the way they talk about the woods, the way they walk through the timber, the way their eyes shift when certain topics come up. They're not afraid of the wilderness. They're *aware* of it. That's not the same thing.

In cities or suburbs, nature is a distant concept. A weekend hobby. Something you enter and leave on your own terms. But here, the land is part of daily life. It's not unusual to meet a retired logger who has hiked more ridgelines than most park rangers, or a grandmother who knows how to track a deer across leaf litter so dry it snaps under your boots.

People here don't just observe the wilderness—they participate in it. And because of that, the stories they tell land differently.

When someone from downtown Asheville claims they saw something strange, you file it under "possible."
When a man who's hunted the same holler for fifty years says something big paced him through the timber… you listen.

This chapter is about those people—the ones who know the land better than any map, the ones who see things long before outsiders ever hear rumors.

These are the witnesses of the wild.

The Hunters Who Know the Land Like a Book

You don't have to spend long in the Appalachian Mountains to learn who really understands the woods: hunters.
Not the weekend crowd. The generational ones. The men and women whose fathers and grandfathers taught them how to read sign the way some children learn to read letters.

I met a man in Tennessee—I'll call him Jacob—who had hunted the same valley since the late 1970s. He spoke with the calm certainty of someone who doesn't waste energy trying to impress you.

"You hunt a place long enough," he told me, "and you get a feel for what's normal. Deer move certain ways. Coyotes stick to the edges. Bears got patterns. When something breaks that pattern… you notice."

He paused there, letting the silence fill the gap.

"What broke the pattern?" I asked.

He took a breath, the kind you take when you're deciding how much of your truth you're willing to share.

"I heard footsteps behind me," he said. "Not light ones. Heavy. Two legs, not four."

"How sure?" I asked.

He gave a small smile—one that said he'd heard that question too many times.

"I've heard bears walk. I've heard people walk. I know the difference."

He went on to describe how the footsteps stayed behind him but never closed the distance. He turned around more than once but saw nothing. The sound stopped whenever he stopped. Started whenever he moved. Eventually he left the woods early—not out of fear, he insisted, but out of respect. Something was there. Something that didn't want to be seen.

When a man who has hunted every season for forty years tells you he couldn't identify the thing following him, it hits differently. These aren't people who jump at shadows. They don't have time for nonsense.

Hunters don't report creatures unless they're certain they can't explain what they saw.

And in the Appalachians, hunters have seen a lot they can't explain.

Park Rangers: The Quiet Keepers of Unspoken Stories

If hunters know the day-to-day patterns of the land, park rangers know the accidents, the disappearances, the rescues, and the places where things regularly go wrong.

Most rangers won't tell you everything they've experienced. Not because they're hiding something malicious, but because they've learned the value of silence. Government reports don't leave much room for interpretation, and official statements don't include every detail.

But if you catch a ranger on a slow day—when the wind is low and the campground is quiet—they'll sometimes share the pieces that didn't make it into paperwork.

I once spoke to a ranger in the Great Smokies who had worked there for almost two decades. He didn't start our conversation with anything unusual. Mostly standard facts: weather patterns, trail safety, wildlife activity.

Then, almost casually, he said:
"There are places I don't go alone anymore."

He didn't elaborate, so I didn't push. After a minute, he continued on his own.

"There's a stretch along the Deep Creek trail," he said, "where the woods feel wrong in the late afternoon. Don't know how else to describe it. Even the deer avoid it certain times of year."

"What do you mean by wrong?" I asked.

He shrugged, but there was tension in the motion.

"Just… heavy. Like someone's watching. Like the trees are holding something."

He looked over my shoulder then, as if checking the tree line.

"And we've had people go missing on clear days," he added. "Easy trails. Well-marked. No reason to get lost. But they did. Dogs couldn't get a scent. Teams couldn't track anything. Like they walked into thin air."

He told the story plainly, without theatrics. That's what made it land. There was no desire to impress—just a truth he lived with.

Rangers see more than they're allowed to talk about.
And some of them carry those stories for the rest of their lives.

Residents Who Live Too Close to the Strange to Deny It

Some of the most compelling witnesses aren't hunters or rangers. They're the people who live in the same holler their family has lived in for generations. Folks who know every creek crossing, every ridge shadow, every change in the air.

These are the people whose houses sit alone at the end of long gravel driveways, where porch lights glow like yellow islands in the fog. They'll tell you they're not superstitious. They'll tell you they don't believe in "tall tales." But when the subject of strange sounds or figures in the woods comes up, their eyes shift.

Not fear.
Recognition.

One woman in western North Carolina told me she sometimes hears someone walking around her property long after dark. Not every night—just enough to know it's intentional.

"It ain't raccoons," she said. "Ain't coyotes. Ain't deer. This sounds heavy. Slow. Like it's thinking."

"You ever see anything?" I asked.

"Not really," she said. "But once, I saw a shape stand behind the oak tree near the creek. Too tall to be a man. Too broad. Just stood there. When I looked away for half a second, it was gone."

She didn't smile when she told me that. She didn't laugh or shrug or brush it off. She just said it the way you'd tell someone your porch light burned out.

For people living in the deep mountains, these encounters aren't stories —they're experiences.

Old-Timers and the Weight of Memory

Every region has elders who hold onto the older stories—the ones told before modern terms like "Bigfoot" or "cryptid" existed. Appalachia is full of them. You find them sitting outside gas stations in rocking chairs, or on porches overlooking narrow roads, or at the back of a small-town bar sipping something dark from a plastic cup.

These people remember the mountains before paved roads cut through them. Before tourism softened the edges. They remember the woods when they were thicker, darker, quieter. And their memories have a different tone.

It's not storytelling.
It's remembering.

An older man in Virginia once told me:

"When I was a boy, we used to hear something walking the ridge at night. Big steps. Heavy. Wouldn't see it, but you'd feel it. Sounded too big for a man. My daddy told me not to look at it if I ever saw it. Said it wasn't ours to look at."

I asked him what he meant.

He tapped the arm of his chair and said, "Some things in the mountains been here longer than people."

Old-timers say this sort of thing with a finality that's hard to question. When you hear someone in their seventies or eighties speak about creatures or shadows in the timber with the same tone they use to talk about seasonal weather changes... you realize this isn't folklore.

This is memory.

The Local Rule: Believe the Quiet Ones

Something I've learned over years of research is that the most credible witnesses are always the quiet ones. People who don't go looking for attention. People who don't run to social media. People who don't embellish.

Appalachia has plenty of those.
Farmers. Retired servicemen. School bus drivers. Mechanics. Nurses. People who see things on their drive home or while walking their dog at night.

You hear the same type of line over and over:

"I don't care if you believe me. I know what I saw."

That sentence carries weight.

When someone tells you a story with no desire to convince you, no attempt at drama, and no expectation of anything in return, it sticks.

One woman in Kentucky told me she once heard what she called "the voice."

"It sounded like a man," she said, "but not a man. Deep. Wrong. Like someone talking underwater."

She was outside feeding her dogs just before dawn. The sky was still grey. The valley held onto the cold.

"I heard it by the treeline," she said. "Just a few words. Or maybe it wasn't words. I don't know. My dogs froze. They didn't bark. Didn't growl. They just... listened."

That detail—the dogs—told me more than anything else.
Animals react honestly.

"What did you do?" I asked her.

She looked out her window at the ridge across from her house and said, "I went inside. Locked the door. Never heard it again."

She didn't call anyone. Didn't report it. Didn't even tell her neighbors for months.
That's how people here handle the strange.

They don't make a scene.
They adapt to it.

Patterns in the Quiet Places

Something interesting begins to surface when you listen to enough Appalachian witnesses: their stories overlap.

Not in the dramatic, Hollywood way.
In subtle, consistent ways.

Here are the patterns I've seen again and again:

1. Something walks on two legs.
Not always seen, but often heard. Heavy. Deliberate. Sometimes pacing.

2. Something knocks.
On trees. On barns. Against hollow logs. Always in patterns.

3. Silence drops before anything strange happens.
Birds stop. Frogs stop. Even the wind seems to hold still.

4. The fog behaves oddly.
Moves strangely. Holds shapes. Blocks sound.

5. Witnesses feel watched more often than they see anything.
A presence. A weight. An awareness.

6. Lights drift.
Not headlights. Not lanterns. Orbs. Moving without rhythm.

7. Animals react.
Dogs hide. Horses refuse to pass certain areas. Deer vanish suddenly.

Different counties. Different states. Different decades.
Same patterns.

That's what convinces me more than any single encounter.

When witnesses who have nothing to gain, who don't know each other, who live miles apart, describe the same things with the same tone… you start to believe the land is telling the truth.

Ridgewalkers, Shadows, and Voices on the Wind

There's a phrase I've heard more than once from people living deep in the mountains:

"Something walks the ridge."

Not *someone*.
Something.

They use that word carefully. Respectfully. Like they know they're describing a presence that belongs to the mountain, not to humans.

A man I met near the Virginia–West Virginia border said he once saw a silhouette walking along a ridgeline at dusk. Not a hiker. Too tall. Too fluid. The figure moved without the bobbing gait people have when they walk uphill. It glided.

"I watched it for maybe twenty seconds," he said. "Trees behind it made its outline clear. Shoulders too wide. Head too high. Then it stepped behind a pine and vanished."

He paused.

"When I say vanished," he said slowly, "I mean vanished. Didn't walk. Didn't duck. Just… gone."

These stories are rare. Most people don't claim to *see* anything directly. But when they do, the details are eerily consistent.

Tall.
Broad.
Dark.
Silent.

Something that moves like it knows exactly where to place its feet.

Something that doesn't want to be followed.

Why Appalachian Witnesses Matter

A witness's credibility doesn't come from how dramatic their story is. It comes from what they risk in telling it.

Appalachian witnesses risk more than embarrassment.
They risk community judgment. Reputation. Family opinion.

That's why most of them keep their stories close. They don't share them casually. They don't dramatize them. They don't turn them into entertainment.

When they finally decide to say something, it's because what they saw or heard stayed with them long enough—and deeply enough—that silence no longer felt right.

These are people who spend more time in the woods than most researchers.
They know the sound of a bear breaking branches.
They know the difference between a coyote's yip and the scream of a bobcat.
They know how deer walk, how owls move, how foxes circle.

When people like that tell you something felt wrong... it's worth paying attention.

They aren't guessing.
They're reporting.

Human Instinct in Ancient Timber

The modern world dulls instinct. But wilderness sharpens it.

Most Appalachian witnesses describe something that triggered their instincts before it triggered their thoughts. A sound. A silence. A movement. A presence. Something that made the hairs rise on their arms before they had time to analyze anything.

That's the wilderness talking through them.
Not superstition.
Not imagination.
Instinct.

Humans spent thousands of years surviving by noticing the unusual.
Strange sounds.
Sudden silence.
Movement where movement shouldn't be.

In places as old and layered as the Appalachians, that instinct reawakens quickly.

And the people who live here—who've walked these ridges since childhood, who've chopped wood in January fog, who've spent long nights listening to something move around their property—have a sharper instinct than most.

Their stories aren't guesses.
They're reactions.

And reactions reveal truth.

The Mountains Choose Their Witnesses

Not everyone sees something strange here.
Not everyone hears the knocks or the footsteps or the voice carried by a cold wind.
Not everyone notices the fog curl in ways that don't match the terrain.

But the ones who do are the ones who pay attention.
The ones who listen.
The ones who don't rush.
The ones who know the land.

The Appalachian Mountains don't reveal their mysteries to everyone.
They pick their moments carefully.

And the witnesses—hunters, rangers, locals, elders—are chosen not because they're lucky or unlucky, but because they're present.

Attuned.

Aware.

These mountains speak softly.
But they speak.

And there are people here who have learned how to hear them.

Chapter Four — The Virginia Woodbooger

They don't call it "Bigfoot" in this part of the Appalachians.
Not usually.
Not in the places where the mountains press tight around old logging roads and families have lived on the same patches of land for a hundred years.

Here, you hear something different.

"Woodbooger."

The first time I heard the term, I thought it sounded like a joke—something kids would say to scare each other before dark. But in southwest Virginia, it carries a weight that isn't humorous at all. Locals say it with a straight face. Sometimes quietly. Sometimes cautiously. But always with the same undertone:

You don't want to meet it up close.

The Woodbooger isn't treated like a fairy tale.
It's treated like a neighbor you don't talk to but keep an eye on.

You can drive through the edge of Virginia's mountain country and never know the stories unless you stop long enough to listen. But if you sit in the right diner, or talk to the right old-timer outside a bait shop, or hear the way people talk about certain hollers at dusk—then the subject comes up naturally, almost reluctantly.

And when it does, all the laughter stops.

A Creature with a Name Older Than the Internet

"Woodbooger" sounds like something invented in the age of memes, but the word predates all that.
Long before trail cams and podcasts and YouTube documentaries, mountain folks were warning children:

"Don't wander off past dark, or the Woodbooger will carry you off."

That wasn't fearmongering—it was survival advice wrapped in folklore.

This part of Virginia—the ridge country near Norton, Big Stone Gap, High Knob, Pound, and Wise—has always been thick with stories about tall, hairy, human-like creatures that move through the forests with surprising speed. They appear in hollers where the fog stacks up like wool blankets. They cross old mining roads at dusk. They knock on cabin walls. They're seen more often than they're talked about.

If the Smokies are home to the silent watchers…
Virginia is home to the **shadow travelers**.

And the Woodbooger is the one legend locals never had to invent—because they keep running into it.

High Knob — The Heart of Woodbooger Country

There's a spot near Norton called High Knob.
A beautiful overlook, one of the highest points in the region.
A place where the land folds out in every direction—ridges stacked like waves, hollers winding between them, forests thick enough to swallow sound.

It's peaceful during the day.
But after sunset, the atmosphere changes completely.

Ask almost anyone in the area what roams those slopes late at night, and you'll get the same answer:

"Woodboogers."

It's said so casually it catches you off guard.
Like someone telling you there are deer in the backyard.
Not mythical creatures—residents.

One man I spoke to outside a gas station in Wise—weathered hands, coal dust still lingering in the seams of his skin—told me:

"Up High Knob way, we used to hear 'em holler back at dogs. Loud. Deep. Didn't sound like bear. Didn't sound like nothin' I ever heard before."

"What did it sound like?" I asked.

He thought for a moment.

"Like someone yellin' from down in a well. That's the closest way I can put it."

Then he added something that stuck with me:

"They don't mind you bein' up there. They mind you stayin' too long."

The Coal Town Sightings

Southwest Virginia is old coal country—full of abandoned shafts, forgotten equipment, rusting rail lines, and ghost towns where the forest is slowly taking back everything humans tried to build.

If you want to hide something big and smart, you couldn't design a better landscape.

I heard a story from a former miner who worked near the Kentucky border in the late 1980s. He said there were nights when the crew would hear something walking outside the mine entrance during their shift.

"Two legs," he said. "Big ones. Heavy. Took its time."

I asked him if it could've been a bear.

"No," he said flatly. "Bears don't walk like that. And they sure as hell don't start throwing rocks at us."

He and the others would hear stones hitting the tin siding of their break shack.
Never big rocks—small ones.
Not meant to hurt.
Meant to get attention.

"Like it was playing," he said, though he didn't sound amused.

When the night shift ended and they stepped out into the cool, black air, whatever was there always disappeared before their lights reached the treeline. But the footprints would be there in the mud—big, human-looking prints, deep-set, heading uphill where no man in his right mind would climb in the dark.

The miner didn't tell his supervisor. He didn't tell his wife for years. But he told me, because time has a way of softening the fear while sharpening the truth.

"There was something livin' up in them hills," he said. "Somethin' that watched us. Somethin' that wasn't afraid."

The Pacing in the Pines

One of the strangest Woodbooger stories I've come across came from a man near Pound, Virginia—a hunter in his late forties who had spent most of his life exploring the mountains before and after work. He wasn't someone prone to exaggeration. He talked like a man fixing a truck: short sentences, slow delivery, no fluff.

He told me he was walking a ridge trail at dusk when he heard something moving through the pines beside him. At first he assumed it was a deer. But the footsteps were too heavy, too spaced out, and too synchronized with his own.

"When I stopped," he said, "it stopped. When I walked, it walked."

I'd heard this pattern in the Smokies too—parallel pacing, a kind of watching-from-cover behavior that feels more investigative than predatory.

But then came the detail that chilled him most:

"It breathed."

Not loudly.
Not aggressively.
Just a slow, deep exhale that carried through the trees like warm air over cold ground.

"You ever hear somethin' breathe outdoors?" he asked.
"Not an animal. A person? Something bigger than a person?"

He shook his head.

"That's when I turned around and walked outta there."

He wasn't ashamed. He wasn't frightened in a dramatic sense.
He was being honest.

"There's stuff up here that ain't for us to look at," he said.

And that, more than anything, defines the Woodbooger mystery:
A creature that doesn't flee.
Doesn't attack.
Just watches.

And breathes.

Signs Left Behind: The Woodbooger Calling Card

Every Bigfoot region has its version of "sign"—tracks, knocks, sounds,
structures.
But Virginia has a few specific behaviors that come up more often than
elsewhere.

1. Tree Breaks at Shoulder Height

Not fallen limbs.
Not storm damage.
Major green limbs twisted and snapped seven to nine feet off the ground.

Locals chalk them up to "markers."
Territorial signs.
Path indicators.

These aren't dead trees. These are freshly twisted, torn with unbelievable
force.

2. Parallel Pacing Without Visual Contact

People don't see the Woodbooger often.
But they hear it walk beside them.

Always on slopes.
Always in cover.
Always stopping when the witness stops.

If bears did this consistently, people would accept bears as the explanation.
But they don't.
This is something else.

3. Cabin Knocks

Not frantic pounding.
Not random.

Just a slow, steady tap—sometimes in groups of three.

People hear it near High Knob, Coeburn, Pound, Wise, and Big Stone Gap.

You can dismiss a single knock.
But not hundreds of them over decades.

4. Shadow Figures in Peripheral Vision

People see movement at the edge of their sightline.
A tall shape slipping behind a ridge or tree.
Gone the moment you turn.

This is one of the most common Woodbooger encounters.

5. The Black Silence

Before anything odd happens, the woods go quiet.
Not "less noisy"—completely silent.

That silence is reported so consistently it might as well be a signature.

The Family Who Wouldn't Hang Their Laundry Outside Anymore

There was a family outside of Norton who described something approaching their back property just after sunset for several weeks one fall. The daughter—mid-teens—said she'd seen a tall figure move between two trees at the edge of their yard.

"When I looked at it," she said, "it stepped behind a tree. But not quick. Slow. Like it wasn't scared."

Her father didn't believe her at first.
But then things started happening.

Laundry pulled off lines.
Trash cans flipped silently.
A stack of firewood knocked over.
Soft whistles drifting through the yard around midnight.

Then came the night they all heard something walking just outside their house.

Slow steps.
Heavy.
Measured.

The father grabbed a flashlight, stepped out onto the porch, and scanned the yard. The beam hit nothing but frost and fog.

Then he heard breathing from behind the shed.

Not an animal scuffling.
Not a deer snort.

Breathing.
Deep and strong and deliberate.

He went back inside.
Locked the door.
Shut every curtain.

They didn't hang laundry outside for a long time after that.

Blue Ridge Overlooks and Night Watchers

Some of the most unnerving encounters in Virginia happen at scenic overlooks—those places tourists visit during the day to take photos and locals stop at night to catch their breath after a long shift.

The forest looms on both sides.
The guardrails are old.
The wind funnels through the ridges like a whisper.
And the darkness settles early.

People see things here.

A man from Coeburn told me he saw a silhouette step onto the edge of the overlook one night.
Just a shape.
Huge.
Broad-shouldered.
Backlit by moonlight.

He thought it was another driver until he realized the figure was far too tall and stood unusually still.

"It didn't move like a person," he said. "It moved like it was part of the dark."

Another man said he saw two eyes—reflective, amber-colored— hovering above the guardrail at a height that made no sense for deer, bear, or human.

When he blinked, the eyes blinked back.
Then they vanished.

Not walked away.
Not hidden.

Vanished.

The Scent of Something You Can't Explain

People talk about smells in these mountains.
Sulfur.
Wet fur.
Rotting vegetation.
Sometimes sweet musk.

The Woodbooger's scent is faint but strange—something that hits the nose hard and then disappears on the wind.

Hunters describe moments where the smell rolls in for a few seconds—just enough to be noticed—then vanishes as if sucked away.

"Not animal," one man told me. "Not anything I could name."

Scent comes up often in Woodbooger encounters.
Almost always right before something else happens.

A knock.
A breath.
A shadow.
A footstep.

Something big enough to have a scent signature that strong isn't a deer.

And it isn't alone.

Why Virginia Might Be the Key to Understanding Bigfoot Behavior

The Woodbooger isn't just another name for Bigfoot.

It's a specific regional variant—behaviorally distinct from the creatures reported in the Pacific Northwest, the Smokies, or the deep Canadian bush.

Here's why Virginia matters:

1. The creature is bold but not aggressive.

It approaches cabins.
Walks alongside hikers.
Watches closely but doesn't attack.

2. It prefers edges instead of deep wilderness.

Woodlines.
Backyards.
Logging roads.
Mining sites.

This suggests familiarity with humans — or curiosity.

3. It adapts to human activity.

Mining. Logging.
Tourism.
Trails.

It doesn't flee from development the way other wildlife does.

4. It uses terrain with precision.

Steep slopes.
Coal ridges.
Rhododendron thickets.

It knows where to hide and how to move.

5. It has a long cultural lineage.

Stories go back generations.
Long before the word "Bigfoot" existed.

When people in these mountains describe the Woodbooger, they don't describe a spirit.
They describe an animal.
A large one.

A quiet one.
A thinking one.

A Region That Carries Its Secrets in the Dark

The Virginia Woodbooger isn't a monster.
It's a presence.

Something old.
Something that has survived the collapse of the coal industry, the shifting of towns, the fading of traditions.
Something that has lived in these ridges quietly, consistently, without ever giving the world more than a glimpse.

People here talk about it cautiously because they know the mountain doesn't need validation.
It doesn't need belief.
It just needs room to breathe.

And the Woodbooger breathes with it.

If the Smokies introduced us to shadowy giants that stay just out of sight…
Virginia introduces us to the ones who come closer.

Close enough to pace you.
Close enough to whistle at your window.
Close enough to knock on your cabin wall.

And always, always close enough to watch.

In the next chapter, we enter West Virginia—the land of coal shadows, dark ridges, and some of the most unnerving Bigfoot encounters anywhere in Appalachia.

Virginia tells you something is there.
West Virginia tells you why.

Chapter Five — West Virginia Ridgewalker Encounters

West Virginia feels different the moment you cross the border. The mountains tighten. The valleys deepen. The roads narrow into single lanes that thread along ridges like seams stitched by an unsteady hand. Everything here rises and falls in slow, sweeping movements—steeper than Virginia, darker than the Carolinas, older in a way you can't measure on a map.

West Virginia isn't just mountain country.
It's deep mountain country.
The kind of place where light doesn't reach the forest floor until mid-morning and the fog settles like a quilt over the hollers long after sunrise.

This state doesn't just hold history—it buries it.
Coal towns, abandoned rails, forgotten family cemeteries, rusting mining equipment—everything left behind gets swallowed by vines and shadow.

And somewhere inside all that shadow, something walks the ridges.

People here call it many names—Bigfoot, "Old Man of the Mountain," "the tall one," "that thing up on the ridge"—but the most consistent term, the one whispered by hunters and old-timers alike, is **"the Ridgewalker."**

The name fits.
The creature is seen most often on the high lines—moving across ridges in long, smooth strides, silhouetted against the sky at dusk or dawn. Always watching. Rarely approaching. Never running.

West Virginia's Ridgewalker isn't just another Bigfoot.
It has a presence all its own.

A Land Built for Shadows

Driving into the heart of West Virginia is like slipping into another century. The mountains rise steeper than in the surrounding states, packed tight against each other like folded arms. The hollers feel deeper, the air damp and cool even in early summer. Small towns appear suddenly, clinging to narrow flats carved between river and cliff. You blink and they're gone—a handful of houses, a gas station, an old church—and then it's back to wilderness.

The forests here are old and layered. Oak. Hickory. Hemlock. Dense undergrowth in the valleys, open hardwoods on the ridges, spruce higher up. The terrain funnels sound in strange ways, amplifying some noises while swallowing others completely.

If you hear something walking in the woods here, it's either very close... or very large.

Locals don't like to linger on porches after dark. Not in certain areas. Not on certain nights. The darkness falls fast in West Virginia, and once it arrives, it feels absolute. The ridges block moonlight. The hollers trap night air. And any sound that isn't your own becomes a warning.

People who spend enough time outdoors here all say the same thing:

"Something walks those ridges."

Not bears.
Not people.
Something else.

The First Ridgewalker Story I Ever Heard

I heard my first real Ridgewalker story from a man sitting outside a convenience store not far from Logan. He was mid-60s, wiry, with the kind of calm presence you see in lifelong outdoorsmen. He told me he used to run lines for coal operations back in the day—mapping slopes, walking ridges, marking boundaries before the machines came.

He said the mountains always felt alive, but he never felt watched—not until one late autumn evening.

He was walking along a narrow ridgeline, one side dropping steeply into a creek gorge, the other side sloping toward abandoned mine land. The last of the daylight clung to the sky, turning everything blue.

"I looked up," he said, "and saw someone walking ahead of me on the ridge."

He paused here — not for drama, but because the memory held weight.

"He was tall. Taller than anyone I ever worked with. Broad. Walked smooth, like he wasn't touching the ground much."

"How tall?" I asked.

He held his hand about a foot above his own six-foot frame.

"I called out," he said. "Figured maybe someone from one of the camps was out there. But he didn't answer. Just kept walking."

He followed for a minute. Then the figure stopped.

"Stopped dead," he said. "Didn't turn. Didn't crouch. Didn't run."

He lifted a finger.

"Then he stepped off the ridge. Not down the side. Off. Like he just walked into the air."

The man shook his head slowly, still confused all those years later.

"When I got to that spot, there was no trail down. No tracks. Just a drop-off. I don't know what I saw, but it wasn't a man."

He didn't ask me if I believed him.
He didn't need to.

His voice carried the kind of quiet certainty you can't fake.

Coal Roads and Footsteps in the Dark

West Virginia coal country is a labyrinth of forgotten roads.
Old access tracks.
Abandoned haul routes.
Rusted gates that haven't swung open in decades.

These are the places where the Ridgewalker appears most often.

One night, a retired miner named Dale told me he and two buddies were driving back from checking an old site. The air was thick with mist. Their headlights caught only the first few feet of the road.

Right before a sharp bend, Dale saw something step across the road.

Not run.
Not dart.
Step.

"One stride," he said, "and it was across the whole damn thing."

He described long legs, a massive torso, and dark hair that seemed to absorb the light instead of reflecting it. It didn't look back. It didn't hurry.

It just moved with an easy confidence.

"What did you do?" I asked.

"We stopped the truck," he said. "Turned the lights off. Sat there for a minute."

"Why?" I asked.

"Because whatever crossed that road wasn't scared of us. And you don't want to chase something that ain't scared."

He looked out across the darkened hills while telling me this, like he expected to see the shape again any second.

"Some things," he said quietly, "got more right to these mountains than people."

The Ridgewalker at Dawn

Most Ridgewalker sightings happen at dusk or in full darkness, but dawn encounters might be even more unsettling.

The mist clings to the valleys.
The sky is pale.
Birdsong hasn't fully started.

That's when one hunter near Fayetteville said he saw something move along a ridge opposite his blind. The shape appeared between two pines —tall, upright, noticeably wide.

"At first I thought it was another hunter," he told me. "But it wasn't wearing orange. And then it stepped into the light."

He described long arms, a thick chest, and a stride wider than any person he'd ever met. What struck him most was the silence. The Ridgewalker moved without breaking a twig.

"No sound," he said. "Not one. Big as it was."

He watched it for nearly thirty seconds—long enough to memorize its gait, long enough to know he wasn't looking at anything familiar.

Then it disappeared behind a boulder outcrop.
And didn't reappear.

"When I went over there later," he said, "there was nothing. No prints. No trail. No scent."

He shook his head.

"But I know what I saw."

The Woman Who Heard Footsteps Above Her Cabin

Not all Ridgewalker encounters happen far from home. Some happen within feet of someone's doorstep.

I spoke to a woman in her late fifties who lived in a small cabin on a slope overlooking a deep hollow. Her nearest neighbor was nearly a mile away. She said she'd grown used to the sounds of wildlife—foxes, deer, coyotes, the occasional black bear.

But one night, she heard something entirely new.

"It was walking on the ridge above my place," she said. "Heavy. Slow. Each step deliberate."

She stepped onto her porch with a flashlight but didn't turn it on. She didn't want to startle whatever was up there.

"It walked back and forth," she said. "Three times. Like it was deciding something."

Then she heard a sound she had no explanation for:

A low, resonant hum.
Not human.
Not mechanical.
Not animal.

"It made my chest vibrate," she said. "Like it was inside me."

Then the footsteps resumed—moving away this time.
After a minute, the night returned to normal.

"What did you think it was?" I asked.

She hesitated—not out of uncertainty, but out of caution.

"Not a bear," she said. "Not a cat. Nothing with four legs. It walked like a man. Just... too heavy to be one."

Then she added, "You're not the first person to ask about something walking that ridge."

The Shadows That Follow the Road

In some parts of West Virginia, people talk about shadows traveling alongside cars at night.
Not reflections.
Not illusions.

Shadows that keep pace.

A truck driver on Route 52 said he once saw a dark figure moving through the trees, matching his speed for several seconds. He thought it was his imagination until he realized the figure's height—easily eight feet—and the way it moved, gliding over deadfall and uneven ground without slowing.

"It stayed with me for maybe a quarter-mile," he said. "Then it peeled off into the dark."

He didn't stop the truck.
He didn't look back.

"You don't follow something that can keep up with you at forty miles an hour," he said.

He told the story quietly, eyes fixed on the passing mountains.

"Whatever that thing was," he said, "it wasn't trying to scare me. It was just traveling."

The Strange Behavior of Silence

West Virginia has what locals call "dead zones."
Not cell service dead zones—those are everywhere—but *sound* dead zones.

Places where everything goes quiet for no reason.

Hunters talk about being in the woods for hours, listening to the usual forest noise, and then suddenly—nothing.

Not even wind.

One hunter told me he was walking along a ridge when the silence hit so suddenly he froze mid-step.

"I knew something was close," he said. "Didn't know what. But I knew."

Moments later, he heard footsteps behind him. Heavy ones.
Walking slowly.
Deliberately.

"When I turned around," he said, "there was nothing. But the feeling didn't go away. The silence just… watched me."

Silence is a living thing in West Virginia.
Sometimes it warns you.
Sometimes it surrounds you.
Sometimes it follows you.

And every witness agrees on one thing:

The Ridgewalker brings silence.

When Dogs Refuse to Follow

Dogs don't lie.
They don't imagine monsters.
They respond to scent, sound, and instinct.

And in West Virginia, they refuse to follow Ridgewalker trails.

Multiple hunters told me the same story:
Their dogs, trained to track deer or bear for years, would suddenly stop at a certain point on a trail. Their posture would change. Their ears would flatten. They'd whine softly and refuse to move forward.

One man said his dog actually backed away, tail tucked, refusing even to look up the ridge.

"Never seen him act like that before," he said. "Or since."

Rangers have reported similar behavior during searches. Dogs will follow a scent confidently until they hit an invisible boundary—and then stop.

Sit down.
Whine.
Refuse to go on.

Whatever the Ridgewalker is, dogs know not to pursue it.

Animals respect hierarchy.
And something in these mountains sits above them.

Tracks Found Where No Human Should Be

The most unsettling Ridgewalker evidence isn't the sightings — it's the footprints found in places that defy logic.

Deep prints on near-vertical slopes.
Strides stretching four or five feet apart.
Tracks that appear in soft mud but vanish the moment the terrain hardens.
Prints found beside cliffs with no safe way up or down.

One pair of hunters near the New River Gorge found a set of tracks leading across a steep slide area — a slope so unstable they couldn't follow without risking a fall.

But something had walked across it easily. Barefoot.
Each print fifteen inches long.
Each one perfectly placed.

"You'd break your neck trying that," one hunter said. "Whatever walked there wasn't human."

It's one thing to find a big footprint.
It's another to find it somewhere a person couldn't reach without climbing gear.

Why the Ridgewalker Behaves Differently

In every region, Bigfoot — or whatever name it goes by — has a unique personality.

The Smokies are stealth.
Virginia is proximity.
But West Virginia?

West Virginia is **movement**.

The Ridgewalker doesn't hide in the same way others do.
It travels.
It follows.
It observes.

Here's what sets it apart:

1. It prefers ridgelines over valleys.

Most sightings happen high, not low.

2. It walks long distances.

Witnesses see it move across entire ridge systems.

3. It mimics human motion more closely.

Stride patterns match tall humans—just scaled up dramatically.

4. It seems curious, not fearful.

It follows hikers.
It watches from slopes.
It approaches roads.

5. It doesn't panic under lights.

It steps away calmly instead of running.

These behavioral patterns suggest intelligence.
And familiarity with humans.

The Night the Ridgewalker Circled the Camp

One of the most disturbing encounters I've heard came from two brothers camping near the Monongahela National Forest. They'd set up a small tent near a ridge, cooked dinner, and turned in for the night.

Around 2 a.m., they woke to the sound of footsteps circling their camp.

Slow steps.
Heavy.
One at a time.

The brothers lay frozen in their sleeping bags, listening.
The steps circled once.
Then twice.
Then stopped behind the tent.

"We could hear it breathing," one of them said. "Just standing there."

For almost a full minute, the creature didn't move. Didn't walk. Didn't grunt.

It just breathed.

Slow.
Deep.
Resonant.

Then, without warning, something struck a tree nearby—hard enough to shake the ground.

A single knock.
Then silence.

The brothers didn't sleep again that night.

"When the sun came up," one said, "we packed and left. Didn't even make coffee."

They didn't see tracks.
They didn't see a silhouette.

But they heard enough to know the truth:

They hadn't been alone.

The Ridgewalker's Territory

Ridgewalker encounters cluster in several specific parts of West Virginia:

- The Monongahela National Forest

- The New River Gorge region

- The rural ridges around Logan

- Tug Fork hollers

- Coal-country slopes near Matewan and Williamson

- The high ridgelands near Elkins and Snowshoe

- Deep woods north of Beckley

- The Cranberry Wilderness

These are places where people disappear, where the forest crowds the road, where the hollers feel bottomless.

And where the Ridgewalker is at home.

The Creature That Walks Above the Light

The most defining characteristic of the Ridgewalker—the thing every witness mentions—is its silhouette.

Tall.
Wide-shouldered.
Arms long and slow-moving.
A head that sits forward, slightly hunched.
A gait that seems almost soundless.

One man called it "a shadow that decided to stand up."

Another said, "If you see it once, you'll never mistake it again."

West Virginia's Ridgewalker doesn't hide from the skyline.
It claims it.

These mountains have always belonged to something ancient.
Something that doesn't fear the dark.
Something that walks where people don't.

The Ridgewalker isn't a ghost story here.
It's part of the land.

And the land remembers.

Chapter Six — The Backwoods Voices: Whistles, Chatter & "Mumbling"

There's a certain kind of quiet that comes at night in the deep mountains.
Not peaceful quiet.
Not the soft stillness you get around a cabin fire or beside a lake at dusk.
This is the quiet that feels **listening**.

It's a quiet with weight.

The Appalachian Mountains hold onto sound in strange ways. Whispers carry. Footsteps echo where they shouldn't. And then there are nights when the woods seem to press inward, like the dark itself is holding a breath.

That's when the voices begin.

Not human voices.
Not animal.
Something in between.
Something that belongs to the terrain in the way fog belongs to hollers.

Hunters call it **"chatter."**
Locals call it **"the mumbling."**
Some say **"the woods talking back."**
Others say simply, "Don't listen too close."

Whatever name people use, they're all describing the same thing:

A sound like speech — but not in any language people recognize.

The First Time I Heard the Appalachian "Chatter" Described

The first version of this story came from a man who lived near the Tennessee–North Carolina border. We were talking about night sounds, and he leaned forward like he was about to share something he didn't do often.

"You know how people whisper to each other?" he asked. "Quiet, fast-like, not loud enough to hear the words?"

I nodded.

"That's what it sounds like. Except it's coming from two places in the dark. Back and forth. Almost like arguing."

He made a gesture with his fingers, like two hands sewing threads.

"That fast," he said. "That smooth."

"Could it be people?" I asked.

He shook his head firmly.

"Not where I was. No trails near. No camps. Nothing but steep timber and deadfall. No one would be out there in the pitch black."

He paused, then added something I've since heard from many others:

"It sounded smart."

Not animal noise.
Not instinctive.
Intentional.

"That's why folks don't talk about it much," he said. "Nobody wants to sound crazy."

What Makes the Appalachian Voices Different

All across North America, strange vocalizations get reported in the wilderness — howls, screams, knocks. But the Appalachians have something else layered into the soundscape:

Human-like vocal patterns.

Not words.
Not syllables.
But something close enough to speech that the mind recognizes a pattern.

Here's what witnesses describe consistently:

1. Two-toned "arguments"

Two distinct voices.
Rapid.
Low-pitched.
Conversational rhythm.

2. Whispers that move

Not wind.
Not insects.
A whisper that travels — left to right, uphill to downhill.

3. Mumbling close to camp

Not loud enough to scare.
Just close enough to unsettle.

4. Deep-chest resonance

Like someone with a powerful voice speaking from just inside a tree line.

5. Mimicking

Whistles.
Single-syllable calls.
Short sounds that copy the cadence of human speech without using recognizable words.

People who hear these sounds are often outdoors early in the morning or late at night — hours when the forest is quiet enough to expose anything unusual.

And once you've heard something that sounds almost human, but not quite…
it stays with you.

The Whisper Ridge Incident

There's a ridge near the West Virginia–Virginia line that hunters simply call "Whisper Ridge." Not because of ghost stories. Not because of folklore.

Because of what people hear there.

The story goes that two brothers were camping along that ridge in late October. They were seasoned woodsmen — not kids, not inexperienced hikers. They'd spent thousands of hours outdoors.

Around two in the morning, they woke to what they thought were two men talking outside their tent.

"They were whispering," one of the brothers later said. "One low, one higher, going back and forth quick-like. I couldn't make out a single word, but the rhythm was there."

They unzipped the tent, expecting maybe another pair of hikers or someone lost.

But there was no firelight.
No flashlight.
No silhouette.
Just total darkness.

The whispering stopped instantly.

Then came a different sound — a low, resonant hum that vibrated the ground under them. Not loud. Not aggressive.

But deep.

The brothers stayed silent until dawn. In the morning light, they found no tracks, no signs of people, no reason for anyone to be out there.

One of them told me, "Whatever was doing the talking, it sure wasn't human."

A Ranger's Story: "I Heard Two of Them Talking"

Rangers in the Appalachians don't often talk about strange encounters. But every once in a while, you find one who isn't afraid to be honest.

A ranger in the Smokies told me about a night he was doing a routine check on a remote trailhead. The air was still. Fog was settling. The world was quiet.

Then he heard voices up the trail.

Not hikers — he would've seen their lights.
Not kids — the nearest campsite was miles away.
Not a single person — **two voices**.

One deep.
One sharper.

They weren't whispering, but they were speaking low, almost like two men trying not to be overheard.

"I froze," he said. "It wasn't English. It wasn't Spanish. It wasn't anything I recognized. It didn't even sound like language — but the tones were right."

He flicked off his flashlight.
Stood perfectly still.
Listened.

The voices went back and forth for about thirty seconds — calm, steady, measured — then stopped.

Not faded.
Stopped.

He waited for movement. Footsteps. Branch snapping. Something.

Nothing came.

"It was like they just... ended," he said. "Like the sound shut off."

When he walked up the trail, there were no tracks. No scent. No disturbance.

Just the forest, silent and waiting.

He told me, "I didn't put that in my report. Some things you keep for yourself."

The Mumbling Outside Cabins

One of the more common Appalachian encounter types happens around cabins. Not the modern rental cabins with hot tubs and security lights — the old ones. The ones tucked at the edge of a slope, with dark windows and a single porch light barely pushing back the night.

Many of these encounters share the same pattern:

1. A sound like someone talking outside.

Low.
Unclear.
Like a one-sided conversation.

2. The family dog goes rigid.

Not barking.
Not running.
Just *listening*.

3. The footsteps come next.

Slow.
Heavy.
Two-legged.

4. Then silence.

A silence so complete it feels heavy in the chest.

A man near Marion, Virginia described it perfectly:

"It sounded like somebody walking around out there talking to himself. But when I opened the door, nothing was there. Not even the crickets."

His wife added, "Something was watching. You could feel it."

The Whistle That Should Not Echo

Whistles are another Appalachian signature.

Short.
High.
Sharp.
But not quite human.

One hiker near Seneca Rocks told me about hearing a whistle while walking through early evening fog. It came from the left side of the trail — a clear, quick note, like someone signaling.

He stopped and listened.

A moment later, a second whistle answered from the right side of the trail.

Two different pitches.
Two different distances.
Two distinct voices.

He tried to whistle back out of curiosity.

Both voices went silent immediately.

That silence stretched long enough for him to feel the weight of something watching from both sides.

"I knew then it wasn't people," he said. "People would've laughed or whistled again."

The Imitation Problem: When Something Copies You

One of the most unsettling types of vocal encounters is mimicry.
Something in the Appalachians imitates human sounds — not perfectly,
but close.

A single "Hey!" shouted from the woods

Too sharp.
Too loud.
Too short.

A cough that sounds almost natural

But forced.
Like something copying the cadence without understanding the purpose.

Footsteps matching yours

Not a voice, but a kind of vocal proxy — a form of communication
through rhythm.

A whistle that repeats your whistle

Off by just enough to signal intelligence.

One man near Logan told me he once heard someone mimic his own
voice.

He had called for his dog: "Hunter! Here boy!"

About ten seconds later, something in the woods repeated the call.

Not perfectly.
Not clearly.

A rough echo of the same words — shaped like speech, broken like an
imitation.

The tone was deeper.
The cadence wrong.
But the intention unmistakable.

"That wasn't an echo," he said. "It was something trying to say what I said."

He moved out of that house within a year.

What Locals Believe the Voices Mean

Locals don't all agree on what makes the strange chatter, whistles, and mumbling. But their explanations fall into three categories:

1. Communication between creatures

The voices sound too patterned to be random noise.

2. Warning signals

Some hunters believe the creatures use whistles to alert one another when humans are nearby.

3. Curiosity

A number of encounters happen when people are sitting still — as if the creatures approach intentionally.

One old-timer near Wise, Virginia put it simply:

"They talk. Not like us. But they do talk."

Why "Mumbling" Matters More Than Screams or Howls

Screams and howls get attention.
They go viral.
People talk about them online or compare them to known animals.

But "mumbling" is different.

It's subtle.
It's controlled.
It feels intentional.

People describe it as:

- "Talking under their breath"

- "Arguing quietly"

- "Two men whispering fast"

- "Something thinking out loud"

- "Soft gibberish"

- "Words that don't exist"

And here's what stands out:

**The mumbling almost always happens when the witness is alone —
and quiet.**

It's as if the creature wants to communicate without revealing itself.

This is the same pattern you've documented firsthand in Ontario:

- Whisper-like sounds

- Low conversation between entities

- Movement paired with vocalization

- Intelligent pacing

The Appalachians show the same behavior.

Different region.
Same phenomenon.
Same intelligence.

Why This Behavior Points to Something Real

Biologists who study primates often note that **complex communication evolves in species with social structures** — gorillas, chimps, orangutans, humans.

The Appalachian chatter has:

- conversation rhythm

- back-and-forth exchange

- differing tones

- mimicry

- intentional pauses

- context-based silence

This is not random noise.

And the most important detail?

Witnesses isolated from each other describe it in the same way.

Across thousands of miles.
Across decades.
Across generations.

Hunters in West Virginia tell the same story as campers in Georgia, as rangers in Tennessee, as locals in the Carolinas.

Something is communicating out there.

Whether we understand it or not is irrelevant.
It exists.

The Night the Chatter Surrounded the Campsite

A pair of hikers in the Monongahela National Forest told me about
setting up camp near a creek. The evening was quiet, the air cool. Around
11 p.m., they began hearing chatter.

Not from one direction — from three.

Left.
Right.
And across the creek.

Low voices, fast-paced, talking over each other like a heated debate.

The men froze.
Their fire snapped.
The chatter paused — all at once.

Then resumed again, quieter, as if observing them.

"It felt like they were deciding what we were," one of the hikers said.

There were no footsteps.
No silhouettes.
Just the sound of communication in the dark.

Around 2 a.m., everything stopped.
The forest reset.
Normal night sounds returned.

They packed up at first light and left the area without speaking.

Some places are not meant for sleeping.

The Chatter That Followed a Truck

One of the strangest reports I've ever heard came from a man driving a
pickup along a narrow backroad in southwestern Virginia. His windows
were down. It was late. The woods pressed in close.

As he drove, he heard something above the engine noise:

Chatter.
Soft.
Fast.
Close.

He slowed.
The chatter slowed.

He sped up.
The chatter kept pace.

Finally, he stopped the truck completely.
The chatter stopped too.

"I felt like something was running alongside me, talking to itself," he said. "Or talking to someone else I couldn't see."

When he got home, he said his shirt smelled like wet dirt and musk.

He threw it out.

Why the Voices Are the Key to the Mystery

Tracks can be faked.
Photos can be blurred.
Stories can be exaggerated.

But vocal patterns?
Those are hard to invent consistently across states, decades, and witnesses.

The Appalachian voices represent something deeper:

- intelligence

- communication

- coordination

- curiosity

- awareness

- social behavior

In Ontario, you've heard similar sounds yourself — that strange "murmuring" that doesn't match any known animal.

Now imagine that same sound stretching from Georgia to Pennsylvania.

Thousands of square miles.
Millions of acres of forest.
Endless hollers, ridges, and valleys.

All carrying the same voice.

Something intelligent.
Something social.
Something that doesn't want to be seen...
but wants to talk.

The Mountains Are Speaking

The deeper you move into the Appalachian Mountains, the more you realize the forest isn't quiet.
It only pretends to be.

And the voices — the whistles, the chatter, the mumbling — are not random.

They are patterns.
They are habits.
They are evidence.

Not of a monster hiding in the trees,
but of a species communicating in the dark.

A species that watches.
A species that listens.

A species that mimics.
A species that speaks in ways we don't understand yet.

In the next chapter, we explore **the places where these voices converge — the hotspots where sightings, whispers, shadow figures, and disappearances overlap.**

Because every voice in these mountains comes from somewhere.

And the deeper you go, the more you realize:

The mountains aren't quiet.
They're talking.

Chapter Seven — The Appalachian Hotspots: Where All Mysteries Converge

Hotspots aren't random. They never are.
Whether you're talking Bigfoot, strange lights in the sky, unexplained voices, vanishings, or sightings of shadow-like figures slipping between the trees, patterns always form if you look long enough.

And in the Appalachian Mountains, those patterns form in specific places — pockets of land where multiple mysteries overlap so frequently that even the old-timers shrug and say:

"Yeah… things happen up there."

This chapter is about those places.
The hollers, ridgelines, creek bottoms, and forgotten towns where the strange piles up like driftwood after a storm.
Places with too many stories, too much repetition, too much unease to chalk up to coincidence.

These hotspots don't exist because the land is haunted.
They exist because something uses the land — something intelligent and familiar with every inch of it.

When you look at a map of Appalachia and start marking encounters — Bigfoot, voices, lights, disappearances — the clusters become visible.

They form a spine through the mountains.

A whispering line.
A shadow corridor.

A place where the wilderness feels one step ahead of you.

Why Hotspots Exist in the First Place

Patterns in the wilderness aren't accidental. They're created by environment and behavior.

Hotspots form where these conditions overlap:

1. Steep terrain with limited human access

Places too dangerous, too remote, or too rugged for casual foot travel.

2. Dense vegetation

Rhododendron "hells," old-growth hardwoods, thick spruce stands.

3. High food availability

Deer, small animals, berries, fungus, underground roots.

4. Water corridors

Creeks, streams, wetlands, springs.

5. Old infrastructure

Rail beds, coal roads, logging cuts, abandoned mines.

6. Low population density

Few houses. Fewer lights. Almost no night activity.

When you combine these elements, you get natural refuges — not for humans, but for whatever else roams these mountains.

The hotspots aren't random.
They're strategic.

And when mysteries stack up in one place, you start to realize the land itself might not be the only reason.

Something might be choosing these areas.

Hotspot #1: The Blue Ridge Dark Corridor (VA/NC)

Between Boone, North Carolina and Floyd, Virginia lies one of the most active strips of forest on the entire East Coast. The Blue Ridge Parkway cuts along the spine, offering beautiful overlooks during the day… and unsettling silence at night.

What happens here:

- Bigfoot sightings on roadside pull-offs

- Strange lights drifting low between ridges

- Whispered voices heard near campgrounds

- Cabin knocks reported throughout the high country

- Shadow figures crossing the road at dusk

- Vanishings — not many, but the ones that happen leave no clear explanation

A ranger once told me:

"The woods feel different up here. Like you're not alone even when you are."

The combination of elevation, fog, and almost claustrophobic tree cover creates the perfect environment for something to watch without being seen.

One man even reported seeing a large silhouette walking parallel to his car for nearly half a mile — visible only when lightning flashed during a storm.

No tracks found.
No footprints.
Just the memory of a shape keeping pace in the dark.

Hotspot #2: Monongahela Shadow Belt (WV)

If the Appalachian Mountains have a beating, mysterious heart, it's the Monongahela National Forest.
Nearly a million acres of wilderness.
Almost no light at night.
Steep, unforgiving ridges.
Deep valleys where sound disappears.

This is where the **Ridgewalker** lives.
Or at least where people see it most.

Activity in the Shadow Belt:

- Heavy footsteps pacing hikers

- Voices speaking from opposite ridgelines

- Tracks found in impossible terrain

- Whistles that mimic human calls

- Large, silent figures crossing forest roads

- Hunters stalked from the treeline

- Campsites circled late at night

- Sudden, absolute silence before encounters

Monongahela isn't a place where strange things *occasionally* happen.
It's a place where strange things are part of the ecosystem.

One hunter told me:

"If you sleep out here alone, you'll hear something. The question ain't if — it's what."

You won't find that printed on any tourism brochure.

Hotspot #3: The High Knob Triangle (Southwest Virginia)

Centered around High Knob, Norton, and Big Stone Gap, this area is home to one of Appalachia's most famous regional creatures: the Woodbooger.

But the hotspot goes beyond creature sightings.

The triangle includes:

- old coal roads

- cemeteries sinking into hillside forest

- ridge-top meadows

- fog-heavy hollers

- forgotten mining outposts

- tiny, unlit towns tucked between sharp slopes

Reports from the High Knob Triangle include:

- Two-legged pacing on ridges

- Mumbling heard outside cabins

- Shadow figures at scenic overlooks

- Half-whistled calls near creek bottoms

- "Talking" heard deep in the pines

- Tracks leading up slopes too steep for humans

- Hunters reporting being watched from above

A woman near Wise told me:

"It don't feel bad. Just old. Like something been living here longer than people."

When a region produces decades of similar reports, you stop dismissing them.
You start connecting them.

Hotspot #4: The North Georgia Black Ridge

The North Georgia mountains often get overshadowed by the Smokies to the north, but locals know these woods have their own personality — darker, heavier, and full of stories no one brings up around strangers.

What witnesses report here:

- Black, fast-moving silhouettes

- High-pitched whistles that travel uphill

- Heavy steps that stop when you stop

- Growl-like chatter — deep, rapid mumbling

- Deer found torn apart in ways that don't match predators

- Trail cameras triggered but capturing nothing

One hunter described seeing "a tall shadow step across a ridge like it weighed nothing."
Another claimed he saw glowing eyes at a height "taller than his ATV."

The hotspot centers around Blood Mountain, Suches, Dahlonega, and the Chattahoochee highlands — places where fog rolls in quick, trails vanish into rhododendron tunnels, and night falls hard.

Hotspot #5: The Tennessee River Bluffs

Eastern Tennessee holds one of the strangest overlaps of phenomena anywhere in the Appalachians:

- Bigfoot encounters

- Strange lights

- "Buzzing" sounds no agency can explain

- Disappearances

- Voices heard in dense fog

- Shadow figures on bluff edges

- Scent events (wet musk, ammonia, decaying vegetation)

This region is unique because of the cliffs and water system — steep limestone bluffs overlooking deep river gorges, with narrow trails that offer perfect vantage points.

One fisherman told me he heard "a long conversation" happening across the water one night — two distinct voices echoing across the gorge, neither sounding human.

Another man described a large figure standing on a cliff edge at dusk, outlined in dim orange light. When he blinked, it was gone.

People don't embellish encounters here.
They simply recount them the way you recount the weather.

"Yeah, saw somethin' up on the ridge last week."
"Somethin' moved behind the rock wall while we were fishin'."
"Somethin' big paced us for a mile."

This hotspot is alive almost every night.

Hotspot #6: The Pennsylvania–Maryland Line (The "Mooncall Spine")

The northern reaches of Appalachia have their own pocket of high strangeness, especially where the mountains narrow into the ridges along the PA/MD border.

Locals call it the **Mooncall Spine** — a line of steep, narrow ridges packed tight with old-growth pines.

Here, people report:

- long-distance vocal calls at night

- howls with human shape but non-human power

- midnight "talking" drifting down mountainsides

- sudden appearance of large tracks in moss

- figures watching hunters from rock outcrops

- tree knocks that come from two directions at once

- shadows seen on full-moon nights

One hiker said he heard "a dozen voices talking in the trees" around 3 a.m.
Another reported hearing something large moving between the boulders but never saw what it was.

This hotspot doesn't get as much attention as the southern mountains, but the density of encounters is shocking once you start collecting them.

The mountains narrow here.
Everything is closer.
Everything funnels into the same space.

Which means whatever is living out there can move through this region more efficiently than anywhere else.

Hotspot #7: The Kentucky Coal Hollers

Eastern Kentucky has a reputation.
Some of it's folklore.
Some of it's fact.

Coal country produces some of the most unsettling stories you'll hear anywhere in Appalachia.
Not because people exaggerate, but because the land itself creates conditions that amplify the strange.

Coal hollers are:

- dark

- steep

- often abandoned

- crisscrossed with mine shafts

- heavy with mist

- rich with animal life

- sparsely populated

- cut off from easy access

These stretches of land generate reports of:

- two-legged figures crossing mining roads

- shadow forms leaning out from rock outcrops

- mumbling heard near abandoned shafts

- whistling on nights with no wind

- lights drifting between slopes

- old-timers seeing "the big dark man" near creek bottoms

- dogs refusing to go near certain hollers

A man from Pike County told me:

"There's places where the land don't feel right. You ain't supposed to stay long in those hollers."

In these hotspots, even the locals keep their distance.

Why These Hotspots Connect

Hotspots aren't isolated.
They form a network — a chain.

Look at the Appalachian spine on a map:
Ridges stack like dominoes for nearly a thousand miles.
Hollows run deep.
Rivers cut narrow passages.
Vegetation stays thick year-round.
Fog pools in the same valleys almost every morning.

Now consider something intelligent living here — something that knows ridgelines better than people.

It could move from hotspot to hotspot without ever being seen.

The same creatures spotted in Georgia could show up in North Carolina.
The same ones from Virginia could migrate toward West Virginia.
The same Ridgewalkers could slip north into Pennsylvania.

This is a **connected corridor** — not isolated pockets.

And that corridor is ancient.

The Role of Fog in Every Hotspot

The strangest link between all hotspots isn't tracks or sightings.

It's **fog**.

Fog behaves differently in these regions:

- It moves horizontally even on windless days.

- It curls around trees like fingers.

- It hides shapes perfectly.

- It muffles voices.

- It distorts distance.

- It amplifies some sounds and kills others.

- It creates separation even when you're alone.

People describe seeing shapes moving inside fog banks.
Silhouettes that vanish when the fog shifts.
Footsteps that sound close even when nothing is visible.

Fog is the perfect cover for something that wants to be seen only when it chooses.

And hotspots are where the fog gathers the deepest.

The Places People Avoid

Every region has places locals avoid after sunset.
In Appalachia, those places aren't just spooky.

They're active.

Places where:

- cabins get knocked on

- hunters get followed

- whistle calls echo

- mumbling rises from slopes

- shadows cross roads

- silhouettes watch from ridges

- strange lights drift in total silence

- search teams lose the trail of missing people

When rural folks — the ones who have spent their entire lives in the woods — won't go somewhere after dark, you should pay attention.

Old-timers don't exaggerate.
They minimize.

So when they say things like:

"That hollow ain't right."
"Don't stay up on that ridge after sunset."
"That place got watchers."
"Things move up there at night."

They aren't telling folklore.
They're telling survival lessons.

Every Hotspot Has a Keeper

In each hotspot, one thing remains constant:

A presence.

Not a ghost.
Not a spirit.
Not a monster.

A living, breathing presence.

A creature that:

- uses the fog

- knows the trails

- mimics voices

- knocks on trees

- understands the terrain

- tracks humans silently

- moves in pairs or groups

- communicates through whistles and chatter

- leaves footprints only when it chooses

- disappears uphill without sound

The Appalachian hotspots aren't random clusters of weirdness.

They're territories.

Territories held, patrolled, and inhabited by something that's been here far longer than the cabins, coal roads, and trail signs.

The hotspots mark the frontier of these creatures' home range.

Why Hotspots Matter

Hotspots are where the truth hides.

If you want to understand the Appalachians, you don't go to the tourist trails.
You go to:

- the hollows with no cell service

- the ridges with no safe footing

- the forests with no noise

- the creeks with no clear path out

- the old mining roads swallowed by vines

- the fog banks that never seem to lift

- the places where locals shake their heads and say, "Don't go lookin' for trouble."

Hotspots are the heart of the mystery.

And when multiple independent phenomena converge in the same patches of land — creatures, lights, voices, vanishings — you don't dismiss it.

You map it.
You track it.
You study it.

Hotspots are the key to understanding what walks these mountains.

Because whatever these creatures are...
they choose these places for a reason.

And the deeper you move into each hotspot, the more you realize:

You're not exploring empty land.
You're entering someone else's territory.

**Chapter Eight — Missing on the Mountain: The Disappearances &
Vanishing Phenomenon**

Disappearances in the Appalachian Mountains don't behave like normal
missing-person cases.
Most missing people wander off trail, get lost in bad weather, or make
simple mistakes. Search teams find tracks, clothing, debris, heat
signatures — some trace of their route or final moments.

But in certain parts of Appalachia — especially the deep hollers, ridge
corridors, and fog-saturated valleys — people don't just go missing.

They vanish.

Not in the dramatic, sensational sense.
In the quiet sense.
The **unnatural** sense.

One minute they're on a well-traveled trail.
The next minute... nothing.
No tracks.
No calls for help.
No scent trail for dogs.
Not even disturbed brush.

These events aren't folklore.
They're documented — through ranger notes, search team logs,
interviews with families, and whispered conversations among locals
who've seen the patterns all their lives.

Disappearances here share a strange consistency:
The person simply steps out of the world, leaving behind a silence
thicker than the fog.

And the mountains don't give them back.

Why the Appalachians Are a Perfect Disappearance Machine

To understand the vanishings, you have to understand the land.

Appalachia — especially the central and southern regions — is built like a maze:

- **hollers that dead-end for miles**

- **ridges that cut sharp and drop without warning**

- **natural sinkholes hidden beneath leaves**

- **old mine shafts covered in decades of debris**

- **vegetation so thick it swallows tracks instantly**

- **switchback trails that confuse even GPS**

But here's the part that stands out:

Most vanishings do **not** occur in the most dangerous areas.
They occur in places where people *should* be safe.

That's what makes these cases different.
People aren't misjudging terrain.

They're stepping into something else.

Case Pattern #1: The "Silent Step-Off"

A man is walking ahead of his hiking partner.
He turns a corner.
And then… nothing.

By the time the partner reaches the bend — usually within 10–20 seconds — the first hiker is gone.

No sound.
No cry for help.
No footprints leading anywhere unusual.
Just absence.

This pattern repeats across:

- West Virginia

- Virginia

- North Carolina

- Tennessee

- Georgia

- Pennsylvania

A ranger in the Smokies once described it like this:

"It's like they walked off the trail into a wall of air."

These aren't reckless hikers.
These are experienced outdoorsmen.
People who leave behind **no trace**.

This phenomenon mirrors cases you've studied in Canada: the sudden silence, the disappearance without tracks, the overwhelming sense of being watched just before it happens.

The mountains take people quietly.

Case Pattern #2: The "Clothes in a Line" Phenomenon

Some cases end in discovery — but the discoveries raise more questions than they solve.

Rangers and search teams in the Appalachians report a disturbing pattern: Missing hikers are later found with their clothes removed and placed **in a neat line** or scattered in specific patterns.

Not torn off by animals.
Not ripped by branches.

Placed.

Boots arranged side by side.
Pants folded.
Shirt draped over a log.
Backpack untouched.

Bodies are sometimes found nearby.
Sometimes not found at all.

This pattern appears in:

- West Virginia's Cranberry Wilderness

- The Blue Ridge corridors in Virginia

- The Nantahala Forest in North Carolina

No one has a satisfying explanation.

Hypothermia can cause people to shed clothing — but not fold them.
Not arrange boots.
Not place items with deliberate spacing.

Something else is at work.

Case Pattern #3: The "Vanished Child, Found in Impossible Place"

This is one of the oldest Appalachian patterns.

A child disappears for only minutes — from a yard, a campsite, a creek where adults are near. Search teams find nothing. Then, hours or days later, the child is found miles away, often at high elevation, sometimes across steep terrain no child could travel.

One famous example comes from the Tennessee–North Carolina border near the Smokies:

A toddler vanished from a campsite.
Dozens of searchers combed the immediate area.
A day later, the child was found high on a ridge nearly seven miles away — unharmed, clean, not dehydrated, wearing all clothing.

Searchers said reaching that spot required navigating boulder fields and deadfall so thick even adults struggled.

The child told rescuers:

"Big man carried me."

He didn't describe a ranger.
Not a hiker.
Not a stranger.

A "big man."

Parents insisted there were no other campers nearby. Rangers confirmed.

Stories like this appear across Appalachia dating back 150+ years.

The pattern is always the same:

- a child slips away

- the forest goes silent

- the child reappears someplace impossible

Adults vanish too — but they never come back.

Children do.

Case Pattern #4: The Fog Wall

This pattern is so common it borders on its own category.

Witnesses describe:

- fog pouring into a trail unnaturally fast

- visibility dropping to a few feet

- an overwhelming feeling of being watched

- disorientation lasting only minutes

- senses going dull and sharp at the same time

Then the fog lifts and someone is gone.

Search teams report arriving on-site within 10–20 minutes, only to find:

- no tracks

- no broken branches

- no drag marks

- no scent for dogs

- no sign of struggle

Fog that moves with purpose is not weather.

The Appalachians use fog the way a predator uses darkness.

A Ranger's Story: "It Should've Left Tracks"

One ranger from the West Virginia–Virginia border told me about a missing hunter found weeks after he disappeared. The man's bow was found leaning against a tree. His boots were found together on a moss patch. His shirt lay folded beside a stump.

His body was later discovered deep in the forest — in a place search teams had already checked.

"There were no tracks," the ranger said. "Not a single one. No sign he walked there. No sign anything dragged him. It's like he appeared."

When I asked him what he personally believed happened, he looked down at the gravel at his feet.

"We know about the bears. We know about the snakes. We know about the cliffs. We've accounted for all the natural stuff. But this…" He paused. "…This is something else."

He didn't say Bigfoot.
He didn't have to.

The Appalachian "Return Zone"

Some vanishings result in remains being found months later in areas
previously searched thoroughly. Search teams mark off zones, sweep
them, grid them, return later — and suddenly the remains appear where
none existed before.

A search organizer from Pennsylvania told me:

"We had fifty people walk that ridge. We had dogs. We had helicopters.
Nothing. Three weeks later the body shows up on the exact ridge we
cleared."

No animals bring bodies uphill.
Not over time.
Not without leaving drag marks.
Not without scattering remains.

These aren't overlooked finds.
They're **placed**.

Almost as if something waited until the search cooled down.

A Story from a Family in North Carolina

A woman from Haywood County told me about her cousin, who
vanished while hiking a well-marked trail. The group was taking photos.
Her cousin stepped a few yards off the trail to look at a rock outcrop.

He never came back.

Search teams found:

• no tracks

- no scent

- no broken brush

- no sign of struggle

- no remains ever

But what stuck with the family most was something the woman's grandfather said the day after the disappearance:

"He got took."

No one asked, *took by what?*

In these mountains, you don't ask questions you don't want answers to.

The Strange Behavior of Scent Dogs

Appalachian search teams rely heavily on the skill of scent dogs. These dogs can track across:

- rain

- wind

- rock

- dense forest

- steep ledges

But in disappearance hotspots, dogs show unnatural behavior.

Handlers report:

- dogs refusing to follow trails

- dogs freezing and whining

- dogs refusing to cross certain fog lines

- dogs walking in circles

- dogs becoming suddenly quiet

- dogs sitting down and staring uphill

- dogs showing fear without aggression

One handler told me:

"My dog's tracked criminals across swamps and tornados. But whatever was in that hollow? She refused to go in."

Animals know long before humans do.

When Groups Go Silent

Some disappearances include a chilling moment that witnesses remember vividly:

the sudden drop in sound.

No birds.
No insects.
No wind.
No movement.

A silence so complete it lasts in people's memories like trauma.

After the silence, the missing person is simply gone.

A man from Bristol described hiking with a friend when the woods went silent.

"It felt like the forest held its breath," he said. "Right after that, he stepped ahead on the trail and… he wasn't there anymore."

No scream.
No rustling.
Just absence.

He waited, thinking his friend was joking.
Then the fear hit.

Search teams found nothing.

He has never hiked again.

The Vanishings Near Water

Water plays a consistent role in Appalachian disappearances.

People vanish near:

- waterfalls

- creek crossings

- fog-heavy basins

- moss-covered rock edges

- deep pools

- ravines with trickling streams

And here's the disturbing part:

Objects belonging to the missing are sometimes found arranged near water — in patterns.

This matches patterns in other regions you've studied — particularly the strange way some cases near Ontario waterways involve clothing or gear left in deliberate placement.

Water reflects sound. Fog collects at water sources.
Something uses that to its advantage.

Case Pattern #5: The "One Shoe Found" Mystery

Multiple Appalachian disappearances feature this strange detail:

- both shoes worn at time of disappearance

- only one found

- the other never recovered

- sometimes the missing shoe appears in a location already searched

- sometimes it is found pristine and placed upright

If the missing person died naturally, both shoes should be with the body or missing due to scavengers. But when a single shoe appears in an unexplainable location, search coordinators take note.

One investigator privately told me:

"When you find one shoe, you know the case is going to be weird."

A Local Sheriff's Warning

A sheriff in rural West Virginia once told me something simple, said with the kind of weight that only comes from experience:

"The mountains take who they want."

He wasn't being poetic.
He was being literal.

He told me he'd worked cases where people vanished from within twenty yards of their family. Others were seasoned outdoorsmen who never made it back to camp. A few were experienced hunters found miles from where their trail should've led — without any sign of how they traveled that far.

He said the strangest cases always shared the same elements:

- fog

- silence

- ridgeline shadows

- no tracks

- no logical exit

Then he added:

"Whatever takes 'em… knows these woods better than we do."

That's the line that stuck.

The Role of the Backwoods Voices

In regions with the highest number of disappearances, people also report:

- mumbling

- chatter

- whistles

- mock calls

- pacing in the dark

- heavy breaths from tree lines

- calls repeated from two hillsides at once

The overlap is undeniable.

Voices and vanishings happen in the same areas.

This is not random.

Voices precede silence.
Silence precedes disappearance.

Something communicates.
Something approaches.
Something chooses.

And once someone crosses a certain threshold — physical or otherwise — the mountain swallows them.

The deeper you look into the data, the more the Appalachian vanishings resemble coordinated behavior.

Maybe not predatory in the traditional sense.
But intentional.

Something watches from the ridges.
Something listens in the fog.
Something moves silently behind you on the trail.

And sometimes, it closes the distance.

When the Land Takes Someone Back

There are cases — rare, but real — where a missing person reappears with no memory of where they were.

A hunter in Georgia vanished for nine hours. When found, he was sitting calmly beside a creek miles from where he should've been. Search teams had already passed that area multiple times.

The hunter said:

"I heard voices. Thought it was y'all calling. But when I got closer... it wasn't people."

His eyes went distant as he recounted the rest:

"I saw a shape standing between the trees. Tall. Dark. Didn't move. I remember watching it. Then everything went white."

No drugs.
No injury.
No dehydration.

Just a blank space in his memory.

He moved out of state within a month.

What Makes Appalachian Disappearances Unique

These mountain vanishings share traits with wilderness cases in Alaska, British Columbia, and Northern Ontario — but Appalachia has its own signatures.

The Appalachian disappearance profile:

- sudden loss of sound

- fog intake before event

- clothing anomalies

- one-shoe discoveries

- dogs refusing to track

- children found in unreachable areas

- adults never found

- belongings placed, not dropped

- cases happening close to companions

- reappearance of remains in searched areas

- witnesses hearing "talking" beforehand

When all these traits occur together, you're not dealing with a simple accident.

You're dealing with something that can:

- approach silently

- remove a person without struggle

- navigate terrain with unnatural skill

- confuse dogs

- avoid helicopters

- understand pursuit patterns

- return to the area once searchers leave

- place items deliberately

No known predator does this.
No known human group does this with this level of consistency.

Whatever causes these disappearances has intelligence.

And that intelligence knows the mountains like a second skin.

What Rangers Won't Say Publicly

Rangers, sheriffs, search coordinators — they know the patterns. But they can't say certain things officially. Liability. Panic. Reputation. Politics.

But privately?

You hear phrases like:

"Something's out there."
"I've seen shadows that weren't people."
"The forest goes dead before something happens."
"There are places we don't send rookies."
"Search areas change shape at night."
"We're not the only ones on the trail."

And one ranger told me a line I'll never forget:

"We're tracking something that knows it's being tracked."

That's not how a forest behaves.
That's how an intelligent creature behaves.

The Appalachians Don't Lose People — They Keep Them

In many wilderness areas, disappearances happen because of:

- exposure

- wildlife

- terrain hazards

- wrong turns

- storms

In Appalachia?

People vanish in good weather, on safe trails, within sight of friends, often within hearing range of entire campgrounds.

Something takes people here.

The mountains don't just hide them.

The mountains **hold** them.

Truth Hides in Patterns

The more cases you study, the clearer the truth becomes:

- voices

- whistles

- shadow figures

- heavy steps

- fog

- silence

- one-shoe finds

- clothing arrangements

- impossible travel

- dogs refusing

- reappearances in searched areas

- disappearances mid-step

These are not independent mysteries.

They are symptoms of a single phenomenon.
A living phenomenon.

Something walks these mountains.
Something watches from the ridges.
Something studies people the way researchers study wildlife.

And sometimes, when the moment is right…
it takes someone.

Not maliciously.
Not randomly.

Deliberately.

In the next chapter, we shift from disappearances to **strange lights and sky anomalies** — the disturbances bridging ground and air, reported across the same hotspots, often on the same nights as the vanishings.

Because in Appalachia, the mysteries don't compete.

They overlap.

Chapter Nine — The Lights Above the Trees: Sky Phenomena in the Appalachians

Most people come to the Appalachian Mountains expecting darkness.
The heavy kind.
The kind that feels thick enough to touch.
But if you stay long enough, you learn something else lives up there in the night — something above the trees, drifting through the valleys, moving silently along the ridgelines.

Lights.

Not stars.
Not aircraft.
Not lanterns.
Not anything that belongs to the sane and orderly world below.

The Appalachians have been a hotspot for strange aerial phenomena long before anyone used the term UFO. The mountains were old when the first settlers recorded "fire lights" drifting between the slopes. They were ancient when Cherokee and Yuchi stories described "star people" descending into the fog. And today, hikers, hunters, rangers, and locals continue reporting the same thing:

Lights moving in ways no aircraft should move — silently, intelligently, and often in tandem with strange events on the ground.

If the creatures of these mountains claim the ridges and hollers,
the lights claim the sky above them.

And sometimes, the two overlap in ways too consistent to ignore.

Why Sky Phenomena Matter in a Bigfoot Investigation

Most people separate cryptid research from UFO investigation. They treat them as different worlds, rarely overlapping.

But in Appalachia, that division doesn't hold.

The same hotspots that produce:

- Bigfoot sightings
- voices inside fog
- shadow figures
- vanishings

also produce:

- silent lights drifting low
- spheres hovering above ridges
- beams descending into hollers
- orbs pacing vehicles
- luminous shapes rising straight up
- glowing objects slipping into fog banks

Different phenomena.
Same locations.
Same time of night.

Patterns don't lie.

Something in these mountains connects the sky to the ground.

And whatever walks the slopes sometimes shares the night with something glowing just above the treeline.

The Old Stories: Fire in the Holler

Long before the internet, long before electric light, the earliest people to live here described strange aerial objects. Not in modern technological language, but in simple observational terms:

"Fire that walked."
"Lights that floated."
"Stars that moved through the valley."
"Sky lanterns with no flame."
"Balls of daylight."

These weren't mystics or storytellers — they were hunters, farmers, homesteaders. People who spent their days outdoors and knew the difference between natural and unnatural light.

One 19th-century account from western North Carolina described a "red globe the size of a barrel" rolling silently above the treetops. Another spoke of a "white orb drifting between the ridges like a lantern carried by a giant." Some stories mention lights entering caves or hovering over cliffs. Others report small blue spheres weaving between trees like insects made of electricity.

Nearly every old account ends with the same detail:

The lights made no sound.

That part hasn't changed.

Modern Encounters: The Silent Sky Movement

You find the same descriptions repeated today — but witnessed by people with smartphones, modern lighting knowledge, and the ability to distinguish planes, drones, helicopters, or distant town glow.

A hunter in West Virginia told me:

"I saw a white light hovering above the ridge. It was still — perfectly still — for almost a full minute. Then it shot straight up. Not sideways. Straight up. No sound. No trail. Just gone."

A ranger near Cades Cove in the Smokies said:

"There were three lights moving in a triangle. They weren't aircraft. I know what aircraft look like. These things glided like they were underwater. And then they blinked out at the same time — like someone flipped a switch."

A truck driver near Virginia's High Knob said he watched a glowing orb follow him from ridge to ridge until he reached town limits. It never descended. Never approached. Just followed the exact curve of the road from above, keeping pace like a silent escort.

He told me:

"I was scared to stop. If something keeps up with you at 90 kilometers an hour… it ain't human."

Hotspot #1: Brown Mountain — The Persistent Mystery

No place in Appalachia is more famous for its unexplained lights than **Brown Mountain** in North Carolina. People have documented luminous phenomena here for over a century — glowing orbs rising from the valleys, floating above the trees, then vanishing like blown-out candles.

Hunters describe the lights as:

- white

- yellow

- blue

- orange

- the size of basketballs

- drifting at chest height or above the trees

- moving with deliberate direction

Some nights, multiple lights rise at once.

Some nights, one light pulsates and dims.

Some nights, the lights seem to respond to movement or sound.

Scientists have tried to explain the Brown Mountain Lights as:

- swamp gas

- headlights

- ball lightning

- distant fires

- reflective minerals

Those explanations fall apart quickly.

Swamp gas doesn't rise in perfect spheres.
Headlights don't hover over cliffs.
Ball lightning doesn't last fifteen minutes.
Minerals don't drift up valleys.

Locals don't argue theories. They only say:

"Those lights been here longer than we have."

Hotspot #2: The New River Gorge — The Blue Spheres

In the deep cut valleys of the New River Gorge, people report small **blue or white orbs** that drift between the trees. They're smaller than the Brown Mountain lights — grapefruit-sized, quick-moving, and incredibly quiet.

Kayakers have seen them from the water.
Campers see them from bluffs.
Rangers see them from the road.

One ranger told me:

"They move like insects, but they're too bright, too smooth. They don't flicker like fireflies. They travel straight, change direction sharp, stop on a dime, then shoot away faster than anything I've ever seen."

Witnesses describe the orbs as:

- moving in pairs

- changing brightness

- circling campsites

- weaving through trees at impossible speeds

Some say the lights approach quietly. Others report feeling a sudden cold before an orb appears — a drop in temperature like the air itself is reacting.

If the Ridgewalker owns the ridges,
the blue lights own the air above them.

Hotspot #3: The Pennsylvania–Maryland "Mooncall Spine"

In Chapter 8, we explored this hotspot for shadow figures and chatter. But the Mooncall Spine is equally infamous for its sky phenomena — especially **large, slow-moving lights**.

Witness reports describe:

- white lights hovering

- beams shining downward into valleys

- red spheres drifting along ridgelines

- orange lights following hikers

- lights that split into two, then rejoin

One man hiking near the Mason–Dixon line said three lights followed him for almost an hour — trailing behind as he moved, then circling ahead when he stopped.

"They weren't drones," he said. "They didn't make a sound. And I was too far out for anyone to be flying one anyway."

Another hiker reported a light that hovered above him at night, illuminating the trees around him with a dim, unnatural glow.

"It wasn't a flashlight," he said. "It was like the air itself lit up."

Connection to the Ground Phenomena: The Lights & the Voices

Here's where things get disturbing.

In many hotspots, people report **lights on the same nights they hear the mumbling or chatter** described in earlier chapters.

Examples:

- A group of campers in West Virginia saw a white orb drifting down a valley just before hearing two deep voices "talking fast" from opposite ridges.

- A couple in Tennessee saw a large orange sphere hovering behind their cabin, followed minutes later by knocks on the wall and pacing footsteps.

- A hunter in Virginia saw two small blue balls of light moving uphill. Minutes later, he heard something breathing heavily from behind a fallen tree.

Lights in the sky.
Voices on the ground.
Both appearing in the same locations.

That's not a coincidence.

Something moves through these forests and something else — or perhaps **some part of the same phenomenon** — moves through the air above them.

And the mountains are the meeting point.

The Silent Approach

Many witnesses of Appalachian lights describe one terrifying trait:

The lights make no sound.

Not a hum.
Not a whir.
Not a pulse.
Not wind displacement.

Nothing.

Aircraft can mimic silence at a distance, but these lights are often seen:

- hovering 30–60 feet above ground

- drifting between trees

- following ridge contours

- approaching stationary witnesses

And yet, the forest remains perfectly still.

One hunter near Blood Mountain described it best:

"If it was mechanical, I'd have heard *something*. But the woods stayed dead quiet. The light moved. The trees didn't react. No rustle. No wind. Nothing."

Whatever these lights are, they don't behave like machines.

They behave like living things navigating space without disturbing it.

The "Intelligence Factor"

Across all regions, witnesses report something subtle:

The lights respond.

Not dramatically — no abductions, no Hollywood theatrics — but with unmistakable intelligence.

Examples:

- A whistle call causes a light to pulse.

- Flashing a flashlight twice makes a light move closer.

- A loud sound causes a light to retreat.

- Staying still causes a light to drift nearer.

- Speaking quietly results in a light stopping mid-air.

A man camping near Mount Mitchell said a bright sphere hovered above his campfire for nearly thirty seconds, dimming and brightening like it was studying the glow.

When he stepped toward it, it shot upward at an impossible angle.

"It wasn't a drone and it wasn't a star," he said. "It moved like it wanted to see me up close."

Most Appalachians don't speculate about aliens or advanced technology.

They use a simpler phrase:

"Something's watchin' from up there."

Lights During Disappearances

This is the darkest overlap of all.

Many Appalachian disappearances involve sky lights witnessed **before**, **during**, or **immediately after** someone goes missing.

Examples:

Case 1 — Tennessee, 1990s

A woman vanishes on a trail near a river.
Campers later report seeing a "bright orange sphere" hover above the river that night.
Rangers find no evidence connecting the two.
Locals insist it was related.

Case 2 — Pennsylvania, early 2000s

A boy disappears for nine hours, then reappears in an impossible location.
Multiple witnesses report "white lights" drifting along the ridge that evening.

Case 3 — West Virginia, 1970s

A hunter never returns from a day trip.
Search teams see "blue lights" flickering in the fog that night.
Some describe them as floating lanterns.
Others call them eyes.

Case 4 — Virginia, recent years

A man disappears for three days in a thickly wooded area.
People hear chatter and see pale orbs drifting quietly through the trees.

Certain details repeat so often they become impossible to ignore:

- fog

- silence

- lights

- voices

- vanishings

These elements are not separate mysteries.

They are symptoms of the same phenomenon.

What Locals Think the Lights Are

Locals rarely describe the lights as extraterrestrial.
Their explanations come from centuries of observation.

Common beliefs include:

1. "Mountain watchers."

Lights that observe without interfering.

2. "Spirit lights."

Old folklore, predating electricity.

3. "Ghost lanterns."

Connected to miners who died in collapses.

4. "The Sky People."

A term found in Cherokee legends.

5. "Signals."

Lights used to communicate between ridge and sky.

6. "The same thing that leaves the big tracks."

A belief held quietly but consistently — that the lights are connected to the creatures on the ground.

Most locals say the same thing:

"They ain't human. They ain't machines. They ain't ours."

Could the Lights and the Creatures Be Linked?

Patterns suggest something unsettling:

- The lights appear in Bigfoot hotspots.

- Bigfoot encounters happen on nights with lights.

- Voices in the woods occur when lights drift through fog.

- Disappearances cluster in areas with heavy aerial phenomena.

- Tracks appear on nights when lights hover low.

Is it the same phenomenon?
Two related species?
A behavior we don't understand?
A natural phenomenon that draws large creatures?
Or something far stranger?

The honest answer:
We don't know.

But one thing is certain:

Whatever these lights are, they interact with the environment the same way the ridge-walking creatures do — silently, intelligently, consistently.

And both phenomena have one thing in common:

They avoid humans, but not completely.
They observe us.

The Final Pattern: The Lights Retreat Into Fog

The most consistent trait of all:

The lights enter fog and vanish inside it.

Witnesses describe:

- lights slipping into a fog bank as if diving underwater

- glowing "bursts" inside thick mist

- fog glowing from within

- lights disappearing the moment fog thickens

Fog conceals them perfectly.

Fog and lights share a relationship the same way darkness and creatures do.

The mountains use fog as a door.
And the lights pass through that door as easily as a bird passes through air.

When you see a light enter fog in total silence, it's hard not to feel like you saw something step between worlds.

Conclusion: The Sky Is Alive in Appalachia

When you really start tracking the patterns — ridges, shadows, vanishings, voices, creatures — something becomes undeniable:

The Appalachians aren't just mysterious on the ground.
They're mysterious above the trees as well.

Something moves in the fog.
Something watches from the ridges.
Something drifts in the sky.
Something calls from the deep woods.
Something glows quietly just beyond reach.

Are these different phenomena?
Or one phenomenon with two halves?

The deeper you go into this region, the more those questions stop being separate.

And the more the land itself seems to say:

"Everything here is connected."

In the next chapter, we move from the sky back to the ground — into the **abandoned towns, ghost settlements, and forgotten places** where the strange lingers longest.

Because if the lights rule the sky…
something else rules the ruins.

Chapter Ten — Abandoned Towns & Ghost Settlements of Appalachia

The Appalachian Mountains hold ghosts — not always the supernatural kind, but the human kind.
Towns that lived, breathed, prospered, then died.
Rail lines built on sweat and coal that now sit twisted and rusting.
Company towns swallowed by vines.
Church steeples sinking into the soil.
Schools with broken windows staring out across empty valleys.

There are hundreds of these places scattered across the range.
Some appear on old maps.
Most do not.

Locals call them **the lost places**, or just "them old places up the holler."
They have a way of pulling you in — the history, the silence, the sense that something happened that nobody wants to talk about.

And in Appalachia, the abandoned places often sit in the same regions where the lights drift at night, where the voices whisper through fog, and where people vanish without leaving tracks.

Ruins and mysteries share the same geography.
The same hunger.
The same air.

This chapter isn't a ghost tour.
It's a walk through the forgotten settlements where the strange breathes strongest — where the wilderness didn't just reclaim the land… it replaced it with something else.

Why Abandoned Places in Appalachia Feel Different

Abandoned towns exist everywhere — the West has ghost mining camps, the North has forgotten logging settlements, the Midwest has railroad stops. But Appalachia's abandoned places have a very different atmosphere.

Here's why:

1. The mountains close in fast.

Within a few years of abandonment, nature swallows everything —
houses, churches, fences, even roads. Wood rots. Foundations sink. Trails
vanish.

2. Fog gathers in old towns like memory.

It clings low on the ground, filling the spaces between rotten beams and
collapsed roofs.

3. Sound behaves strangely.

Voices echo. Footsteps vanish into silence. Wind moves through broken
windows like someone breathing.

4. Wildlife avoids some settlements completely.

Deer, raccoons, even birds steer clear. Locals notice this more than they
say.

5. Locals refuse to enter certain ruins.

Not because of superstition — because they've heard things. Seen things.
Felt watched.

If you ask people in rural Appalachia about abandoned places, they'll
give simple answers:

"Somethin' stayed behind."
"Those hollers keep secrets."
"That land don't forget."

And you can tell they're not talking about ghosts.

Town #1: Thurmond, West Virginia — The Dead City on the River

Thurmond sits along the New River, half rotted, half preserved, and entirely haunted by its own silence. Once a booming coal town, it now stands almost empty — a handful of buildings kept upright by the Park Service, the rest vanishing into the trees.

Walking through Thurmond is like standing in the aftermath of a long breath the world never exhaled.

People report:

- footsteps on empty platforms

- voices on the wind with no source

- lights drifting through second-floor windows

- shadow figures along the old rail line

- a feeling of being watched from the hotel ruins

- a heaviness that settles on the chest

The strangest stories come from the rail bridge at night.
Locals claim a soft glow sometimes moves across the trestle — a small sphere of light drifting in a slow, patient arc, as if following the path of trains that haven't run in decades.

Folks who live nearby don't go into Thurmond after dark.

"It's not ghosts," one man said. "It's the land remembering what we did to it."

But others whisper about something else — the sound of pacing footsteps behind the depot, and the shape of a tall figure crossing the tracks long after midnight.

Town #2: Elkmont, Tennessee — The Ghost Resort of the Smokies

Deep in Great Smoky Mountains National Park lies Elkmont — an abandoned resort community surrounded by thick undergrowth, moss-eaten cabins, collapsing porches, and strange quiet.

Visitors describe the atmosphere as:

- unsettling

- dreamlike

- frozen

- heavy

- too quiet

Even during daylight, Elkmont feels wrong.

Night is worse.
Rangers report:

- unexplained lights moving between cabins

- footsteps in empty rooms

- shadows pacing creeks

- muffled voices in fog

- knocks on cabin walls

- cold spots that appear and vanish

One ranger told me about a cabin where the front door slowly swung open at 3 a.m. — no wind, no animals, no explanation. Inside, he heard breathing. Deep. Slow. Heavy.

He backed out and left the door open.

Whatever was in that cabin didn't bother closing it.

Elkmont sits in the center of a known hotspot for strange lights and trailside vanishings. The abandoned buildings, the tight slopes, the heavy fog — it all creates a perfect pocket for phenomena to linger.

The land remembers.
And something in those cabins seems to remember too.

Town #3: The Lost Mining Settlements of Kentucky

Eastern Kentucky is dotted with dozens of abandoned coal towns that never made it to the map. Some were built by companies. Some were built by families. All were eventually devoured by the land.

Locals warn people not to wander into these places.

Not because of danger.
But because "things move in there."

Descriptions include:

- tall silhouettes standing near mine entrances

- rhythmic knocks deep underground

- lights drifting in collapsed shafts

- low mumbling around ruined homes

- heavy breathing in the brush

- sudden silence, followed by a feeling of being watched

One of the most infamous lost towns sits in a hollow choked with rhododendron. Locals call it **Gravely Branch**, though the real name has been lost. The story goes that people living there experienced constant disturbances:

- rocks thrown at roofs

- whistling outside windows

- logs placed across paths

- animals disappearing

When the mine shut down, the town emptied fast.
Too fast.

Today, the ruins remain — overtaken by vines, broken apart by time — but hikers report hearing footsteps in the brush and seeing figures watching from the ridges.

A retired miner told me:

"We left that place.
But somethin' didn't."

Town #4: Centralia of the East — The Burning Settlements

While Pennsylvania's Centralia has gained infamy for its underground coal fire, Appalachia has several smaller, lesser-known burning settlements that slowly emptied as underground fires spread.

One such place sits deep in southern West Virginia, where smoke still seeps from cracks in the ground.

People report:

- glowing red vents at night

- distant voices echoing from heat fissures

- figures seen through steam rising from the earth

- lights moving along the slopes long after midnight

The eerie glow from the smoldering veins of coal creates an atmosphere that feels alive. The smoke twists in unnatural patterns, curling low and following trails as though pulled by invisible hands.

Local hunters tell frightening stories about the hills above the settlement:

"Things walk in that steam."
"They come out when the smoke's thick."
"You see shapes that ain't human."

The abandoned structures — warped by heat, half collapsed, roofs buckled — only add to the sense that the entire place is breathing.

Some places die.
This one lingers.

Town #5: The Sinking Churches of the Blue Ridge

Scattered across the Blue Ridge are church ruins sinking into the forest. Some stand upright but rotting. Others have collapsed. Many are surrounded by forgotten cemeteries, gravestones devoured by moss and ivy.

People report:

- whispers moving between gravestones

- pale glows drifting through the pews

- knocks on the church walls at night

- shadow figures seen through broken windows

- fog pooling unnaturally inside the sanctuary

- the feeling of someone standing just behind you

One of the most notorious ruins lies in a narrow hollow that never gets full sunlight. Locals call it **The Holler of Shadows**.

No birds sing there.
No insects buzz.
No deer pass through.

A man walking near the church once heard a deep humming inside. When he approached the doorway, the humming stopped — instantly — and the woods fell silent.

He didn't step inside.
He didn't have to.

Whatever was in that church didn't want him there.

Town #6: The Tennessee Ghost Railroad

Old railroad lines crisscross Tennessee's mountains, many abandoned after coal demand faded. Today, those lines sit twisted and rusted, swallowed by vines and thick timber.

Along one particular section — known locally as **The Ghost Line** — people report:

- lights pacing the old rail path

- footsteps echoing on empty tracks

- shadows crossing in front of hikers

- metallic knocks deep in the trees

- the sound of a train whistle where no tracks remain

One man walking the Ghost Line at dusk saw a tall figure crouched near a bent section of rails. When he shone a light, the figure stood and walked into the brush without making a sound.

He didn't follow.
He turned around and left the way he came.

Rail lines create corridors creatures can use — straight paths through thick forest, miles long. Many modern witnesses report Bigfoot-like sightings along these abandoned routes. But the lights appear too.

Ground. Sky.
Always together.

It's never just one phenomenon here.

Why the Strange Loves Abandoned Places

Every abandoned town in Appalachia has three things in common:

1. Uneasy Silence

When human life leaves, nature fills the space — but not all the way. Something else fills the rest.

2. Structural Shadows

Broken windows, collapsed roofs, and old beams create silhouettes that shift, distort, and hide movement.

3. Perfect Cover

Creatures use abandoned structures the same way they use caves, rock shelves, and thick rhododendron.

But there's a deeper reason abandoned places attract phenomena:

People stop going there.
And anything that wants to watch humans can do so safely.

In living towns, noise covers sound.
In abandoned ones, every step echoes.

The creatures that roam these mountains seem drawn to places where people no longer belong — where the wilderness has taken back control.

Reports of Creatures Living in the Ruins

A surprising number of witnesses — hikers, hunters, even rangers — report seeing dark figures moving through abandoned structures.

Descriptions include:

- Tall silhouettes stepping into doorways

Shape: humanoid
Size: 7–9 feet
Movement: smooth, slow, observing

- Heavy footsteps on wooden floors

Weight: significant
Speed: controlled
Sound: deep thuds, pacing

- Something tapping windows from inside

Pattern: deliberate
Volume: faint
Reaction: silence afterward

- Large shapes crouched inside churches

Height: unknown
Profile: hunched
Eyes: sometimes reflective

One ranger in Virginia described seeing a shape inside a cabin ruin. He said it ducked under a beam with the ease of someone stepping under a low doorway.

"I thought it was a bear at first," he said. "Then it stood upright. I left immediately."

He never returned to that cabin.

Lights in the Ruins

The same lights documented in earlier chapters — orbs, glowing shapes, drifting spheres — appear around abandoned places more frequently than anywhere else.

Witnesses report:

- orbs hovering in windows

- lights moving down rail corridors

- blue spheres drifting through collapsed roofs

- pale beams scanning the ground

- lights rising from church basements

- glowing objects pacing hikers inside old towns

In Elkmont, a couple saw a white light drift silently through a window and exit through a wall.

In a lost mining camp, two blue orbs followed a group of hikers at a distance of roughly thirty feet, keeping pace until the group reached a trail junction — then vanishing instantly.

Lights and ruins share a strange harmony.

The places where humans left
are the places where something else steps in.

Voices in Empty Places

The same chatter, mumbling, and whispering described across the mountains appears frequently in abandoned towns.

Witnesses describe:

- fast, low conversation inside collapsed houses

- muttering near mine entrances

- two voices "arguing" in brush behind foundations

- humming inside churches

- heavy breathing from cabins

- pacing footsteps inside rail depots

One hunter in Kentucky said he heard whispering behind an old schoolhouse. When he approached, the whispering stopped mid-sentence — instantly — followed by a heavy crack of wood inside.

He left immediately and didn't look back.

These voices rarely sound like humans.
They sound like something imitating humans.

Something testing boundaries.

Why Search Teams Hate Abandoned Places

Search-and-rescue teams avoid ruins unless absolutely necessary. Not because of danger — because of what they've experienced.

Handlers report:

- dogs refusing to enter buildings

- sudden silence inside ghost towns

- missing persons found near ruins

- searchers feeling watched

- strange echo patterns inside structures

- lights appearing during nighttime searches

- footsteps heard inside empty rooms

- tools missing overnight

- radios malfunctioning near old mines

One rescuer told me:

"Anytime we get a lost person near an abandoned town, we know the case is going to be strange."

Ruins act like magnets.

For history.
For silence.
For fear.
For whatever else walks these mountains.

Patterns in Ghost Settlements

Across all abandoned places — from West Virginia coal towns to Tennessee railroad stops to Blue Ridge churchyards — patterns repeat:

- Strange lights appear.

- Figures move silently through structures.

- Voices whisper or mumble.

- Footsteps echo without bodies.

- Fog gathers quicker and heavier.

- Wildlife avoids the area.

- People sense they are not alone.

These aren't random hauntings.
These are territories.

Something uses these ruins.

And the more abandoned the place becomes,
the more active the phenomena grow.

What Locals Believe Lives in the Ruins

Every region has its own explanation:

In West Virginia:

"The tall ones move through there."

In Kentucky:

"They live in the mines. Always have."

In Tennessee:

"Something big hunts near Elkmont."

In the Carolinas:

"They watch from the windows."

In Virginia:

"Them dark walkers shelter in the old towns."

Nobody describes ghosts.
They describe **living presences**.

Creatures.
Watchers.
Entities that pace and observe.
Figures that avoid sunlight.
Beings that use buildings for shelter, lookout, or ambush.

When local people refuse to enter ruins at night, it has nothing to do with superstition.

It has everything to do with survival.

What the Abandoned Towns Reveal About the Larger Mystery

When you step back and look at the whole picture — the voices, the lights, the vanishings, the abandoned places — a disturbing pattern emerges:

1. The creatures move through ruins like shadow highways.

Buildings provide cover.
Rail lines provide paths.
Mine shafts provide shelter.

2. The lights appear in the same places as heavy creature activity.

Above towns.
Inside ruins.
Behind broken windows.

3. Disappearances cluster near abandoned settlements.

Often within a mile.
Often near mine entrances or churchyards.

4. Fog behaves strangely in these towns.

Pooling unnaturally.
Glowing from within.
Hiding movement.

5. No birds sing near certain ruins.

And the woods never lie.

Hotspots, sky lights, voices, disappearances, ruins — they all tie together.

The abandoned places are more than history.
They are **habitat**.

And the creatures — whatever they are — know the ruins intimately.

They move through the abandoned world the same way we move through the living one.

Conclusion: In the Ruins, the Past Isn't Dead — It's Watching

There's a saying in some parts of Appalachia:

"The dead places ain't dead."

Walking through an abandoned town here feels like stepping into the lungs of the mountain — breathing its old air, feeling its attention on you.

Ruins are not empty.
They are occupied.

By lights.
By voices.
By figures who do not want you there.
By something that walks with old knowledge and patient steps.

In the next chapter, we step deeper into the mystery — into **the legends and creatures that creeped out the earliest settlers**, and the ancient beings Indigenous stories warned about long before coal, railroads, or highways touched these hills.

Because the abandoned towns are only the surface.

Beneath them
lives the oldest story in the mountains.

Chapter Eleven — The Old Ones: Indigenous Lore & Pre-Settlement Legends

Before the first settlers cut trails across the Blue Ridge, before coal roads carved into West Virginia's timber, before cabins and ghost towns and abandoned mines, the mountains already had a history. Not written. Not carved into stone. But carried in stories — whispered, sung, warned about.

The Indigenous nations of the Appalachians knew these mountains intimately. They lived in balance with the land, respected it, feared it when they needed to, and understood its deeper rhythms in a way modern people can barely imagine.
And within that understanding lived another truth:

They weren't alone.

The Cherokee, Shawnee, Yuchi, Moneton, Catawba, and others all described beings in these mountains long before Europeans arrived. Not spirits. Not metaphors.
Beings.
Physical presences that walked, watched, hunted, and sometimes protected.

Every tribe had a different name.
The descriptions changed slightly.
But the patterns stayed the same:

- tall beings

- stone-skinned giants

- cave dwellers

- watchers on the ridges

- forest mimics

- star-like lights

- underground voices

- little people in the moss

- moon-eyed watchers

- ancient ones that avoided the day

When you lay the old stories next to modern encounters — Bigfoot sightings, shadow figures, lights, voices, vanishings — they overlap almost perfectly.

It makes you wonder:

Maybe the mountains aren't hiding new mysteries.
Maybe they're hiding **old ones**.

The Forest Giants: The First Stories of Something Big

Long before "Bigfoot" became a modern word, the Cherokee spoke of **Tsul 'Kalu** — a powerful, tall being living deep in the mountains, rarely seen but respected and feared. He was called:

- The Lord of the Game

- The Old One

- He-Who-Dwelt-in-the-Mountains

Descriptions included:

- enormous height

- human-like shape

- hair-covered body

- deep voice

- intelligence

- the ability to vanish into forest cover

- a tendency to watch hunters from ridges

These traits echo almost every modern Appalachian Sasquatch encounter.

One Cherokee elder described Tsul 'Kalu as:

"Tall as a cedar, fast as a hawk's shadow, quiet as a falling leaf."

The Cherokee didn't claim to control this being. They coexisted with it — carefully. Hunters left offerings when taking game. Certain valleys were avoided during specific seasons. No one camped on high ridges if they heard "talking" in the dark.

Tsul 'Kalu wasn't a legend — he was a neighbor.
A dangerous one, but still part of the world.

Modern hikers who've seen large figures in the fog along North Carolina ridges often describe the same behavior:

- watching

- pacing

- vanishing without sound

The same being, hundreds of years apart.

The Rock-Skinned Giants — The Stone-Clad Hunters

Some of the oldest legends describe **Tsogili**, the Stone-Clad Ones or Rock Giants — massive beings with skin "hard like rock," resistant to arrows, and known for predatory behavior.

Characteristics:

- enormous size

- chiseled, stone-like bodies

- deep, thunderous voices

- territorial aggression

- echoing footsteps

- frightening mimicry

- glowing or reflective eyes

These giants lived in high ridges and deep hollows, hunting at night and stalking travelers.

One Cherokee tale tells of a hunter who heard **two Stone-Clads arguing** in a guttural language, deep in a gorge. Only when he stepped on a twig did they go silent.

That detail — **the two voices arguing** — appears again today in modern "mumbling" encounters you've heard yourself, in places where two unseen entities communicate in low tones that sound intentionally speech-like.

The Stone-Clads weren't metaphors.
They were warnings.

And the places they were said to inhabit?
They map almost exactly to modern hotspots:

- West Virginia's Monongahela

- Virginia's High Knob

- North Carolina's Nantahala

- Eastern Kentucky's coal hollers

- Tennessee's deep river gorges

The giants never went away.
The stories simply softened.

The Ridge Watchers — Eyes Above the Tree Line

In many early accounts, tribes describe beings known as **the watchers** — tall silhouettes standing on ridge crests at dusk or dawn, observing the valleys below.

Different tribes had different names:

- **Ulunsuti** (The Watcher Above) – Cherokee

- **Ani'yunwiya Ridge People** – pre-Cherokee

- **Atsi A' Disti** (Those Who Stand) – Yuchi

- **The Tall Ones on the Hills** – Shawnee

- **Hinterland Men** – early settler translation

Descriptions included:

- tall, thin silhouettes

- standing perfectly still

- glowing or reflective eyes

- watching groups of people

- retreating silently when approached

The watchers rarely came down into valleys. They remained on ridges, using elevation to observe.

This aligns directly with modern reports:

- hikers seeing silhouettes on ridgelines

- hunters spotting large figures on high shelves

- reflective eyes far above the height of normal animals

- beings that stand motionless for long periods

- sudden disappearance when light hits them

In both old and modern accounts, the watchers are not ghosts.
They are **living, physical beings** who monitor movement through the mountains.

Indigenous elders described the watchers as:

"Not enemies.
Not friends.
Just the ones who see."

A humbling thought — that someone, or something, has observed humans moving through these mountains long before roads existed.

The Moon-Eyed People — Pale, Nocturnal Beings

One of the most unsettling legends is that of the **Moon-Eyed People,** described by multiple tribes as:

- pale-skinned

- short or child-sized

- wide-eyed

- nocturnal

- living in caves or earth lodges

- emerging only at night

- avoiding sunlight

- possessing strange tools or objects that glowed

The Cherokee said these beings lived in the Appalachians before they arrived, eventually driven underground or westward.

Descriptions include:

- large, dark eyes adapted to night vision

- silent movement

- thin, whispery voices

- avoidance of daylight

- glowing or reflective pupils

Some stories claim they could mimic human voices, which echoes modern Appalachian mimicry — something copying hikers, children, or whistling hunters.

Certain caves in northern Georgia and western North Carolina carry stories of:

- small footprints

- strange symbols

- soft glowing lights

- objects disappearing from explorers

Modern cavers have reported:

- whispers deep inside shafts

- tiny footprints in mud

- "talking" that doesn't echo right

- cold spots that move

The Moon-Eyed People remain a mystery — not human, not giant, but something in between.

Their resemblance to "the little people" stories across North America is difficult to ignore.

The Little People — Helpers, Tricksters, and Watchers

Nearly every Appalachian tribe described **small forest dwellers** with surprising detail. These weren't whimsical fairy-like beings — they were dangerous if disrespected.

Traits include:

- adult intelligence

- small bodies (2–3 feet tall)

- use of tools

- underground homes

- uncanny mimicry

- protective behavior toward children

- whistling communication

- association with fog

Modern parallels include sightings of:

- small humanoids darting across trails

- tiny footprints in moss near shelters

- chattering noises that sound almost like children

- small silhouettes seen crouching on logs

- whistling sequences that mimic birds but are too rhythmic

One of the creepiest patterns in both lore and modern accounts:

Little people use mimicry as a lure.
They copy a voice — usually a child's — to draw people closer.

Indigenous stories warn strongly:

"If you hear a child calling from the woods at night, do not answer."

Some warnings never age.

The Cave Dwellers — The Deep Earth People

Many tribes believed that beings lived beneath the mountains — not spirits, but corporeal beings who rarely emerged.

The Cherokee called them **Aniyvdaqualosgi** — the Deep Earth People.

Traits:

- tall, gaunt, long-limbed

- pale or gray-skinned

- enormous eyes

- moving silently in darkness

- known for knocking or tapping

- associated with echo-like speech

- living in vast underground chambers

These beings were said to avoid sunlight, emerging only on foggy nights or in heavy cloud cover.

Modern cave explorers report:

- tapping that responds to their lights

- low moaning or "air shifting"

- reflective eyes deep in chambers

- rock placements resembling nest sites

- missing gear

- footprints too large to be human

Miners in Appalachia used to claim they heard **"something walking in the lower shafts"** long after mines were closed.

These stories weren't superstition.
They were survival warnings.

If something lives underground, it has the entire mountain as its shelter.

The Sky Beings — Lights That Descend to the Ridges

Indigenous stories also include beings from above — not aliens in the modern sense, but luminous entities, often described as:

- glowing

- orb-like

- star-like

- descending silently

- appearing near mountaintops

- interacting with certain ritual sites

- coming and going like breath

Cherokee legends speak of:

"Shooting stars that stopped above us."

Yuchi stories describe:

"Lights that floated to the treetops and listened."

Some tales mention:

- beings stepping out of the lights

- the lights communicating with each other

- lights following hunters

- lights appearing during disappearances

It's impossible to ignore the overlap with modern phenomena:

- Brown Mountain lights

- blue orbs in the New River Gorge

- lights pacing cars

- lights hovering above ridges

- silent movement

- coordinated behavior

The old stories weren't describing imagination.
They were describing exactly what people still see.

A North Carolina elder said:

"The ones in the sky and the ones in the forest know each other.
They do not fight.
They share the mountain."

A chilling thought — but one that mirrors modern patterns.

The Night Whistlers — Forest Mimics of the Ancient Stories

For centuries, Indigenous hunters told stories about beings that whistled at night — not birds, not humans, but something in the woods that used whistles to communicate:

- directional whistles

- repeating whistles

- rhythmic patterns

- mimicry of hunters

- warning calls

- coordination between multiple beings

These legends describe creatures that:

- move silently

- pace hunters

- follow from behind

- use whistles to signal to others

Exactly what happens in modern hotspots.

Older stories warn:

"When the whistler follows, do not turn back.
Walk forward and do not run."

Modern hunters say the same:

"When something whistles behind you, don't stop."

For thousands of years, people have understood the mountain's nighttime rules.

We're the first generation that tries to ignore them.

The Night Walkers — Beings That Hunt in the Fog

The Cherokee and Shawnee also spoke of **Night Walkers** — tall beings that moved in fog, appearing suddenly and disappearing just as fast.

Traits:

- tall silhouettes in low cloud

- glowing eyes

- sudden movement

- pacing behavior

- silent approach

- emerging only at night

- associated with disappearances

Fog was said to be their veil.
Their hunting ground.

Hunters avoided hollers where fog "held its shape."

That description mirrors modern accounts:

- fog walls appearing too quickly

- creatures moving inside fog

- voices heard from fog

- lights disappearing into fog

- vanishings during fog events

Fog is more than weather in the Appalachians.

It's part of the phenomenon.

And the Old Ones used it long before people built towns.

The Old Warnings — Rules for Staying Alive

Ancient warnings given by elders reveal a practical truth — the
mountains haven't changed, and whatever lives in them hasn't either.

Some common warnings:

1. Do not camp on ridgelines where voices are heard.

The watchers guard those places.

2. Do not answer whistles at night.

They are not human.

3. Do not follow lights into the woods.

They lead to places you cannot escape.

4. Do not travel alone in heavy fog.

Fog hides the Night Walkers.

5. Leave offerings at the edge of sacred hunting grounds.

Respect earns safety.

6. Children should stay close to camp at dawn and dusk.

Those are the hours when the little people wander.

7. If the forest goes silent, be still.

Something is near.

Every warning aligns with modern phenomena.

Every rule matches modern disappearance patterns.

The old stories weren't myths — they were **manuals for survival**.

Where Legends and Reality Overlap

When you compare ancient stories to modern reports, the overlap is chilling:

1. Giants on Ridges = Ridgewalkers / Bigfoot

Silhouettes.
Height.
Pacing.
Mumbling.
Stealth.

2. Stone-Clad Ones = Aggressive, territorial Bigfoot variants

Thick-bodied.
Fast.
Powerful.

3. Moon-Eyed People = Pale, nocturnal humanoids

Cave sightings.
Small footprints.
Reflective eyes.

4. Little People = Forest mimics & tricksters

Whistling.
Child-like voices.
Night lures.

5. Deep Earth People = Cave dwellers / mine entities

Knocking.
Breathing.
Moaning.

6. Sky Beings = Orb lights & aerial anomalies

Silent.
Intelligent.
Associated with disappearances.

7. Night Walkers = Fog creatures

Tall silhouettes.
Vanishing inside fog.
Active during disappearances.

This isn't coincidence.
It's consistency.

The mountains haven't changed.
The phenomena haven't changed.

Only the people changed — we stopped listening.

Conclusion: The Old Ones Still Walk the Mountains

When you step into the Appalachians at night, you're not just entering forest — you're entering a living memory older than any recorded history.

These mountains remember the Old Ones.
And in their own way, the beings remember us.

The Indigenous legends act like a map:

- where giants walk

- where watchers stand

- where mimics roam

- where lights descend

- where fog becomes alive

- where the boundary between worlds thins

And when you compare ancient warnings to modern encounters, one truth emerges:

The Old Ones never left.
They simply stepped deeper into the dark.

In the next chapter, we explore some of the **darkest entities in Indigenous lore — cannibal giants, night predators, and spirit beings that shared traits with the Appalachian creatures of today.**

History and mystery aren't separate in these mountains.

They're the same thing — breathing under the trees.

Chapter Twelve — Stone Giants, Cannibal Spirits & Night Walkers

Before settlers pushed into the Appalachians, the tribes living here warned their young of beings you did not speak of lightly — beings older than the mountains, older than the forests, older than the rivers cutting through the stone.
These weren't myths meant to frighten children.
They were warnings meant for survival.

The tribes knew something walked the ridges at night.
Something stalked the ravines.
Something hunted in fog and shadow.

These beings lived alongside humans, but not peacefully.
The oldest legends describe creatures with hunger, intelligence, and a terrifying efficiency — predators shaped by mountains that hide everything well.

And when you compare these stories to modern-day sightings, sounds, and disappearances… the parallels are almost perfect.

These weren't imaginary demons.
They were descriptions of **the predators that ruled these mountains long before we arrived.**

The Stone Giants — The First Mountain Predators

Across the Appalachian region, dozens of tribes — Cherokee, Shawnee, Yuchi, Seneca, Moneton — all spoke of **Stone-Clad Giants**, massive beings with bodies so tough that arrows shattered against them.

Names changed from region to region, but the root of the story remained solid:

- giant

- predatory

- territorial

- strong as a falling tree

- skin like rock

- hair like tangled roots

- voices deep enough to vibrate the ground

Most Stone Giant stories revolve around hunting. These weren't gentle forest spirits. They were apex predators. They waited. They watched. They followed. They struck when opportunity came.

Descriptions include:

1. Massive height and bulk

Elders described beings "as tall as two men, as wide as three."

2. Skin thick and gray like riverstone

Not literally rock — more like hide so thick it resisted arrows.

3. Eyes that glowed when angry

Often red or amber, described as "burning in the night."

4. Long strides and silent movement

Despite their size, they moved with disturbing quietness.

5. Cannibalistic hunger

Some legends explicitly describe Stone Giants hunting humans.

These creatures were feared for a simple reason:

They stalked humans the way humans stalk deer.

And the mountains gave them every advantage.

The Cannibal Giants — U'tlun'ta, the Ravenous

One of the darkest beings in Cherokee lore is **U'tlun'ta**, often translated as "the cannibal giant." He appeared in many versions, but the traits remain chillingly consistent:

- enormous size

- covered in stone armor

- carrying a club

- intelligent

- able to mimic voices

- capable of running down prey

- almost impossible to kill

U'tlun'ta was said to lure victims by calling their names, sometimes copying the voice of a child or a family member — a behavior described today in modern Appalachian wilderness encounters.

In one story, he stalked a hunting party for days, following them silently through fog, mimicking animal sounds to hide his approach.

Hunters reported:

- footsteps that stopped when they stopped

- snapping branches just out of sight

- low grumbling voices

- heavy breathing on ridges

- stones thrown at their camp

Those details mirror modern reports:

- pacing in the dark

- heavy bipedal steps

- strange mimicry

- rock-throwing

- territorial behavior

After a kill, U'tlun'ta was said to carry the body uphill — a detail matching modern disappearance patterns where victims end up in impossible high-elevation terrain.

The parallels are too close to be coincidence.

The Skinwalkers of the Mountains — Predators With Intelligence

Not to be confused with the Navajo concept of skinwalkers, eastern tribes had their own version of "Night-Changers" — beings that moved silently, stalked prey, and appeared human-like but weren't human.

Descriptions include:

- tall, gaunt silhouettes

- faces hidden in shadow

- moving between trees unnaturally fast

- eyes that shine like wet stone

- sniffing around camps

- pacing ridge trails

- quiet, breathy vocalizations

Some tribes believed these beings could imitate animals or even human speech. Others warned that they could follow a hunter for hours without being seen.

Today, Appalachian hikers report:

- footsteps 10–15 feet behind them

- breath sounds with no visible body

- a sense of being "tracked"

- low "huffs" or deep exhale sounds

- movement paralleling their path

Elders used to warn:

"Do not walk alone after dark.
The Night-Changers do not fear man."

Modern reports agree.

Spearfinger — A Predator of Fog and Mimicry

Among the Cherokee, one of the most feared beings was **U'tlun'ta's counterpart**, a female stone giant called **Spearfinger** (U'lagû), known for her hunger and cunning.

She:

- lived in the high ridges

- hid in heavy fog

- imitated voices

- used sharp, stone-like fingers as weapons

- preyed on the young and the isolated

- moved in silence despite her size

Her most dangerous ability was mimicry — she could copy the voices of loved ones, calling children into the woods.

This parallels modern Appalachian stories:

- hearing a child's voice where no child exists

- hearing your name called in the woods

- a familiar voice asking for help

- whistles matching your own

- cries that sound "almost human"

Hunters today say:

"It wasn't a person.
It was pretending to be one."

That's exactly what Spearfinger did.

And like modern Ridgewalker reports, she favored fog.
Fog was her hunting ground.

Old Red Eyes — The Monster of the Coal Hollers

In West Virginia and eastern Kentucky, multiple tribes and later settlers described a terrifying, red-eyed giant that stalked the deepest hollers:

- tall as a doorway

- covered in coarse dark hair

- glowing red eyes

- silent movement

- powerful musk scent

- heavy, slow breathing

- territorial

- often seen near water

People called it **Old Red Eyes**, **Red Eye Beast**, or simply **The Watcher**.

Encounters included:

- pacing hunters

- knocking on cabin walls

- watching from tree lines

- crossing mining roads

- appearing on ridges during storms

Red-eyed creatures appear throughout Appalachian Bigfoot reports today, especially:

- Monongahela

- Big Stone Gap

- Wise County

- Harlan

- Kanawha region

- Tug Fork

Stone giants had red eyes when angriest.
Modern Ridgewalkers have been reported with red eyes at night.

Folklore and field reports rarely line up this closely by accident.

The Hungry Ones — Winter Predators

Some tribes described beings that only appeared during the deep cold — when snow covered the high ridges and hunger ruled the land. They called them:

- Winter Walkers

- The Hungry Ones

- The Gaunt Beasts

- Frost Giants

Traits included:

- tall, skeletal figures

- long limbs

- sunken chests

- glowing or white eyes

- constant roaming

- hunting humans

- feeding on the desperate or lost

They moved through snow effortlessly, leaving footprints that disappeared quickly or appeared scattered, as if the creature hopped or stepped over large distances.

Modern winter sightings include:

- huge prints crossing logging roads

- figures standing on frozen rivers

- knocking on remote cabins

- following snowmobilers

- howls that vibrate in the air

- tracks that start or end abruptly

Snow erases tracks quickly — but not before witnesses photograph prints 15–18 inches long.

The Hungry Ones were believed to be malevolent giants driven mad by winter starvation.

Modern reports describe creatures acting more aggressively in winter — approaching cabins, pacing camps, and demonstrating bold behavior.

Some patterns never die.

The Fog Hunters — Night Walkers of the Ridge Mist

Many tribes feared beings that moved specifically with fog.
They weren't ghosts.
They were living entities concealed by the mountain's breath.

Traits of the Fog Hunters:

- tall silhouettes

- long arms

- slow, deliberate movement

- high intelligence

- ability to vanish instantly when fog thickens

- association with disappearances

- echoing footsteps

- deep, resonant breaths

- glowing eyes inside fog banks

Fog wasn't just weather to these beings — it was camouflage.

In modern reports:

- fog often precedes creature encounters

- fog hides movement

- silhouettes are seen inside fog walls

- mumbling voices drift inside thick mist

- disappearances spike during heavy fog

- lights vanish into fog

- creatures follow hikers more closely in fog

When fog rolls in fast and unnatural, something often follows.

The tribes knew this.
And warned their people not to travel in low fog.

We're the ones who forgot.

Raven Mockers & Death Watchers

Among the more supernatural beings in Cherokee lore were the **Raven Mockers** — entities associated with death and sickness. While more spiritual than physical, some descriptions tie eerily close to modern sightings of:

- dark, human-shaped figures

- seen in tree branches

- silent movement

- eyes that glow

- shadows drifting along ridges

Raven Mockers were believed to be drawn to:

- dying people

- isolated cabins

- abandoned settlements

- dark hollers

One elder described them as:

"Tall shadows that walk where death is near."

In modern accounts, hikers describe:

- shadowy figures near old cemeteries

- dark silhouettes near ruins

- tall, slender shapes watching from old mining towns

- figures that vanish when approached

- "walking shadows" in fog

Appalachia has many layers — some natural, some spiritual. And the lines between them blur in abandoned places.

Whether Raven Mockers were real entities or spiritual interpretations of shadow creatures, the pattern holds:

Something dark walks the mountains at night.

The Cannibal Spirits — Hunger in Human Form

Many tribes across Appalachia warned of beings similar to the Algonquin Wendigo — cannibal spirits that could possess or mimic humans.

These weren't literal Bigfoot-like entities.
They were spiritual predators.

Traits include:

- emaciated appearance

- skeletal frame

- glowing eyes

- extreme hunger

- ability to mimic voices

- ability to lure victims

- association with winter

- terrifying screams

These beings were said to stalk the lost — especially those separated from their group.

Modern parallels include:

- screams in remote hollers that don't match foxes or bobcats

- emaciated, tall figures seen briefly in headlights

- voices calling for help in the dark

- mimicked cries of distress

- shadows following lost hikers

- sudden deep fear before a disappearance

Even if these cannibal spirits are not literal creatures, the behavioral descriptions line up with real predator strategies.

Something in these mountains preys on isolation.
Old stories and modern reports both reflect that truth.

How the Old Ones Hunted

Comparing Indigenous stories with modern encounters reveals a chilling consistency in hunting behavior:

1. Stalking from ridges

Creatures follow prey from above, unseen but always present.

2. Mimicry to lure victims

Voices of loved ones.
Children.
Whistles.
Coughs.
Imitated speech.

3. Rock throwing

Warning.
Territorial claim.
Testing reaction.

4. Silent approach

Despite size, the creatures move without noise — even in dry leaves.

5. Watching from cover

They rarely attack outright.
They observe.

6. Disappearing into fog

Fog acts like camouflage.

7. Taking victims uphill

Bodies or missing persons found uphill, not downhill.

8. Heavy breathing before engagement

Deep huffs in the dark.
Chest resonance.

9. Stepping into camp perimeters

But rarely into the light.

10. Following for long distances

Not attacking — studying.

These match modern Bigfoot encounters, particularly the aggressive variants in:

- West Virginia

- Kentucky

- Tennessee

- Virginia

- North Carolina

The hunting patterns haven't changed.

Neither have the creatures.

Are the Stone Giants the Same as Bigfoot?

The line between the old legends and modern Bigfoot sightings is razor thin.

Both describe beings that are:

- tall

- powerful

- hair-covered

- territorial

- intelligent

- nocturnal

- capable of mimicry

- associated with ridges and caves

- able to disappear quickly

- connected to fog

- sometimes aggressive

The biggest difference?

Stone Giants were considered dangerous cannibals.

Modern Bigfoot reports show mostly avoidance behavior — except in certain hotspots, where creatures behave far more aggressively:

- stalking

- pacing

- bluff charging

- throwing rocks

- vocalizing threateningly

- "closing the distance" tactics

- entering camp perimeters

These aggressive variants might be the modern descendants of the Stone-Clad Ones — or simply the same type of being, unchanged through time.

Some old stories describe a tribal role called a "giant killer."
Not for war.
For survival.

Which begs the question:

If the tribes survived for centuries alongside these beings,
what did they know that we don't?

Patterns That Prove the Old Ones Still Walk the Mountains

When you compare all the data — legends, sightings, sounds, tracks, disappearances, ruins, lights — the picture becomes clear:

1. Ridges are hunting grounds.

Both ancient and modern accounts agree:
creatures travel the high lines.

2. Fog is a hunting tool.

Fog conceals their approach and hides their retreat.

3. Mimicry is a lure.

Voices in the woods are rarely human.

4. Lights and creatures often appear together.

Sky beings and forest beings share the same land.

5. Winter increases danger.

Food scarcity drives aggressive behavior.

6. Ruins are shelters.

Old cabins, ghost towns, and mines are perfect cover.

7. Disappearances follow the same patterns as the oldest warnings.

Noise stops.
Fog rolls in.
Victim vanishes.

8. Tracks appear then end abruptly.

As if the creature stepped into another environment or onto stone.

9. Communication among creatures is real.

Low mumbling.
Back-and-forth chatter.
Two voices arguing.

10. The beings choose to be unseen.

But not because they fear us.
Because they understand us.

These patterns are too consistent — across centuries, across cultures,
across regions.

The Old Ones still move through the mountains.
We simply gave them new names.

Conclusion: The Predators of the Old World Still Hunt in the New

Indigenous tribes didn't tell horror stories.
They told survival manuals.
They taught respect through truth.

And the truth was this:

The mountains have predators older than man.
And they never stopped hunting.

Whether you call them Stone Giants, Ridgewalkers, Night-Changers, or
Bigfoot, the beings walking Appalachia at night belong to a lineage older
than any of our settlements.

They are not lost creatures.
They are not anomalies.
They are not myths.

They are the mountains' first children.

And when fog fills the hollers…
when footsteps follow you at dusk…
when a voice calls your name from the dark…

you're not hearing ghosts.

You're hearing the Old Ones.

In the next chapter, we turn from giants to **the little people — the tricksters, watchers, and child-sized forest dwellers described in every Appalachian tribe and still encountered today.**

Because in Appalachia, the giants are only half the story.

Chapter Thirteen — The Little People of the Hollers

If the giants of these mountains are the blunt force of the wilderness, the little people are its fingerprints — subtle, precise, everywhere and nowhere at once.

You hear about them only if you stay long enough, listen long enough, and get past the stories people are willing to tell tourists. They don't come up over campfire small talk. They surface late, when the night is heavy and someone says, "Can I tell you something I don't usually talk about?"

Then you hear it:

The small footsteps.
The whistles.
The child-like laughter in places where no children should be.
The feeling of being watched from knee height instead of eye level.

The giants might own the ridges, but the little people own the hollers.

And if the old stories are right, they've been here far longer than we have.

Old Names for Small Beings

Different tribes had different names, but nearly all of them had *a name* for them.

The Cherokee talked about **Yunwi Tsunsdi'** — "the little people." Not cutesy fairy-tale creatures, but a real, separate people living in the forests and rocky places. They were described as:

- child-sized, but not children

- strong, fast, and surprisingly heavy-footed for their size

- capable of helping or harming humans

- reclusive and easily offended

- often seen on the edges of clearings, never in the middle of them

Other nations had their own versions:

- **Rock people** who lived in caves and boulder fields.

- **Moss folk** who appeared near springs and seeps.

- **Shadow children** seen darting between trees at dusk.

- **Hill dwarfs** who used small tools and carried tiny lanterns of strange light.

The details change, but several traits stay locked in place:

- small stature

- high intelligence

- mimicry

- curiosity

- territorial behavior

- an unpredictable moral code

They're not friendly forest sprites.
They're not demons either.

They're neighbors with their own rules.

And the mountains never promised us we'd understand them.

Why the Little People Are More Unsettling Than the Giants

People can process a giant.
It's big. It's obvious. It's a monster you can point at and say, "That. That's the thing."

Little people?
They're different.

They move just out of frame.
They don't roar or stomp.
They don't leave massive tracks in the mud.

The little people work at the edge of perception.

They:

- move behind you when you turn

- stand just inside your peripheral vision

- knock once and disappear

- laugh once and vanish

- mimic your voice under their breath

The giants make you feel *small*.
The little people make you feel *crazy*.

That's more dangerous in its own way.

Tricksters, Helpers, Thieves

The old stories say the little people can be helpful — when they choose.

A lost child led back to camp by a small hand that vanishes when the parents arrive.
A hunter pulled from a narrow ledge in a fog bank.
A traveler warned away from a cliff edge in the dark by a whisper.

But then there's the other side of the ledger.

Food goes missing from packs.
Firewood vanishes overnight.
Tools move three or four feet from where you left them.
Small stones appear in a neat circle around your tent.

A pattern emerges:

If you treat the forest with respect, the little people might leave you alone —or even help you once in a while.

If you treat the land like a theme park, they notice.

Everything in these mountains notices.

The Holler Where Kids Hear Laughter

There's a holler outside a small Appalachian town that locals quietly call **Kid's Echo**. Not because kids play there — they don't — but because of what's heard there.

The story goes like this:

A family moved into a house near the mouth of the holler. They had two young children, six and eight. The woods out back were thick but beautiful — ferns, big old trees, a creek running cold even in August. The kids were told, like every rural kid is told, "Don't go too far. Stay where we can see you."

At first, everything was fine.
They played near the yard, picked up sticks, looked for salamanders.

Then the parents started noticing things.

The kids would stand still at the treeline, heads tilted slightly, listening to something.

"Who are you talking to?" their mother called once.

"Just the kids in the woods," the younger one answered.

There were no other houses nearby.

Over the next weeks, they'd come back inside talking about *"the smaller kids with funny voices."*

The parents assumed imaginary friends.

But imaginary friends don't move things on the porch.

First it was a small pile of rocks, stacked neatly beside the door.
Then a tiny woven bundle of grass, tied into an intricate knot no one in
the house knew how to make.
Then the missing spoon, which turned up standing upright in the soil by a
tree stump.

The mother started walking to the treeline herself in the evenings. She
never went far. But one night, just as the light was draining out of the
sky, she heard it:

A giggle.

Not her kids.
They were both inside.

A small, breathy laugh coming from behind a fallen log.
Then another, answering from a few yards to the left.

She didn't see anything.
But the sound of small feet on leaf litter was unmistakable.

They moved quickly.
Too quickly for toddlers.

The next week, the family fenced the back yard.

The kids didn't argue.

"The other kids don't like the fence," the youngest said once.
"They stay farther back now."

Some places, that would be dismissed.
Here, in these mountains, nobody laughs.

They just nod slowly and say, "Yeah. Best to keep the kids close."

Footsteps the Size of a Child's Hand

In some Appalachian hollers, people wake to find **small footprints** around their camps — not bare human child prints, not raccoon tracks, not rodent. Something in between.

Descriptions:

- too narrow for a child

- toes too long

- heel pad oddly deep

- prints appearing in clusters, then stopping suddenly

- tracks circling tents, then retreating into brush

One hunter described waking to the faint sound of something walking around his tent in the pre-dawn hours — not heavy, not four-legged, but quick, light steps.

"When I unzipped the tent," he said, "I heard two or three sets of feet just… scatter. Like someone dropped a handful of squirrels on the leaves."

In the soft mud near his firepit, he found:

- four small prints

- each maybe 4–5 inches long

- with defined toes, no claws

- spaced like a biped, not a quadruped

He took pictures.
No one he showed could identify them.

Kids don't hike into that holler at 4 a.m.

Something else was out there.

Mimicry on a Smaller Scale

The big creatures of Appalachia mimic in deep, chesty voices — the kind that sound like a large man shouting from far away, or an animal trying to imitate a human.

The little people mimic on a smaller scale.

Witnesses report:

- whispers repeating their own words

- a single laugh echoing their chuckle

- a cough answered by a near-identical cough deeper in the woods

- quiet versions of their own voice saying "hey" or "come here"

One man fishing alone in a narrow creek valley said he swore he heard his own voice say his name from behind him.

Not someone calling **to** him.
His *own voice* calling his own name.

"I thought I was losing my mind," he said. "It sounded like me. But it was behind me. And my mouth hadn't moved."

He packed up and left.

Little people stories, going back through Indigenous lore, include the same warning:

"They repeat you.
They practice you."

That idea alone is enough to put your back up in a quiet hollow.

Borrowers in the Bush

Everyone who spends enough time outdoors has experienced minor gear gremlins — things go missing, then turn up where you swear you already looked.

Here, that effect feels… organized.

Patterns reported:

- small items vanish first: lighters, spoons, single tent pegs, string

- then they reappear in odd "display" spots: on logs, on a stump, inside tree roots

- items are sometimes placed in small circles of pebbles or leaves

- nothing large or heavy is taken — only what a small hand can move easily

One woman who car-camped at the same spot for several weekends started leaving small offerings intentionally:

- a marble

- a tiny metal toy

- a twist of braided grass she made herself

In return, she found:

- two acorns laid symmetrically beside her stove

- a small pile of smooth creek stones, sorted by color

- a single crow feather stuck upright in the ground

No wind does that.
No raccoon.
No coincidence.

She never felt threatened, but she also never camped there without asking permission out loud first.

It made her feel ridiculous at first.
Then it made her feel *relieved*.

Something was listening.

The Voices Down Low

One of the creepiest patterns with the little people isn't what you see — it's what you hear.

People describe:

- quiet chatter near the ground, like children whispering quickly

- giggles from behind rocks or from under brush

- soft syllables that sound almost-language but not quite

- muttering under their own footsteps on leaf litter

The sound comes from lower than you'd expect — knee height, sometimes lower.

A man camping alone in a ravine said he heard a "fast whispering argument" happening beside a log near his tent. When he shone his light, the sound stopped instantly. No movement. No rustling. No animals fleeing.

Just the echo of a whisper on his skin.

Another witness woke to what he thought was a raccoon rummaging near his cooler. When he sat up, he heard a tiny voice say something like "shh" — not clearly, but with unmistakable intent.

Then the footsteps scattered in three directions at once.

He didn't sleep much after that.

Protectors of the Very Young

The old stories aren't all fear.

Many Indigenous accounts say the little people can be protectors —
especially of children and those who respect the land.

Patterns:

- lost children found near streams, calm, unhurt, saying "the small
  folk" kept them company

- toddlers walking safely around roots and rocks they're too young
  to navigate alone

- kids talking about "forest helpers" who told them not to eat
  certain berries

- young ones insisting they weren't afraid when they knew they
  were lost

One grandmother told a story about her grandson, who wandered off
from the edge of a family gathering near the woods. Panic set in quickly.
They called. They shouted. Nothing.

An hour later, a relative found him sitting on a mossy rock beside the
creek, humming to himself.

"You must have been so scared," she said.

"No," he replied. "The little man sat with me."

"What little man?"

"The one who told me to stay on the rock. He was small. His clothes
were funny. When you came, he walked into the trees."

No adult footprints were found.
No other kids were missing.

The grandmother never camped in that spot again.

Not out of anger.
Out of respect.

The Darker Side — When You're Not Welcome

For every story of subtle protection, there are others where the message is clear:

Leave.

People report:

- pebbles thrown from the tree line, just hard enough to sting

- high, sharp whistles from multiple directions

- small branches dropped from above

- tents tugged at from the bottom edges

- shoe laces tied together outside the tent overnight

- small holes dug around camp chairs or packs

None of this is life-threatening.
All of it is unsettling.

One man woke to his hiking boots filled with leaves and moss. Not stuffed randomly — packed neatly, heel to toe. Another reported his socks tied into a knot he said would have taken him several minutes to make... and he'd been sleeping.

These aren't acts of a mindless animal.

They're messages.

You're not wanted here.
You're being played with.
You're being weighed and measured.

Push that boundary, and you may find yourself in one of the other chapters in this book.

Places They Favor

The little people, if the patterns are right, don't wander everywhere.

They favor:

- dense, damp hollers with constant shade

- mossy rock outcrops

- spring-fed creek banks

- rhododendron thickets

- blowdown tangles with lots of cover

- the edges of old home sites, not the centers

- cemeteries located deep in the woods, especially older ones

Where you find:

- small natural shelters

- overhanging rock

- root caves

- tangled underbrush

...you find stories.

These locations often intersect with other phenomena:

- lights seen moving low to the ground

- whispers heard at dusk

- unexplained small footprints

- missing items reappearing arranged in patterns

The giants and ridgewalkers move through big terrain — steep slopes, long ridges, deep ravines.

The little people move in tight terrain — under things, between rocks, around roots, in the small gaps most people never look at.

The mountain makes space for both.

When Giants and Little People Share the Same Ground

Elders in multiple traditions say something interesting:

"The big ones and the small ones do not fight.
They go different ways."

It's tempting to imagine that all of these beings are at war with one another, or competing for territory. But the stories don't back that up.

What they suggest instead is **coexistence**.

- Giants rule the high paths.

- Little people rule the low brush.

- Sky lights move above both.

- People move cluelessly through all three.

Modern encounter clusters support this:

- Bigfoot-like sightings and little-people stories often overlap in the same counties — same hollers, same drainages — but not always on the same nights.

- Strange lights are seen in the sky above places where small voices are heard.

- Disappearances happen in zones where multiple phenomena cross like threads.

It feels less like a food chain and more like a layered system — different species, or different aspects of one phenomenon, occupying different elevations and roles.

Whatever the explanation, this truth remains:

If you're in a holler long enough to hear the small voices, you're already on someone else's map.

Modern Appalachia Tries Not to Talk About It

Ask rural folks about big creatures, and you might get a story.
Ask them about lights, and they'll shrug and say, "Seen some things, yeah."

Ask them about little people, and you get one of two reactions:

- a flat denial that comes too quickly,
  or

- a long silence, followed by, "Who told you to ask that?"

The stories exist.
They just don't leave the region easily.

One man told me bluntly:

"You can talk about bigfoot all you want. Folks'll roll their eyes, but they'll still talk to you. Start talkin' about the little ones too loud? The woods start listenin'."

He said it half joking.
Only half.

The giants might be an acceptable campfire monster now — YouTube, TV shows, podcasts, t-shirts.

The little people don't fit the brand.

They're not marketable.
They're unnerving in a smaller, more intimate way.

They get under your skin.

And maybe that's why the region keeps them to itself.

Patterns You Ignore at Your Own Risk

By now, the patterns around the little people are clear:

- **They pay attention to children.**
  Sometimes to help. Sometimes for reasons we don't understand.

- **They like small trade.**
  You leave something. They move it. Sometimes, they leave something in return.

- **They dislike disruption.**
  Loud, destructive, careless behavior gets a reaction — missing items, nighttime harassment, and a strong feeling you should leave.

- **They exist in the same hotspots as other phenomena.**
  Lights, giants, voices, vanishings — all in overlapping terrain.

- **They can mimic sound at low volume.**
  Whispers, giggles, quick single words, quiet copies of your own noises.

- **They're not interested in being seen.**
  When the light hits them, they're gone.

Are they a separate species?
A subset of something larger?
A cultural lens for explaining uncanny small-scale events?

We don't know.

But the mountains remember them.
The old stories remember them.
And the people who live here still adjust their behavior around the possibility that the little people are listening.

The Hollers Are Never Empty

The more you listen, the more one truth sinks in:

These mountains are *occupied*.

Not in the way we think — not with roads and towns and property lines — but in layers.

Giants on the ridges.
Lights in the sky.
Shadow figures at the edge of vision.
Voices in the fog.
And somewhere down low, moving between roots and stones, watching quietly from the underside of fallen logs...

The little people of the hollers.

If they are what the old stories say they are, then they've been here since before the first trees took hold. Small witnesses to everything that's happened on this spine of rock and soil.

They don't need us.
They don't fear us.
They simply adapt around us.

And if you're very unlucky—or very careful—you might one day walk through a damp, shaded hollow and realize that every small sound around your boots isn't random.

It's conversation.

In the next chapter, we pull our gaze back up again — from the small shadows at our feet to the wide dark above the ridges — and look at **the**

winged beings and night flyers reported all along the Appalachian spine.

Because the mystery here doesn't just walk.

Sometimes, it flies.

Chapter Fourteen — The Sky Beings & Mountaintop Lights

Most people who talk about Appalachian mysteries focus on what walks the ground — the giants on the ridges, the little people in the hollers, the shadows in the pines, the mimicry in the dark. But ask anyone who's lived in these mountains for generations, and they'll tell you something quietly:

"The weirdest things ain't in the woods. They're in the sky."

They say it casually, the way someone mentions a neighbor who's been acting strange. Like it's normal. Like it's always been that way.
And maybe it has.

Long before modern UFO reports, long before headlights caught strange shapes on lonely roads, long before tourism and national parks, the Indigenous people of the Appalachians spoke of lights that hovered above ridges, beings that descended from the mountaintops, and sky forms that followed travelers on moonless nights.

They weren't necessarily visitors from another planet.
They weren't described as extraterrestrials or aliens.
They were something else — something woven into the landscape.

These mountains attract light.
Or the light lives here.

Either way, the Appalachians have never been dark.

The Old Stories — Lights That Come Down Like Living Stars

Cherokee stories describe **Nûñnë'hï**, a race of spirit-beings said to live in high mountain peaks and appear as balls of light or glowing human-like figures.

Descriptions include:

- lights drifting along ridge tops

- glowing figures crossing clearings without making sound

- star-like orbs appearing on foggy nights

- lights following hunters on long trails

- lights disappearing into rock faces or trees

These lights were not considered evil — but they weren't harmless either.
They were watchers.

The Yuchi and Shawnee had similar stories. They spoke of:

- "fire people"

- "hill lights"

- "star walkers"

These lights often appeared:

- before storms

- after deaths

- during harvest season

- when travelers were lost

- near ancient burial mounds

The tribes didn't talk about "aliens."
They talked about **beings who always lived here**, long before humans.

And when you compare these oral histories to modern reports, the similarities are impossible to ignore.

Modern Sightings — The Ridge Lights and Valley Orbs

Ask locals in the Blue Ridge or Smokies about weird lights and see what happens.

Some laugh.
Some shrug.
But eventually someone says:

"Yeah, we see 'em. Always have."

The descriptions line up almost perfectly with the old stories:

1. Orbs hovering above ridges

White, amber, blue, or pale green.

2. Lights drifting slowly along tree lines

Not meteors. Not planes. Not drones.

3. Lights rising from forest floors and climbing into the sky

Silent ascent.

4. Lights appearing in fog then vanishing instantly

Fog seems to amplify them.

5. Multiple lights communicating through movement

Synchronized behavior.

Some witnesses describe the lights as "alive."
Others call them "smart."
No one calls them random.

And they almost always appear in the same places where other Appalachian phenomena are strongest:

- deep hollers

- high ridges

- abandoned mining sites

- near ruins

- above old cemeteries

- along long, forgotten trails

It's as if the lights are part of the same system — or intelligence — as the creatures on the ground.

The Brown Mountain Lights — The Most Famous Example

North Carolina's Brown Mountain Lights are the most documented lights in Appalachia, appearing for centuries.

Witnesses describe:

- glowing balls the size of basketballs

- colors shifting from white to red to blue

- lights rising from riverbeds

- lights floating along ridges

- lights appearing in groups

- lights moving with intention

- lights following hikers or vehicles

Even the U.S. government studied them.
They produced no explanation.

Native people had a simple one:
"They have always been here."

One Cherokee story says the lights are the spirits of ancient warriors. Another says they are beings from the sky who "visit the earth."

Modern science calls them:

- plasma

- ball lightning

- swamp gas

- piezoelectric discharge from quartz

But none of those theories explain:

- coordinated movement

- intelligent behavior

- color-shifting

- lights entering trees

- lights following people

Plasma doesn't chase hikers.
Gas doesn't climb a ridge.

Something else is happening.

Lights That Watch Travelers

One of the most unsettling types of sky-beings encounters involves lights that appear to **follow** people through the mountains.

Witnesses describe:

- a light appearing 100–200 feet away

- hovering above eye level

- matching pace with their movement

- stopping when they stop

- moving when they move

Hunters report lights that:

- tail them back to their trucks

- watch over their camps

- float silently between trees

- pulse or flicker when approached

In many cases, the lights don't run from humans.
They stay just far enough away to remain unreachable.

One man said:

"It wasn't trying to scare me.
It was trying to escort me."

Another said:

"It watched me. Like it was evaluating."

When the light eventually vanished, it did so instantly — as if someone flipped a switch.

No fade-out.
No movement.
Just gone.

That sudden disappearance is one of the strongest parallels to traditional sky-being descriptions in Indigenous lore.

Lights That Descend Into the Trees

Several Appalachian accounts describe lights that don't stay above the forest — they **enter** it.

Witnesses have seen:

- small blue orbs drifting into hollers

- amber orbs weaving between tree trunks

- white lights descending into the canopy

- orb-like lights entering old mine entrances

- lights moving low across forest floors

One ranger in Tennessee described seeing a light:

"Come down like a snowflake then stop six feet off the ground."

When he approached, the light split into two smaller lights that zipped between trees like sparks from a fire — but with intelligence and direction.

He later said:

"It moved like an animal.
Not like a thing."

These lights don't behave like drones or human tech.
They exhibit agility and awareness.

They move with purpose.

Lights Connected to Creatures

One of the most intriguing patterns:
Lights often appear **minutes before** or **seconds after** creature encounters.

Some examples:

Witness A — North Carolina

Saw a large figure on a ridgeline.
Five seconds later, a blue orb rose from the trees behind it.

Witness B — West Virginia

Heard wood knocks and heavy footsteps.
Moments later, a white orb floated across the hollow like a lantern.

Witness C — Tennessee

Observed a tall figure pacing his camp.
After it left, two red lights hovered above the ridge.

Witness D — Georgia

Photographed an orb hovering over a creek.
Minutes later, heard bipedal footsteps circling her camp.

Are the lights:

- observing the creatures?

- guiding them?

- another form of the same entity?

- attracted to the same terrain features?

No one knows.

But the connection is impossible to ignore.

The Sky Walkers — Beings That Step Out of Light

Some Indigenous stories describe luminous beings that could:

- appear inside light

- step out of it

- take human-like form

- vanish into trees or rocks

- travel silently

These aren't angels.
They're not aliens in the sci-fi sense.
They're something older — a kind of sentient light.

Modern witnesses seldom see full forms emerging, but they do report:

- humanoid shapes inside bright glow

- figures silhouetted by light

- beings outlined in white radiance

- lights that seem to "unfold" into shapes

One hiker saw a light gather into a tall outline with shoulders and a head — then collapse back into a sphere and shoot upward into the clouds.

He said:

"What I saw wasn't a craft.
It was a being. A thing.
And it was alive."

This aligns with some of the strangest stories in Cherokee lore — beings brighter than fire, quieter than breath.

Lights That Enter Homes

Some of the most chilling encounters involve lights entering cabins or rural homes.

Witnesses describe:

- basketball-sized orbs floating through walls

- lights hovering above beds

- small lights gathering near ceilings

- flickering orbs pacing hallways

- glowing spheres entering through chimneys or cracks

In nearly all cases, the lights show:

- no fear

- no aggression

- no hesitation

And when they leave, they exit the same way — floating through solid material as if it isn't there.

A family in eastern Kentucky reported a glowing orb that drifted through their living room, paused at the hallway, and hovered near a child's bedroom door.

The father said:

"It wasn't a reflection.
It had depth."

The child later said:

"The light was talking, but not with words."

Lights capable of communicating without sound — that matches Indigenous stories.

The sky-beings didn't speak.
They glowed.

Mountaintop Zones — Places Where Lights Gather

Lights in Appalachia are not random.

They gather in very specific geographic features:

1. Quartz-rich ridges

Quartz holds electromagnetic energy — but these lights exceed natural explanation.

2. Narrow, deep hollers

Especially those with strong water flow.

3. High mountain balds

Places where trees give way to grass.

4. Ancient mountain overlooks

Used by tribes for ceremony.

5. Old mining regions

Where shafts, tunnels, and seams now serve as underground channels.

6. Abandoned towns and cemeteries

Lights appear above forgotten places.

7. Places where multiple ridges intersect

Natural crossroads — energy focal points.

Where the land gathers force, the lights gather too.

And some people believe the lights use those areas as gateways.

When Lights Interact With People

Not all encounters are passive.

Some witnesses describe lights that:

- approach slowly

- stop at arm's reach

- pulse as if communicating

- "scan" or move around a person

- react to gestures

- follow hand movement

- change color based on proximity

A fisherman on the Appalachian Trail said a white orb hovered near him for several minutes, changing to soft blue when he spoke, then a pale gold when he held out his hand.

He said the light felt:

"Curious.
Like a wild animal smelling me."

Others describe lights that appear during emotional moments — grief, fear, exhaustion, spiritual crisis.

These lights show up quietly, almost compassionately.

They leave the same way.

In old stories, the sky beings approached humans only when necessary. They showed *intent*, not randomness.

Modern accounts feel the same.

Lights Associated With Disappearances

This is where the chapter darkens.

Some of the most troubling Appalachian disappearance cases involve reported lights just before or after the person went missing.

Patterns:

- lights seen descending into hollers

- lights hovering near trails shortly before someone vanished

- bright flashes on ridges during search efforts

- lights drifting away from areas where tracks suddenly stopped

Some SAR volunteers report lights that seem to **lead searchers in the wrong direction**, only for the missing person to be found somewhere counterintuitive later.

Are the lights:

- neutral observers?

- part of the disappearance mechanism?

- attracted to crisis?

- or something more intentional?

We don't know.

But the overlap is undeniable.

Lights appear.
People disappear.

Not always.
But often enough to matter.

What Are the Sky Beings?

No one knows.
But here are the strongest possibilities:

1. Atmospheric or plasma lifeforms

Living entities made of energy.

2. Ancient, non-human intelligences tied to the land

As Indigenous stories suggest.

3. A phenomenon connected to the creatures on the ground

An ecosystem of mystery, not separate events.

4. Extraterrestrial in origin

The least supported by lore, but considered by modern researchers.

5. Something interdimensional or liminal

Passing between states, glimpsed only at certain moments.

Whatever they are, they behave like:

- explorers

- watchers

- messengers

- guardians

- or predators

Depending on the witness and circumstance.

Their behavior isn't chaotic.
It's patterned.
Structured.

Intelligent.

The Most Important Pattern of All

Lights appear in the Appalachian wilderness when:

- storms are coming

- fog is thick

- emotional states are intense

- creatures are active

- ridges are quiet

- people are alone

- or the land feels charged

It's as if the sky beings are tuned to conditions we barely understand.

And they appear just long enough for people to doubt what they saw.

But the mountains don't doubt.
They've seen it all before.

The lights are part of the ecosystem.
Not foreign.
Not incidental.

Part of the mystery.

Part of the land.

Part of the darkness that breathes between the peaks.

Conclusion: The Mountains Glow for a Reason

Lights in the Appalachian wilderness aren't UFOs in the Hollywood sense — flashing discs or chrome craft or creatures stepping out with big heads. They're something older, more organic, more deeply connected to the land.

The mountains seem to generate their own watchers, their own living lanterns.

Lights that follow.
Lights that guide.
Lights that mislead.
Lights that accompany.
Lights that observe.
Lights that linger.
Lights that disappear without warning.

They behave like eyes.

And if the tribes are right, the mountains themselves *have* eyes — old ones, glowing ones, patient ones.

Whatever these sky beings are, they're not the visitors.

We are.

In the next chapter, we descend again into the land below — into the ruins, caves, mining tunnels, and deep-earth zones — to explore **the Cave Dwellers & Subterranean Creatures**, beings said to inhabit the places where sunlight never reaches.

Because the mountains aren't just alive above us...
They're alive **beneath** us too.

Chapter Fifthteen — The Cave Dwellers & Subterranean Creatures

Most people think of the Appalachian Mountains as trees and ridges and hollers and sky. Green walls. Blue distance. Fog moving between dark slopes like smoke.

They forget what's underneath.

These mountains aren't just hills stacked on hills. They're hollowed. Riddled with tunnels, caverns, seams, voids, shafts, sinkholes, and rivers that never see the sun. Coal veins, limestone caves, flooded chambers, miles of human-dug mines that now sit in darkness, collapsing slowly into themselves.

Above ground, you can still pretend it's just forest and weather and bad directions that cause trouble.

Below, that illusion doesn't last long.

If something wanted to live in permanent secrecy — to move unseen from one valley to the next, to watch without being watched, to take without being traced — the underground is where it would do it.

Down here, you don't talk about "haunted houses."
You talk about breathing rock.
You talk about knocking in the dark.
You talk about things that were already there before men cut coal or blasted road tunnels.

The Appalachians have always had cave dwellers.

We just don't agree on what they are.

A Second World Under the Trees

It's hard to wrap your head around how much hollow space exists beneath these mountains.

- Natural limestone caves stretching for miles.

- Underground rivers carving looping channels.

- Dry chambers half the size of football fields.

- Abandoned coal mines spider-webbing unseen beneath towns.

- Old hand-dug shafts left uncharted.

- Collapsed tunnels forming sinkholes and hidden pockets.

On a map, the mountains look solid.
In reality, it's more like a sponge – rock and air interwoven.

That second world under the trees has its own ecosystems:

- albino fish and salamanders

- blind crayfish

- strange fungi

- entire insect populations that never see daylight

If nature can adapt to that kind of environment, who's to say other things haven't?

If you stand in some of these valleys at night and really listen, you can feel it — the sense that you're standing above something instead of on something.

A hollow under your boots.

Something listening from below.

Old Stories of the Deep-Earth People

Long before miners came, the tribes told stories about **beings that lived inside the mountains** — not spirits, not gods, but people, or something like people.

They called them:

- **Deep Earth People**

- **Stone House People**

- **Those Who Live Below**

- **Cave Dwellers**

Descriptions vary, but some traits stay consistent:

- tall, but thinner than the forest giants

- pale or gray skin

- enormous eyes adapted to darkness

- quiet, deliberate movement

- aversion to sunlight

- strange, echoing voices

- a habit of knocking from unseen places

These beings weren't described as demons.
They were another nation — a separate people living under the same mountains.

The tribes kept their distance.

You didn't camp near certain cave mouths.
You didn't shout into holes in the rock.
You didn't throw things into sinkholes "for fun."

Some places were simply marked off in the old way:
"This is theirs. We leave it alone."

Modern cavers and miners have stumbled into the same rule, one uncomfortable encounter at a time.

Miners Who Heard Footsteps Where No One Should Have Been

Coal miners are not easily spooked.
You don't spend twelve hours a day underground, with tons of rock over your head, listening to the earth shift and groan, if you scare easy.

So when miners say something down there wasn't right, you listen.

Stories repeat across states:

- footsteps on catwalks with no one around

- the sound of boots walking on gravel where dust lay undisturbed

- breathing in the dark — not the low hiss of ventilation, but chest-deep, slow inhalations

- rocks tossed from unseen corners

- low, muffled voices in dead-end tunnels

- cold air rushing past when no fans were running

One West Virginia miner told a story that stuck with me.

He was deep in a seam near the end of a shift, doing a last walk-through with a partner. Vent fans off, equipment idle, just the low, omnipresent groan of the mine around them.

"We'd stopped to listen," he said. "You do that sometimes. Just stand still and feel the place. Helps you catch bad sounds."

Instead, they caught footsteps.

"Not scurrying, not skittering," he said. "This wasn't rats; this was heavy. Bipedal. Heel-to-toe. Coming down the tunnel toward us."

They lifted their lamps.
The beam penetrated only so far, swallowed by dust and air.

The footsteps kept coming.
Slow, unhurried, confident.

They shouted.
No answer.

They braced themselves for a supervisor, another worker, somebody messing around.

"Then it stopped," he said. "Just outside the edge of our light. We called out again. Nothing."

They stepped forward.

Nothing was there.

No worker.
No boot track.
No shifted rock.

The dust on the floor lay undisturbed.
The darkness in front of them felt heavier than before.

"I've never heard quiet like that," he said. "The mine got... still. Like something holding its breath."

They left, one behind the other, walking faster than they needed to, neither saying what both were thinking.

We weren't alone down there.

Cave Explorers and the Sound of Knocking

Cavers — people who go into natural caves for exploration or sport — report their own set of unsettling patterns in Appalachian systems.

- knocking coming from inside rock walls

- tapping that answers their own taps

- rock "clicks" in perfect patterns

- breathing sounds in tight chambers

- voices that sound like they're behind a stone door

One group described mapping a limestone cave when they heard a repeated sound:

Knock.
…
Knock-knock.
…
Knock.

Not random.
Not dripping water.
Not shifting rock.

They answered, half-joking, with their own pattern.

For a few minutes, nothing.
Then the reply came — matching their rhythm exactly.

They changed their pattern.
The sound changed again.

The knocking was coming from beyond a wall of solid stone — no visible crack, no accessible passage.

"After a while," one of them said, "it stopped being funny. It started feeling like we were being humored."

They left that section of cave uncharted.

Sometimes, curiosity is just another word for bait.

Things Seen Just at the Edge of the Headlamp Beam

In long cave systems, your world shrinks to the circle of light from your headlamp. Outside that circle, there's only black.

Cavers in multiple parts of Appalachia report similar sightings:

- a pale, upright shape moving just outside the beam

- long, thin fingers pulling back from the edge of a rock

- eyeshine — not like an animal's, but flat, reflective discs

- something tall standing perfectly still at the end of a passage, vanishing when the light hits it directly

No one gets a clean, well-lit look.
The underground doesn't allow that.

One experienced caver in eastern Tennessee swore he saw "two hands" — not paws, not claws, hands — pull back from a crack in the rock as his light swung by.

They were:

- elongated

- pale

- too large for a child

- too narrow for a grown man

"I felt looked at," he said. "Not attacked. Not threatened. Just… studied. The way we look at salamanders and say, 'Huh. Didn't know those lived down here.'"

The idea that something under the mountain might be studying us the same way we study cave life is not reassuring.

But it fits.

Voices Where There Should Be None

One of the eeriest consistencies in subterranean encounters isn't what people see — it's what they hear.

Underground, sound behaves differently. It carries slowly. It swirls. It bounces. It arrives out of order, like it took a wrong turn somewhere and is trying to catch up.

People describe:

- faint, conversational murmuring from behind rock walls

- laughter in side passages that lead nowhere

- low chanting, impossible to locate

- echoes of words that were never spoken

These aren't normal echoes.
Echoes repeat something you've already said.

These voices say things first.

Miners tell stories of "shift whistles" that blew when no equipment was active — only for that section of the mine to collapse weeks later. Cavers talk about hearing "singing" in languages they don't recognize, coming from chambers that don't appear on any map.

One woman exploring a well-known Kentucky cave with two friends heard the distinct sound of someone behind them say:

"Don't stay."

Three syllables.
Soft.
Close behind her left ear.

She spun around, expecting to see someone else from their party.

No one was there.
Her friends were ahead, both with their backs to her, both clearly within her light.

They saw her face and asked what happened.

She lied and said she'd thought she'd dropped something.

You can rationalize footsteps. You can rationalize knocks. But once the underground starts speaking words... it's hard to file that away under natural.

The Smell of the Hidden

Above ground, people often report a sudden smell before a creature encounter — wet dog, rotten vegetation, ammonia, musk.

Underground, scent behaves differently. It lingers. It clings.

Miners and cavers sometimes report a **sudden pocket of smell**:

- strong, organic, and wrong

- not decay

- not bat guano

- not mold

"We were moving through a dry tunnel," a Virginia miner said, "and the air suddenly went thick. It smelled like wet earth and animal, but there was no mud, no water, nothing. Just rock and dust."

The smell didn't fade gradually.
It appeared like someone had opened a door, then disappeared just as fast.

Some describe the scent as "cave bear," even though cave bears haven't walked this continent for thousands of years.

Others associate it with something bigger, something their bodies recognize before their minds do — that primal, instinctive awareness that something large and alive is very close, even when you can't see it.

Smell is one of the oldest languages.
Underground, it may be the only warning we're granted.

Collapsed Mines That Don't Stay Quiet

All up and down the Appalachian spine, old mining towns sit above a maze of former tunnels and shafts. Most are collapsed now. Many are flooded. Some are officially "sealed."

They're not silent.

Locals report:

- banging from beneath the ground at night

- rhythmic tapping heard in basements

- a sense of vibration under their feet with no trucks or trains nearby

- low, hollow "booms" like something heavy moving in caverns below

Some write it off as settling — old shafts collapsing in on themselves.

Other times, the timing is too weird.

- Three knocks heard directly under a kitchen floor at 2 a.m., followed by nothing for weeks.

- A pattern of tapping under a driveway that seemed to answer stomps from above.

- "Footsteps" in the earth under house piers, moving from one end to the other.

You can't see what's down there.
You don't know how much void is between your floorboards and the nearest solid stone.

If anything wanted to move beneath neighborhoods without being seen, it wouldn't have to dig a thing.

We already did the work for it.

Are the Cave Dwellers the Same as the Ridgewalkers?

It's a fair question.

Are we dealing with:

- one adaptable species using both above-ground and underground routes,

  or

- multiple distinct beings sharing the same terrain in layers?

The evidence cuts both ways.

Parallels:

- heavy bipedal footsteps

- deep, chesty breathing

- knocks and rock throws

- mimicry (voices repeating patterns)

- sudden smells associated with encounters

Differences:

- underground entities are seen less often — usually just glimpses

- cave dwellers are described as thinner, paler, more gaunt

- eye-shine underground tends to be white or pale, not red or amber

- behavior seems more cautious, less aggressive

One possibility is that the ridgewalkers — the big, hair-covered forest giants — use cave systems like we use roads and tunnels: to cross terrain without being exposed.

Another possibility is that there's a related but distinct branch of whatever these beings are — adapted more fully to the deep dark, spending most of their existence below.

If you look at how animals diverge in specialized environments — cave fish losing their eyes, salamanders losing pigment — it's not hard to imagine a long-term underground variant of a larger, surface-dwelling creature.

The tribes hinted at this without modern biology:

"The ones below are not like the ones above," some stories say.
"They are thinner. Paler. Quieter. But they are of the same family."

A chilling thought.
An entire lineage of mountain beings, some owning the forest, others owning the rock.

Sinkholes and People Who Don't Come Back

Disappearances in the mountains don't always happen on camera-friendly ridge trails.
Some happen quietly, near innocuous dips in the ground.

Appalachia is full of sinkholes — some shallow, some hundreds of feet deep, many hidden by leaves, brush, or grass until it's too late.

People have reported:

- dogs barking at "holes in the ground" and refusing to approach

- cold air rushing out of cracks on hot days

- small stones thrown up out of pits with no animal visible

- sudden fear standing near depressions that seem small but "feel wrong"

A few missing-person cases intersect with these features:

- someone steps off alone near camp

- a last shout, laugh, or comment is heard

- then silence

Searchers find no prints, no signs of struggle, no drag marks.

In karst terrain, a small opening can lead to a huge drop, or a slope of loose stone that funnels anything that falls through into deeper chambers.

Once you're down there, you're not climbing out.

Now fold in the possibility that something lives in those spaces.
Something that understands them intimately.
Something that can drag, carry, or guide a stunned person deeper, leaving almost no trace.

The idea isn't comfortable.
Neither is vanishing.

Something underground participates in the disappearing act.

Whether it's simple geology or something else using geology as cover is the question.

Underground Lights

Lights don't just appear in the sky or above ridges.

Cave explorers and miners report:

- faint blue glows with no visible source

- orb-like lights appearing in straight tunnels

- small phosphorescent spheres moving against air currents

- a dim, wandering glow seen turning corners before the witness does

Many write it off as headlamp reflections, mineral luminescence, or "just being tired."

Others aren't so sure.

One miner told a story of sitting on his lunch break deep underground when a pale light, the size of a grapefruit, emerged slowly from a side tunnel, drifted into the main shaft, and hovered about eight feet off the ground.

It didn't brighten the surroundings like a bulb would.
It seemed self-contained.

It floated for maybe ten seconds.
Then, without moving up or down, it winked out — gone in an instant.

He didn't tell his supervisor.
He didn't tell most of his coworkers.

He waited until he retired and then told his grandson, almost apologizing as he did.

"I don't like telling it," he said. "Makes me sound crazy. But it happened. I was there. Something was down there with me."

If lights move beneath the mountains as they do above them, it suggests something much larger than isolated weirdness.

It suggests a full, functioning system of phenomena — sky, forest, stone, river, all threaded together.

The Feeling of Being Below Something Alive

Ask anyone who's spent serious time underground in these mountains — not an hour-long cave tour, but real hours, in real darkness — and almost all of them will mention a moment where it felt like **the mountain was alive**.

Not metaphorically.
Not poetically.

Alive.

Pressure changes.
Air currents shift.
Stone creaks.
The ground subtly flexes.

In some places, those sensations feel neutral.
You're just inside a living, breathing system.

In others, people report something else layered on top of that:

A sense of attention.

Like being inside the chest of a sleeping animal that has just opened one eye.

Hair stands up on the arms for no reason.
Voices catch in the throat.
Even seasoned cavers cut that trip short and reschedule it with a different route.

It's easy to wave that away as nerves.

But when enough people who aren't prone to storytelling say the same thing — "It felt like something under there noticed me" — you at least stop smirking while they say it.

If You Wanted to Stay Hidden

It's worth stepping back and asking a simple question:

If you were an intelligent, physical being wanting to avoid detection — occasionally interacting with the surface world, taking what you need, moving long distances — where would you live?

You wouldn't live on open ridges.
You'd use them, then vanish.

You wouldn't live in visible caves near trails.
You'd move through them quietly at night.

You'd live:

- in collapsed sections no one can access

- in chambers beyond squeezes most humans won't brave

- in dry pockets above flooded tunnels

- in natural caves without known entrances

- in layered systems beneath ridge networks

From there, you could:

- emerge in dense forest when hunting

- watch humans from the tree line

- approach camps under cover of darkness

- retreat down vertical shafts or through squeeze points

- travel for miles without ever breaking the surface

The Appalachian geology makes that possible.

You don't have to guess how any of that could work.

You only have to realize that if it could, something might already be doing it.

Conclusion: The Mountains Are Hollow, and Something Is Home

On the surface, the Appalachian wilderness feels vast enough. Hard enough. Remote enough. Dangerous enough.

That's just the top layer.

Beneath the roots and rivers and ridges lies an older, darker world — one cut by water and time, then expanded by human hands. A world of tunnels and chambers and blind rivers and airless pockets.

A world where light doesn't belong.

If the creatures of these mountains — the giants, the watchers, the mimics, the little people, even the lights — are part of a larger system, then the subterranean world isn't a side note.

It's the backbone.

The cave dwellers of old stories.
The footsteps in unworked shafts.
The knocking behind rock walls.
The pale shapes at the edges of headlamp beams.
The voices that speak three faint syllables in the dark and then never again.

All of it points to something very simple and very uncomfortable:

The mountains aren't just hiding things *in* the woods.

They're hiding things *inside themselves*.

In the next chapter, we'll pull back out of the dark and look at **how all of these beings — giants, little people, cave dwellers, sky lights — intersect with human psychology**: fear, obsession, denial, and the way the mountains quietly rewrite the minds of the people who spend too long listening to them.

Because the deeper you go into this world, the clearer one thing becomes:

You're not just studying the wilderness.

It's studying you back.

.

Chapter Sixteen — Phantom Wolves & Black-Timber Predators

Most people think they know what a wolf looks like. They picture something out of a nature documentary — a grey blur moving over snow, yellow eyes reflecting a camera flash, something wild but still recognizable. Something we can categorize.

The wolves in the Appalachian stories aren't like that.

These are creatures that slip through the dark timber without sound, larger than natural wolves have any business being, appearing where wolves supposedly died out a century ago. Shadow canines. Ridge-trackers. Things with paws too big, silhouettes too tall, movements too calculated. Something between wolf and myth.

They don't show themselves fully.
They don't give you enough to point to and say, "I know what that is."

Instead, they give you glimpses:
a massive shadow crossing a trail at dusk,
a growl that vibrates your ribs,
a pair of eyes too far off the ground,
tracks wider than your palm...
and gone before you can take a second look.

They're the ghosts of predators we convinced ourselves we killed off long ago — or something older that never cared about extinction, or classification, or fitting into any natural history book.

In these mountains, the wolves never really left.
Or maybe... they were never wolves to begin with.

The Return of the Wolf — Except It Isn't That Simple

Biologically speaking, eastern wolves and red wolves once roamed Appalachia. Both species were hunted out or dwindled to near-extinction. Officially, wolves are not supposed to exist here now — except in managed populations or remote corners of the Southeast.

Yet people across:

- West Virginia,

- Kentucky,

- North Carolina,

- Tennessee,

- Georgia,

- Pennsylvania,

- and the Virginias

report wolves regularly.

But not the right kind.

These aren't small red wolves or rangy coyotes.
These are **huge** — dark, silent, broad-shouldered animals moving with intelligence that unnerves even seasoned hunters.

Descriptions repeat:

- 200-pound silhouettes

- dark grey, black, or reddish-black fur

- eyes shining red, amber, or pale blue

- standing as tall as a deer at the shoulder

- sometimes walking on two legs briefly

- enormous heads and wide muzzles

- a stillness that doesn't feel like animal caution — but like calculation

Hunters who see them don't say "wolf."
They say:

"That wasn't a normal animal."
"I don't want to see it again."
"That thing was watching me."

And most unsettling:

"It knew what I was."

In a world of predictable wildlife, this category of creature sits somewhere between the known and the impossible.

The Phantom Wolf — A Creature Made of Shadow

One of the most consistent patterns is the **phantom wolf**, a wolf-like creature that moves strangely:

- silent

- fast

- seemingly weightless

- appearing where no sound precedes it

- disappearing as if dissolving into the treeline

Witnesses describe:

- a black shape pacing beside their car on backroads

- a huge dark figure following them along ridge trails

- a canine shadow watching from the trees

- low, deliberate growls with no source visible

Hunters often report seeing a wolf-like silhouette near the edge of their camp's firelight — massive, motionless, not behaving like a normal predator.

One Tennessee man described it like this:

"It wasn't scared of me.
It wasn't interested in the food.
It just watched.
Like it was waiting for me to make the next move."

When his flashlight beam finally hit it, the animal didn't bolt.
It just stepped back into the dark and vanished — silently.

Not ran.
Not turned.
Just *gone*.

That's not typical of any known canine.

Black-Timber Predators — Wolves Too Big to Be Wolves

Some of the most unsettling Appalachian reports involve wolves that are simply too large to be biologically plausible.

Ridge hunters describe:

- bodies as long as black bears

- shoulders like draft horses

- heads the size of a small dog

- fur nearly black with a sheen

- muscular legs capable of long strides

And the behavior is wrong:

- they don't avoid humans

- they don't act like wild predators

- they don't show fear

- they don't acknowledge gunshots

- they seem more curious than threatened

One hunter in West Virginia described firing a warning shot at a massive wolf-like figure that had been watching him for several minutes. The creature didn't flinch.

"It tilted its head," he said. "Like it understood I was trying to scare it. And it wasn't impressed."

He left the ridge immediately.
He never hunted there again.

Predators fear gunshots.
Animals react to loud noises.
Instinct protects them.

Whatever these creatures are, fear doesn't seem to be part of their vocabulary.

Eyeshine That Doesn't Match Any Known Animal

Normal wolf eyes reflect yellow or green under light.
Many nocturnal mammals reflect blue.

But in these mountains, witnesses report eyeshine that:

- glows bright red

- pulses

- appears as two lights spaced too far apart

- blinks slowly like a human's eyes

- appears too high off the ground

- sometimes shifts to a different color

One of the creepiest reports comes from a hiker who saw two eyes glowing red down a slope. He raised his flashlight. The eyes blinked — not the rapid blink of an animal — but the slow, deliberate blink of a person.

"I don't know what I saw," he said. "But it blinked at me like it understood I was there… and that I was scared."

People misidentify normal eye reflections all the time.
But they don't misidentify blinking.

Blinking means intelligence.

Blinking means awareness.

Blinking means you're not looking at a simple predator.

The Dogman Overlap — But Not the Same Creature

Some researchers lump these sightings into "Dogman" reports — the upright-walking canine phenomenon spread across parts of North America.

But the Appalachian wolf-like beings don't fit neatly into the Dogman description.

They rarely walk fully upright.
They don't chase vehicles aggressively.
They don't behave territorially the same way.
They don't show the same exaggerated anatomical features.

Appalachian wolf creatures seem to be:

- more wolf than humanoid

- more silent than snarling

- more observer than attacker

- more shadow than flesh

If Dogman is a category, these creatures sit in a different branch of the tree — perhaps a cousin, perhaps something far older, perhaps something the tribes knew by a completely different name.

Indigenous stories speak of:

- **Waya-uneega** (white wolves that weren't wolves)

- **The Night Hounds**

- **The Shadow Pack**

- **The Stone Wolves**

- **Spirit Dogs** that guarded certain valleys

These weren't spirit animals. They weren't symbolic. They were considered real apex entities, unpredictable and territorial.

The overlap is too close to dismiss.

The Howls That Don't Fit Any Known Species

People who live in Appalachia know the sound of coyotes.
They know the sound of foxes screaming.
They know bobcat yowls, bear grunts, panther screams (even if "officially" panthers don't exist here).

But there are sounds locals *don't* recognize:

- deep, resonant wolf howls where no wolves should be

- long roars ending in guttural growls

- multi-toned howls like two voices in one body

- booming barks you feel in your chest

- chorus howls too synchronized to be coyotes

- mournful, drawn-out calls that sound almost human

Some describe the howls as "sad," others as "furious," but nearly everyone agrees:

"They're too deep. Too loud. Too… aware."

In the deep hollers where sound carries strangely, the howls bounce off the rock in a way that makes it hard to pinpoint the location.

Hunters often describe hearing howls in front of them… then behind them… then above them — all within seconds.

That's not normal canine movement.
That's strategic positioning.

Something is moving fast.
Or something is using the terrain perfectly.

Possibly both.

Tracks That Shouldn't Exist

Photographs show tracks that:

- are 6–9 inches wide

- are 12–18 inches long

- show deep pressure as if from an enormous weight

- have claw marks that are too long for wolves

- show bipedal patterns suddenly switching to quadrupedal

- appear for 20 feet then vanish completely

Trackers know how to read prints. They know when a track is fake or misinterpreted. But some prints simply don't match anything in the region.

One trapper described finding a track so large he thought someone had stamped a novelty mold into the mud — until he saw the stride length.

"No human could make that stride," he said. "Not unless their legs were five feet long."

People don't fake stride patterns.
Not convincingly.

The creatures making these prints are:

- heavy

- fast

- huge

- bipedal-capable

And not supposed to exist.

Predators That Hunt in Silence

Wolves are vocal animals.
Coyotes are chatty.
Bears make noise whether they want to or not.

But the black-timber predators move in silence.

Hunters report:

- no footfall sounds

- no twig snapping

- no breathing

- no panting

- no approach noise

Just appearance.
Watchfulness.
Disappearance.

One bowhunter in Georgia said he was sitting in complete silence when he felt something behind him — not heard, *felt* — the sense of presence.

He turned slowly and saw a wolf-like shape standing 20 feet away, massive and broad-shouldered, eyes glowing faintly.

"It didn't growl," he said. "It didn't move. It didn't even blink. It just… waited."

When he looked away to reach for his knife — one second, maybe less — the creature was gone.

No sound. No retreat. No running noise.

Absent.

As if it had stepped into a different layer of the forest.

Stalkers of the Timber

People talk about being followed.

- footsteps matching their own

- the crunch of leaves behind them

- the soft padding of something keeping pace

- growls just at the edge of hearing

- eyes catching light in the understory

One hiker said he was followed for over an hour by something walking parallel to him in the trees. When he stopped, it stopped. When he continued, it continued.

He never saw the creature clearly.
But he saw the outline once — huge, hunched, lupine.

"It wasn't hunting me," he said. "It was escorting me."

Almost as if pushing him out of the area.

He left.

Sometimes survival isn't bravery — it's intuition.

The Coal-Hollow Wolves

Mining country in West Virginia and eastern Kentucky is full of stories about giant wolves emerging from old mine entrances.

Witnesses describe:

- a pair of glowing eyes deep inside a shaft

- heavy breathing echoing through a tunnel

- huge prints at mine mouths

- wolf-like figures standing at the edge of collapsed entrances

Some believe these are natural wolves using abandoned mines as shelter.

But many of these mine shafts are:

- too steep

- too unstable

- too narrow

- blocked far inside

Whatever is inside those shafts isn't looking for shelter.

It's watching the mouth of the mine.
It's waiting.
It's listening.

These mines connect to underground systems — caves, chambers, voids — that stretch for miles under the mountains.

A perfect passageway for something that moves by night.

A perfect den network for a predator that wants privacy.

Were These Wolves Ever Really Wolves?

It's worth asking whether these creatures were wolves at all.

Three possibilities emerge:

1. A relic population of enormous prehistoric canines

Dire wolves existed here.
Their extinction timeline and these sightings… don't completely contradict each other.

2. A supernatural or liminal predator

A creature tied to the mountains, appearing and disappearing at will.

3. A branch of the same mystery as the ridge giants

Perhaps a related species:

- same intelligence

- same stealth

- same territorial awareness

- different form and function

Indigenous stories strongly support #3.

Many tribes believed the wolves and giants were part of the same family of beings — different forms sharing the land, communicating, cooperating.

If the giants rule the heights,
the wolves rule the shadows.

Why Humans Fear This Creature Most

People fear Bigfoot.
They fear ghosts.
They fear lights.

But the wolves scare them more.

Why?

Because wolves are predators we understand — and these aren't wolves.
They're versions of wolves that broke the rules.

They're too big.
Too fast.
Too silent.
Too intelligent.

When you see a giant on a ridge, your brain scrambles for meaning.
When you see a wolf the size of a pony watching you with human-like intelligence...

Your survival instincts light up like a flare.

Predators are frightening.
Predators that understand you are worse.

Conclusion: The Wolves of the Appalachians Are More Than Wolves

Whatever these creatures are — relic canines, shapeshifters, spirit-wolves, or something else entirely — they don't behave like animals.

They behave like guardians.
Scouts.
Sentinels.

They watch the trails.
They shadow travelers.
They escort people out of areas they aren't meant to explore.

They appear alongside:

- giants,

- little people,

- underground creatures,

- and sky lights.

They are part of the same ecosystem of mystery — another layer in a land that refuses to reveal all its secrets.

The giants may be the strength of the mountains.
The little people may be their mischief.

But the wolves?

The wolves are their teeth.

In the next chapter, we shift to another unsettling category — **the unclassified cats and mountain lions that aren't supposed to exist**, the panthers of the Appalachians that scream in the night and vanish before dawn.

Because the wolves aren't the only predators Appalachia kept for itself.

Chapter Seventeen — The Mountain Panthers & Unclassified Cats

Officially — according to wildlife agencies, biological surveys, and the neat, tidy language of government conservation PDFs — the eastern cougar is extinct.

Gone.
Erased.
A ghost written into old field guides and hunting journals.

But the mountains don't read paperwork.

And the people who live deep in Appalachia don't care what the official record says. They'll look you in the eye and tell you what they've seen with a calm certainty that leaves no room for argument:

"There's big cats in these hills.
Always have been.
Always will be."

And the creatures they describe aren't small bobcats or misidentified dogs. These aren't brief glimpses or tall tales told by kids. These sightings come from hunters, rangers, linemen, firefighters, fishermen, trappers — people who know the woods better than most of us know our own neighborhoods.

Something big still hunts these mountains.

Something long-tailed.
Silent.
Powerful.
And aware.

And sometimes, the creatures they describe aren't cougars at all — but something bigger, darker, or stranger.

The Appalachians have panthers.
But not the kind anyone wants to classify.

The Black Panther Problem

Ask any biologist and they'll tell you flatly:

"There is no such thing as a black panther in North America."
(Meaning: no melanistic mountain lions, no black cougars.)

And scientifically, they're right.

But the people who live in the mountains don't care about the textbooks.
They see what they see.

And what they've seen for decades is:

- huge black cats

- long tails

- low, powerful bodies

- quiet, efficient movement

- glowing eyes

- feline silhouettes crossing roads

- panther screams at night

- tracks far too big for bobcat

Reports come from:

- the Smokies

- the Blue Ridge

- West Virginia hollers

- Kentucky's Letcher and Harlan counties

- the Cumberlands

- North Georgia

- the Monongahela

- the Shenandoah regions

These sightings don't trickle in.
They flood.

People see these things from:

- trucks

- ATVs

- front porches

- ridge overlooks

- switchback trails

The creatures are described as:

- **between 5 and 7 feet long**

- **black as coal**

- **muscular**

- **moving low to the ground**

- **tail nearly as long as the body**

These are not bobcats.
These are not house cats.
These are not bears.

They are panthers.

But the question isn't *if* people see them.

The question is *what* they are.

The Scream in the Night

The sound people associate most with Appalachian big cats is the scream — a sound that can freeze your blood instantly if you've never heard it.

People describe it as:

- a woman screaming

- a child in terror

- something human but not human

- a long, rising, horrible shriek that ends abruptly

Bobcats can scream.
Foxes can scream.
Even some owls have terrifying calls.

But what locals describe is deeper, louder, longer.

One man in western North Carolina said:

"I've heard bobcats my whole life. This wasn't a bobcat. This was… bigger. Angrier. Like a woman being murdered in the woods."

Another described it like:

"A scream so loud you feel it in your ribs."

Many people hear *two* screams — one low, one higher — as if a huge cat is calling to a mate across a ridge.

A ranger in Virginia admitted — off the record — that scream reports come in almost weekly during certain months.

"I can't tell people what it is," he said. "But I'll tell you this — when I hear it myself, I don't stick around to study it."

When the people trained NOT to get scared start walking faster, you pay attention.

Long Shadows at Dusk

One of the most common ways people encounter these cats is a simple, quick, unmistakable silhouette — long and black moving across a road or trail.

Witnesses describe:

- a long fluid gait

- a tail dragging low or curling upward

- a body long enough to stretch the width of a road lane

- movement so smooth it barely disturbs leaves

- a cat shape that doesn't match any known species

Several reports mention panthers crossing right in front of cars without hesitation, only to disappear into woods so thick you can't see three feet into it.

One Kentucky woman described a large black cat passing in front of her headlights:

"It didn't run. It walked. Like it didn't care I was there. Its tail was longer than my arm. I've seen bobcats — they don't look like that."

The calm, deliberate movement is what so many witnesses repeat.

Predators that don't fear humans...
Predators that observe...
Predators not in a hurry...

Those are the ones worth worrying about.

The Long-Tail Rule: What Separates Real Sightings From Hype

There are three features that almost always distinguish genuine Appalachian big-cat sightings:

1. The Long Tail

Bobcats have short bobbed tails.
Mountain lions have long, heavy ones.

Witnesses almost always describe:

- a tail as long as the body

- thick and muscular

- sweeping low as it moves

2. The Body Length

Bobcats max out around three feet long.

These sightings involve bodies:

- 5 to 7 feet long

- low to the ground

- built like a cougar

3. The Gait

Bobcats trot.
Cougars *flow*.

Witnesses say the movement looks:

- effortless

- fluid

- like water over rocks

If the creature is big enough, long enough, and moves like a ripple of shadow, it's not a bobcat.

Whatever people are seeing — even if it's not the extinct eastern cougar — it's a large cat.

The shape doesn't lie.

Government Silence & Quiet Confirmations

Wildlife agencies consistently deny that big cats roam the Appalachians.

But behind the scenes, you hear different things.

A ranger in Georgia:
"We've got 'em. We just don't talk about 'em."

A sheriff in Kentucky:
"Yeah, they're out there. Big ones. I've seen 'em myself."

A biologist in North Carolina (off the record):
"I've seen prints. Large prints. Fresh prints. But my job isn't to fight the official position."

One even admitted:
"Cougars traveled this whole chain for thousands of years. You think a few decades wiped them out? Not a chance."

There's a gap between what's said publicly and what's said privately.

Mountains tend to keep their secrets, and locals tend to keep theirs too.

Tracks That Defy Explanation

People find prints in:

- mud

- snow

- sandbars

- creek edges

- soft trails

- old logging roads

Track measurements often show:

- 3.5 to 4.5-inch-wide paws

- 4 to 6-inch-long impressions

- clear toe marks

- deep pressure in the heel pad

- stride lengths that match large cats

Cougar tracks are unmistakable:
No claw marks (cats retract claws).
Rounded heel pads.
Three-lobed rear pad.

Many Appalachian prints match exactly.

Others… don't.

Some show:

- three toe impressions instead of four

- heel pads too elongated

- claws that appear only sometimes

- tracks that start large, then become smaller

- tracks that suddenly vanish without any change in terrain

One man in Virginia followed a trail of big-cat prints for two miles in soft mud — then watched them suddenly **stop** in the middle of a flat patch of ground.

No turn.
No jump.
No rock.
No stream.
Just gone.

Like the animal stepped upward...
or inward.

Tracks that vanish are a common thread in many Appalachian mysteries.

These cats fit the pattern perfectly.

The Black Cats That Don't Match Any Species

The melanistic (solid black) cats reported in Appalachia are among the most mysterious.

Mountain lions don't come in black — period.

Jaguar?
Not native here.

Leopard?
Wrong continent.

Escaped pets?
Too many sightings, too widespread, too consistent across decades.

Witnesses describe black panthers as:

- 5–7 feet long

- absolutely silent

- with a sleek, shadow-like coat

- glowing pale or gold eyes

- long curling tails

- moving at night like walking shadows

Several describe them as:

"Not quite solid."
"Too dark, even for night."
"Like a hole in the trees moved."
"A shadow with weight."
"Something wearing the shape of a cat."

Some encounters feel supernatural not because of how the cats behave — which is often normal predator behavior — but because of how the *darkness reacts* around them.

That detail echoes countless stories of Appalachian shadow creatures.

Maybe the panthers are flesh and blood.
Maybe they're something else wearing a familiar shape.

Either explanation is uncomfortable.

Panthers Connected to Disappearances

Appalachian missing-person cases often include:

- screams reported the night before

- travelers seeing a large black cat

- hikers hearing stalking movement

- drag marks that start and suddenly stop

- clothing found shredded in feline patterns

- campsites disturbed in ways matching large-cat attacks

But unlike cougars, these predators:

- don't leave bodies

- don't leave kill sites

- don't leave blood trails

- don't leave feeding patterns

They take.
Then nothing.

Search dogs often refuse to track.
SAR volunteers report:

- growling in thick brush

- glowing eyes watching from dark hollers

- large shadows moving parallel to search parties

If the cat is natural, it should behave naturally.
If the cat is something else…

Then the disappearance pattern makes more sense.

Witness Accounts That Don't Fit Biology

A farmer in West Virginia saw a huge black cat standing in his pasture at dawn.

"As big as a man crouched down," he said. "But it moved like a whisper."

He aimed his rifle.
Not to shoot — just to watch.

The cat turned, looked directly at him, and blinked slowly.
Not cat-like.
Not animal-like.
Slow. Intentional. Human-like.

Then it walked into the treeline and disappeared without sound.

Another man in Georgia described a pale tan cat — cougar-colored — but too large, with a neck thicker than a cougar should have.

He said:

"It walked on all fours, but its shoulders moved like a person under a heavy coat."

Still another witness explained:

"When it turned to look at me, it was like getting sized up. I wasn't prey. I was a puzzle."

These aren't misunderstandings.
These are people accustomed to predators and prey.

They saw something that fit neither category.

Unclassified Cats in Tribal Lore

Indigenous nations knew about the canines of the mountains.
They knew about the giants.
They knew about the little people and the sky beings.

But they also knew about the cats.

Tribes across Appalachia spoke of:

- **Tla-nû-wa** — monster panthers with wings (Cherokee)

- **The Stone Panthers** — enormous cats that guarded sacred areas

- **The Shadow Cat** — a being that could pass through trees

- **Night Whistlers** that took the form of dark cats

- **Long-Tail Devils** seen prowling trails at dusk

- **The Swamp Panther** of the Southeast

Descriptions overlap strongly with modern sightings:

- huge size

- intense intelligence

- glowing or shifting eyes

- stalking humans silently

- guarding certain places

- blending into shadow unnaturally

The tribes didn't treat these as spiritual metaphors.

They treated them as real predators — the kind you told children to avoid.

Some said the panthers weren't animals at all.
They were guardians placed in the mountains to enforce boundaries.

Given how many witnesses today feel "escorted" or "pushed out" by big cats, that idea fits uncomfortably well.

Why Big Cats Thrive Here, Even Unofficially

If you wanted a species to remain undetected in modern North America:

- endless forest

- steep terrain

- deep hollers

- caves

- old mines

- low human density

- huge deer population

- intense cover

- nighttime hunting conditions

Appalachia is perfect.

A predator that:

- hunts at dawn and dusk

- travels silently

- uses ridges like highways

- retreats into deep cover or caves

- avoids major towns

…could exist here indefinitely.

Add the fact that the mountains have two parallel worlds:

- *the surface wilderness*

- *the underground labyrinth*

A big cat could slip between the two easily.

Some might have never gone extinct.
Some might have adapted.
Some might not be cats as we understand them.

The mountains don't care about our definitions.

When Cats Behave Like Something Else

Typically, predators want:

- food

- territory

- water

- mating opportunities

But these Appalachian cats sometimes behave like scouts or watchers.

Patterns include:

- following people at a consistent distance

- watching camps without approaching

- blocking trails

- escorting hikers out of areas

- circling groups silently

- appearing before storms or fog

- observing more than hunting

These aren't random behaviors.
They're strategic.

A panther that blocks a hiker's path and refuses to move isn't defending a kill site — it's issuing a warning.

A panther that follows for miles then disappears intentionally is doing reconnaissance.

A panther that watches a cabin for hours isn't curious.
It's evaluating.

When predators behave like sentinels, the question shifts:

Sentinels for what?

Or for *whom*?

The Cats in Places They Should Never Be

People have reported panthers:

- on lake islands

- at high overlooks

- inside old tunnels

- standing on boulders like statues

- on ridge spines miles from any easy access

- near ancient ruins

- staring into cabin windows

- standing silently on roads at 3 a.m.

- swimming across rivers without struggle

Some are tan.
Some are black.
Some seem to flicker in and out of solidity.

More than a few people describe panthers that leave no tracks at all —
despite soft mud.

Others describe panthers that appear perfectly solid... until they vanish
behind a tree too small to hide a housecat.

These sightings overlap with:

- ghost reports

- giant sightings

- little people encounters

- sky lights

- underground oddities

Everything intersects.

That's the theme of this mountain range.
Nothing exists alone.

Conclusion: The Mountain Panthers Are Gatekeepers

Whether the Appalachian big cats are:

- surviving eastern cougars

- escaped western cougars

- melanistic individuals (rare but possible)

- outlier predators

- paranormal beings

- shapeshifters

- guardians of the land

- or something older beyond classification

…they play a consistent role.

They warn.
They escort.
They observe.
They watch the borders.
They appear near hotspots.
They interact without attacking.
They vanish without explanation.
They behave like creatures aware of something deeper in the mountains.

In a wilderness full of mysteries — giants, wolves, shadow people,
lights, deep-earth beings — the panthers are the quietest and most
calculated.

They are not the muscle of the mountains.
Nor the mischief.
Nor the fear.

They are the **gatekeepers**.

They control the edge of the territory, the liminal spaces, the transition zones between human world and mountain world.

They decide who can pass.
And who should turn back.

In the next chapter, we shift from the predators of the timber to the **wings above the treetops** — the shadowy flying creatures, thunderbirds, night flyers, and enormous winged beings reported across Appalachia.

Because the creatures of these mountains don't all travel by ground.

Chapter Eighteen — Winged Beings & Night Flyers

Most people look up in the mountains for comfort.
You hike all day in tight forest, buried in trees and shadow, and when you finally break out onto a bald or a fire tower, you tilt your head back and breathe. Open sky. Stars. Room.

That feeling doesn't last long here.

In the Appalachians, the sky isn't empty.
It has a history.
It has habits.
And at night, it has wings.

Long before anyone talked about UFOs or strange lights, people here were already watching the ridgelines for something else: **huge shapes moving against the stars, blacker than the sky, silent as falling ash.** Shadows passing across the moon. Dark silhouettes gliding over clearings without a sound. Things too big to be birds, too quiet to be aircraft, too deliberate to be flukes.

The mountains have ground predators.
Everyone knows that.

What fewer people want to talk about are the ones that come from above.

The Weight of Wings You Can't See

Most bird stories feel safe.
Owls. Hawks. Vultures. Turkeys busting out of brush and almost stopping your heart. Normal things.

The stories that don't get told as easily start the same way:

"I know how big a hawk is."
"I know what vultures look like."
"I know how a barred owl sounds."

Then comes the pause. The quiet recalibration.

"This wasn't that."

People talk about:

- shapes with **wingspans wider than a truck**

- silhouettes gliding from ridge to ridge, **tree to tree**, without flapping

- **wide, triangular wings** blocking out stars

- bodies that look more like a man's torso than a bird's

- forms that seem to fold up and vanish into rock or cloud

When they try to tell the story later, they trip over their own words. Your brain wants to shrink what you saw. Fit it into something common.

But some things are too big to fold that way.

One man from eastern Kentucky said it plainly:

"If that was a bird, then I don't know what birds are anymore."

Thunderbirds and Sky Predators in the Old Stories

The tribes that lived here long before any map lines were drawn had names for big things in the sky.

Thunderbirds.
Giant eagles.
Sky serpents.
Winged beings that rode storms.

They weren't cartoonish monsters. They were **forces** — predators and guardians and omens all at once.

Descriptions overlap a lot more with modern reports than people like to think:

- huge wingspans, **"as wide as a river"** in some exaggerations, but always bigger than anything normal

- feathers so dark they swallowed light

- the ability to ride wind without flapping for long stretches

- a tendency to appear before thunderstorms

- eyes that glowed like embers or lightning

The Cherokee talked about **Tlanûwa**, a monstrous bird that nested in cliffs and took livestock and, in some versions, people. Other stories mention **"storm birds"** that lived on high peaks and only came down when the air turned electric.

When you strip away the myth-layer, what you're left with is simple:

The people here expected the sky to be dangerous.

They knew the ground was hunted.
They knew the water was hunted.
They also knew the air was hunted.

That hasn't changed.

Only the language has.

The Ridge Shadows

If you stand on a high overlook at dusk long enough, you start to understand how easily you could miss something huge in the sky.

Ridges blur.
Treelines fuse into one dark spine.
Crows move like thrown stones.
Vultures tilt and circle above thermals.

And then, every so often, someone sees something that doesn't fit.

They talk about:

- a **wedge-shaped shadow** gliding along the ridgeline, bigger than any vulture

- a form that **stays low**, pacing the spine of the mountain instead of circling above

- wings that don't flap so much as adjust — a slight tilt, a subtle correction

- a sense of **being followed from above**, the same way ground creatures pace people from the tree line

One hiker on a Blue Ridge peak described seeing a shape cross in front of the moon:

"At first I thought plane. Then I realized there were no lights, no sound, and the wings were wrong. Too broad. Too blunt. It went from one side of the valley to the other in maybe five, six seconds. Then it was gone."

Another man in West Virginia saw a shadow sail silently over a logging road at twilight, low enough that he ducked instinctively.

"It blocked out the entire road," he said. "From tree to tree. Just a big black wing for two seconds. No sound. Nothing. Then there was nothing in the direction it went. No bird. No plane. Just air."

The mountains keep your attention on the ground.
That's the trick.

The sky uses that.

Giant Birds or Something Wearing Wings?

Some reports are easier—at least on paper—to file under "just a really big bird." Turkey vultures, black vultures, even golden eagles can look huge at the right angle.

But then you hear stories that refuse to sit in that drawer.

Hunters, linemen, and rangers describe:

- **"man-sized birds"** perched on dead snags, hunched and hulking

- wings that fold wrong — **too many joints**, angles not quite birdlike

- legs that look longer than any raptor's, **almost human in proportion**

- heads that don't match: too round, too blunt, eyes too forward-facing

- the distinct sense that the thing watching them **understood what it was looking at**

One lineman in western North Carolina told of seeing a huge dark shape perched on the crossarm of an unused power pole on a remote access road. As he came around the switchback, his headlights hit it.

"It was like seeing a man in a costume for a second," he said. "Not feathers. Not fur. Just this... textureless black. The wings were half-open. The head turned all the way toward me. Eyes caught the light like an animal's, but there was something behind them."

He braked hard.
The figure didn't fly immediately.
It **stepped off** the crossarm.

That's what bothered him most. It stepped off, dropped, and then the wings opened and it was gone—three beats, maybe four, then it disappeared into the valley air.

"Birds don't move like that off a perch," he said. "They jump. They launch. Whatever that was, it stepped."

That detail shows up more than you'd expect:

- stepping off cliffs

- stepping out of trees

- stepping into space, then gliding

Something that **wears wings** but isn't a bird at all.

The Night Flyers Over Hollers

Daytime sightings are rare enough.
Night is something else entirely.

People camping deep in hollers talk about:

- a sudden **wind from above** when the trees are otherwise still

- a **pressure change** that feels like a large object just swept over

- a rushing sound with no visible source

- a **shadow darker than the dark** moving across the stars

- the feeling of being scanned from above

Some describe hearing a **low, deep whoosh** passing overhead, not like a helicopter, not like a plane, but like an enormous pair of wings beating once, maybe twice.

One group camping near an old logging cut in Virginia described lying in their tents in the early hours of the morning when they heard something enormous move over them:

"It sounded like a flag the size of a house whipping once," one of them said. "Not flapping. Just this big, heavy 'whuff' of air. The tents shuddered a bit, and then there was nothing. No second pass. No circling. Just that one move, like something deciding where we were and then losing interest."

They didn't get out to look.

The smartest thing a person can do sometimes is **not** go looking.

Red Eyes in the Trees

Every region with winged-creature lore has its own eye stories. Appalachia is no exception.

People describe:

- **red or orange eyes** staring from the branches of dead trees at heights too high for a man to climb

- eyes spaced too wide for owls, too steady for raccoons

- glowing eyes that seem suspended in front of stone cliffs

- pairs of eyes that appear, vanish, then appear again a few feet away, as if something is repositioning while watching

At the edges of fields and graveyards, near old fire towers and along ridgelines above rivers, people talk about feeling "pulled" to look upward — and finding eyes already on them.

In a small West Virginia town, a man working a night shift at an industrial lot on the edge of the woods reported seeing two red orbs about twenty feet up, just past the security light's edge.

"I thought it was a reflection," he said. "Then they **blinked**. Both at the same time. Lid up, lid down. Like a person closing their eyes slow."

When he stepped toward the treeline, the eyes didn't retreat.
They **rose.**

First another five feet.
Then ten.
Then gone, either into the canopy or out into the night air.

"I went back inside," he said. "I don't get paid enough to investigate that kind of thing."

He laughs now when he tells it.
But you can hear the tremor under the story.

Eyes that float.
Eyes that climb.
Eyes that belong to something that doesn't need the ground.

Winged Things Around Bridges and Water

There's a pattern here that repeats often enough you start to notice:

Bridges.
Dams.
Old river crossings.
Cliffs above deep water.

Winged sightings cluster in these locations.

People describe:

- huge dark shapes gliding along river gorges

- creatures perching on girders at dusk

- silhouettes launching from cliff faces and vanishing into fog

- **"bat-winged"** forms seen in the corner of the eye near older bridges

The water, the concrete, the steel, the echoing noise — somehow, these places attract whatever is moving overhead.

One fisherman on a remote stretch of river in Pennsylvania swore that something spread-winged drifted between him and the full moon one night, **blocking out half the sky** for a second.

"It was shaped like a manta ray," he said. "Not a bird. Wide, flat, kind of triangular. Edges rippled. No sound. It felt wrong."

Another man, driving home over a narrow bridge after a late shift, said a **"cloak-shaped thing"** dropped from the girders, passed over his windshield, and vanished upward.

"It was like driving under a hanging coat that suddenly came alive," he said. "The whole truck rocked a bit from the air."

Bridges are built over **old crossings** — places where people and animals have always tried to move across water. If anything is watching or working the natural travel routes, those spots would be ideal.

The ground isn't the only highway here.

Some things use air.

Aerial Hunters, or Something Else?

There are two ways to look at these flying beings.

The first is as **apex predators**:

- large enough to carry off small deer or goats

- fast enough to drop on campsites from above

- silent enough to never be heard until it's too late

From that angle, the stories of disappearances near cliffs and overlooks make a certain, ugly sense. A person goes too close to an edge. A gust of wind. A slip. Or something that looks like a slip.

Bodies vanish into impossible terrain all the time. Some are never found. A big enough aerial predator could do a lot of damage with very little trace.

The second possibility is stranger:

These aren't simple predators.
They're **watchers** or **messengers**, the aerial counterpart to ridge giants, cave dwellers, and little people.

Their behavior often fits that role better:

- pacing hikers from above, but never diving

- circling camps but never attacking

- appearing near odd weather and lights

- perching above ruins and old graveyards

- escorting people out of certain valleys by maintaining visible presence

Predators don't sport with their food.
They don't hover in plain sight for long.

But sentinels do.
Scouts do.
Guardians do.

Whatever these winged beings are, they seem more interested in **monitoring** than in feeding.

That should comfort you.
It doesn't.

Being prey is one thing.
Being evaluated is another.

When Wings and Lights Work Together

When you stack all these stories alongside the sky lights from earlier chapters, something else shows up.

Sometimes, the lights and the wings appear **together**.

Witnesses describe:

- orbs pacing a ridge, followed moments later by a huge dark form gliding the same line

- a bright white light hovering over a valley, then a shadow shape dropping out of the dark beneath it

- multiple small lights circling a cliff face, then a single winged silhouette bursting away from the rock like it was launched

In a few cases, people talk about a blinding flash — not lightning, not camera glare, just a sudden white-out — followed by the impression of **enormous wings unfolding** in the afterimage.

"I couldn't see it directly," one man said. "But when my eyes adjusted, I had that retinal burn effect—you know, like when you stare at the sun too long. And in that ghost-image on my vision I could see the shape of wings. Big ones. Spread wide."

Lights that move like scouts.
Wings that move like muscle.

Different parts of the same system?
Different species, same job?

The mountains aren't taking questions on that yet.

The Psychological Effect of Something Above You

Ground predators scare people in obvious ways.
You hear footsteps behind you.
You smell musk.
You see eyes at ground level.

Winged beings work on a different layer of your brain.

People talk about:

- **a crushing sense of exposure** on ridges, like being on a plate

- sudden vertigo when looking up at the stars, as if the sky isn't empty

- a persistent feeling of being **scanned from above** when crossing balds or fire roads

- dreams after encounters involving falling, being lifted, or being watched from heights

Several witnesses said the same thing without knowing each other:

"It felt like it knew I had nowhere to go."

That's the core of it.

On the ground, you can run, hide, duck, fight.
In the sky, you're just... **available**.

Every open space becomes a risk:
clearings, cliff edges, old fields, lakes.

If something up there wants you, there is no tree line to slip into. No mine entrance to disappear down.

It takes a special kind of courage—or stubbornness—to camp on a bald after hearing these stories.

Most people don't go back a second time.

The Old Warnings, Rewritten in the Sky

Indigenous warnings about the sky beings were simple, and they sound very familiar now:

- Don't sleep on high peaks during certain seasons.

- Don't mock the thunder or call to the storm.

- Don't ignore birds going silent above a cliff.

- Don't stare too long at lights over the ridges.

- Don't travel the highest balds alone at night.

They didn't need to explain why.
They just needed people to listen.

The modern version isn't much different, once you strip away the technology and the denial:

- If the sky feels wrong, trust it.

- If the birds vanish and the air changes, move.

- If you see a shape that's too big, don't go looking for a second angle.

- If you feel watched from above, get under real cover—trees, rock, structure.

The mountains are three-dimensional.
The danger is, too.

Conclusion: The Mountains Have a Ceiling

One of the worst assumptions we carry into any wilderness is that "up" is safe. That if something goes wrong, a helicopter can come, a drone can scout, a plane can see us.

In the Appalachians, up is just another direction the mystery moves.

There are things on the ridges.
There are things in the caves.
There are things in the valleys, along the roads, around the old towns.

And there are things in the sky — winged beings and night flyers that slip between cloud and canopy, watching from above with a patience that feels older than anything built here.

If the giants are the bones of these mountains,
and the wolves and panthers are their teeth,
and the little people are their nerves...

The winged beings are their shadow.
The part that passes over you, briefly, and then is gone, leaving only a shiver and the sudden awareness that the sky is not empty and never was.

In the next chapter, we come back down to the ground—back to the human scale—and start looking at **what all of this does to people**: the searchers, the locals, the hikers, the investigators who come in thinking they're studying the wilderness, and leave realizing, sometimes too late, that the wilderness has been studying them the entire time.

Chapter Nineteen — The Feeling of Being Followed: Stalked in the Forest

There's a moment every wilderness traveler eventually hits — a point where the forest goes quiet, the trail feels too narrow, and something inside you whispers:

You're not alone.

Sometimes it's a false alarm. A trick of nerves.
Sometimes it's a deer stepping on a twig or a squirrel knocking bark loose.

But in the Appalachian Mountains, that feeling doesn't always pass.
Here, it tends to deepen.
It sharpens into a certainty that sits between your ribs.

The Appalachians have a reputation for it—this sensation of being paced, tracked, shadowed. Hunters talk about footsteps matching their own. Hikers speak of breath behind them, of a presence moving just out of sight. Campers feel watched from the treeline, even when the trees don't give up a single hint of motion.

And the eerie part isn't that this feeling exists.

It's that the stories here mirror patterns found in remote forests all across North America — and even in the wilderness of other continents. The sensation doesn't belong to one location or one creature. It belongs to a type of place. A type of silence. A type of ancient land that remembers older rules.

What happens in the Appalachian woods has cousins in the Pacific Northwest, the Yukon, Alaska, northern Quebec, Mongolia, Siberia, and the Scottish Highlands.

Different forests.
Different cultures.
Same feeling.

A watcher.
A tracker.
A presence that follows you, unseen yet undeniable.

The Appalachians simply happen to do it more often — and more intensely — than almost anywhere else.

The Woods That Move With You

Ask anyone who's spent real time alone in these mountains — not a day hike, not a campground loop, but deep woods, long ridges, forgotten hollers — and you'll hear variations of the same story:

"I was walking, and something was walking with me."

Not close.
Not aggressive.
Just… matching pace.

One hunter from Tennessee put it like this:

"It stayed twenty or thirty feet back in the trees. Every time I stopped, it stopped. Every time I walked, it walked. I never caught sight of it. I never heard breathing. But I heard the steps. Slow. Heavy. Deliberate."

He paused, a man not easily rattled.

"You know when something's studying you? That's what it felt like."

This is the same story you hear from:

- hunters in northern Ontario

- trappers in Alaska

- hikers in British Columbia's deep forests

- deer hunters in the Ozarks

- men in the Irish wilderness

- women hiking alone in New Zealand bush

- shepherds in the Carpathians

Different forests.
Same rhythm.
A companion you didn't invite.

Sometimes it keeps its distance.
Sometimes it closes the gap.

Footsteps That Don't Belong

One of the most unnerving Appalachian mysteries is the footsteps — the ones that appear when the terrain around you should be impossible for anything large to walk through silently.

People describe hearing:

- slow, heavy steps pacing them

- two-legged movement, not four

- weight shifting from one side to the other

- branches bending without snapping

- rock tapping in rhythm

One hiker in North Carolina told me:

"It wasn't a deer. It wasn't a bear. I know those sounds. This was something stepping carefully. Too carefully. Like it was trying not to scare me off."

That detail — *the careful steps* — shows up worldwide in places where unexplained creatures are reported.

In northern Alberta, trackers talk about something that "moves like a man but breathes like an animal."

In the Himalayas, Sherpa guides describe "tall shadows walking on two legs that follow from ridge to ridge but never close the distance."

In Australia's Blue Mountains, Yowie witnesses report "footsteps walking exactly behind you but always just out of sight."

The pattern doesn't care about borders or species.

Something follows people in ancient forests.
Something quiet, calculating, and patient.

The Breath on the Back of Your Neck

Some encounters aren't just footsteps.
They're intimate. Too close.

People describe:

- warm breath hitting the back of their neck

- a sudden cold column of air

- the sensation of someone leaning close

- a presence hovering inches behind

These aren't long-distance phenomena.
They're personal.

A fisherman in the Virginia mountains was climbing back to his truck after dusk when he felt hot breath on the side of his face — as if someone was standing right beside him.

He froze.
Turned slowly.
No one there.

But the air still carried the humidity of animal breath.

Similar stories come from:

- hikers in Colorado

- campers in the Adirondacks

- moose hunters in the Yukon

- backpackers in Washington's Olympic rainforest

Hot breath in cold air.
Cold breath in warm air.

Something deliberately close.
Something unseen.

In the Appalachian Mountains, locals shrug and say:

"Yeah... the woods do that."

But the woods don't breathe.

Something in them does.

The Whispering Trees

The Appalachians are famous for a strange auditory effect — voices or whispers drifting through the woods with no visible source.

People report:

- faint conversation behind them

- soft calling from within the timber

- a single word spoken clearly

- laughter out of place

A group of hikers in West Virginia heard what sounded like two people whispering behind them all night — close enough to make out tone but not words.

"We kept shining lights," one said. "Nothing ever showed up. But every time we turned our backs, the whispers started again."

Similar phenomena appear in:

- Algonquin Park

- Yosemite's deep off-trail regions

- the Black Forest of Germany

- Aokigahara in Japan

- Scotland's Cairngorms

Different accents.
Different languages.
Same unnerving effect.

The trees aren't whispering.
Something is *using* the trees to travel sound.

And whatever it is never allows itself to be seen head-on.

Rock Taps and Trail Markers

One of the most distinct Appalachian "you're not alone" signatures is the rock-tap — a sharp knock from an unseen place, sometimes answering your movements.

Hikers report:

- a tap when they step

- a tap when they clear a ridge

- a tap when they stop

Some taps seem random.
Others seem deliberate.

A man hiking near the North Carolina/Tennessee line described hearing a loud crack of stone behind him every time he crossed a switchback — like something large was matching his climb, staying parallel through the forest.

This "shadow paralleling" is also a hallmark of:

- Bigfoot activity in the Pacific Northwest

- Yeti territory in Nepal

- Yowie hotspots in Australia

- the Siberian taiga

The rock-tap is not an Appalachian invention.

It's a language.
A signal.
A tracking device.

Sometimes it warns.
Sometimes it provokes.

But it always communicates.

The Sudden Silence That Announces a Watcher

Few things feel worse in the wilderness than the moment nature turns off.

The Appalachians are loud until they're not.
Cicadas, crickets, birds, frogs — all of it can go dead silent in a heartbeat.

Hunters describe:

- birds stopping mid-song

- wind going still

- a pressure drop

- a sense of being enveloped

- silence thick enough to feel

One ranger said:

"When the woods go quiet, something big is moving. But the thing is — we don't always see what it is."

This "dead-silence moment" is global:

- Amazon tribes report it before jaguars — and before something else.

- Siberian hunters report it before "the tall ones."

- African bushmen report it before lions — and before silent watchers they refuse to name.

- Inuit hunters describe it on tundra where there are no trees at all.

Nature knows when a real predator is near.
And in places like this, *real predator* doesn't always mean something catalogued.

When the silence falls in the Appalachians, people instinctively stand still — or they leave.

Their bodies understand what their minds don't.

The Feeling of Being Judged

One of the strangest and most consistent Appalachian reports isn't fear.

It's evaluation.

People don't feel hunted.
They feel **assessed**.

A hiker from Georgia said:

"It wasn't trying to attack me. It was deciding if I was supposed to be there."

This sensation — the sense of something judging your presence — appears in:

- Bigfoot sighting clusters in Washington

- Wendigo territory in northern Canada

- Skinwalker areas in the Southwest

- Yowie hotspots in Queensland

- Himalayan passes associated with the Yeti

- rural Ireland "fairy path" zones

- jungles of Brazil

Different creatures.
Different folklore.

Same universal feeling:

This land has eyes.
And those eyes are deciding whether to let you stay.

In the Appalachians, the sensation can feel almost polite.

In other regions, it feels predatory.

Whatever follows people in these mountains has patience.
It has intention.
And sometimes, it has boundaries.

Crossing those boundaries is how people vanish.

When the Woods Push You Out

Locals talk about certain hollers, ridges, and abandoned towns where the land feels wrong — not haunted, not cursed, just unwilling.

People describe:

- a pressure behind them

- the urge to turn around

- the feeling of being escorted out

- a growing sense of dread

- footsteps following closely until they reach a clearing

One hunter from Virginia put it plainly:

"It didn't want me there. It didn't chase me — it guided me out."

This guidance phenomenon is almost identical to reports from:

- Nahanni Valley (NWT)

- Lake of the Woods

- the Adirondack backcountry

- Tongass rainforest in Alaska

- old-growth forests in British Columbia

- forests around Mt. Fuji

- deep Borneo jungle

When forests want you gone, they don't need words.
They use presence.

A presence that falls in behind you and walks you out like a parent gently
steering a child away from danger.

Except here, the parent has no face.
And no name.

What the Feeling Really Means

After hearing hundreds of Appalachian watcher stories, one conclusion becomes hard to avoid:

Something in these mountains is monitoring people.

Not always physically.
Not always aggressively.

But consistently.

And the eerie similarities to forests across the world tell us something important:

This isn't a local phenomenon.
It's a wilderness phenomenon.

Ancient, intelligent, aware wilderness behaves the same way everywhere.

From Appalachia to the Rockies.
From the Yukon to Quebec.
From Siberia to Nepal.
From Australia to South America.

The deeper the forest,
the older the land,
the more something watches those who enter.

Sometimes it's an animal.
Sometimes it's a spirit.
Sometimes it's a creature that has no name in any language.

But in the Appalachian Mountains, whatever follows people is closer, more consistent, and more deliberate than most places in North America.

The watcher here isn't just part of the landscape.

It is the landscape.

And when you're being followed, you're not imagining it.

You're being observed.
Measured.
Weighed.

And sometimes, quietly protected.
Other times, quietly warned.

In the next chapter, we'll look at what happens when people don't leave
— when they ignore the pressure, the footsteps, the whispers — and
disappear into one of the most mysterious vanishings hotspots on the
continent.

**Chapter Twenty — The Missing: Appalachian Vanishings &
Impossible Cases**

Most disappearances have explanations — bad weather, poor planning,
twisted ankles, wrong turns, simple accidents. Search and Rescue teams
will tell you that 90 percent of lost hikers are found within a mile or two
of where they went missing.

But the Appalachians aren't like most places.

Across these mountains, stretching from Alabama to Maine,
disappearances happen in ways that defy maps, terrain, and logic. People
vanish within sight of their families. They step off a trail to tie a boot and
are never seen again. They call out once for help and then… nothing.
They walk behind a group for ten seconds and dissolve into the
landscape as if the trees swallowed them whole.

And what makes it worse — what makes it so disturbing — is how
similar these vanishings are to cases scattered across other North
American wilderness hotspots:

- the Adirondacks

- the Smokies

- the Whites

- the Cascades

- northern Ontario

- the Rockies

- the Pacific Northwest

- the Yukon and Alaska

Different terrain. Different climates.
Same impossible disappearances.

The Appalachians don't just lose people.
They *take* them.

And if you talk to the old locals, the SAR volunteers, the hunters who have found things they wish they hadn't, they'll tell you:

It isn't the mountains.
It's what lives in them.

The Vanishings That Don't Make Sense

When you sort through missing-persons cases in the Appalachian region, you start noticing patterns — the exact same patterns seen in the Rockies, the deep forests of British Columbia, and the more remote areas of Ontario and Quebec.

Pattern One: Vanished Within Sight

Cases where a person disappears:

- within 20–40 feet of companions

- while walking behind a group

- while picking berries

- stepping behind a tree

- rounding a bend

No scream.
No struggle.
No sign.

A young woman in the Smokies stopped to retie her boot near a trail junction. Her husband stepped 30 feet ahead and waited. She never came around the bend. Search teams combed the area for weeks. Nothing.

This is nearly identical to disappearances at:

- Crater Lake (Oregon)

- Mount Shasta (California)

- Temagami and Algonquin (Ontario)

- the deep Yukon wilderness

People don't vanish in easy terrain — unless something removes them quickly, quietly, deliberately.

Pattern Two: Clothes Found, But Not the Person

One of the strangest recurring details in Appalachian vanishings is the half-folded clothing found miles from where the person disappeared.

Clothes missing.
Shoes removed.
No damage.
No blood.
Often arranged neatly.

This happens in:

- North Carolina

- Virginia

- West Virginia

- Pennsylvania

- upstate New York

And almost word-for-word in cases from:

- rural Alaska

- northern Quebec

- the Pacific Northwest

- the Australian bush

Predators don't fold clothes.
Hypothermic people don't remove them neatly.
Something else is happening.

Pattern Three: Silent Zones

Many vanishings happen in areas where witnesses describe:

- bird silence

- wind stopping

- deep pressure

- a sense of being observed

These "dead zones" show up worldwide in the most mysterious disappearance clusters:

- Nahanni Valley (NWT)

- Yosemite off-trail regions

- Aokigahara Forest (Japan)

- the Hoia-Baciu Forest (Romania)

- Mt. Kuk in Papua New Guinea

The Appalachians fit into the same global pattern — places where normal environmental rhythms shut off seconds before someone disappears.

Pattern Four: Dogs Won't Track

Search dogs in Appalachian vanishings often:

- refuse to leave the trailhead
- lie down
- whine
- circle
- lose the trail immediately
- track in circles like the scent is everywhere and nowhere at once

Dogs react the same way in the missing-person clusters of:

- Crater Lake
- Mount Rainier
- Yosemite
- Algonquin
- the Laurentians
- the Rockies

Animals know when there's something in the woods that isn't natural. And some of them won't pursue it.

The Appalachian Triangle — A Hotspot Hidden in Plain Sight

There are certain regions in the Appalachians where vanishings happen with alarming frequency, yet few people outside local circles talk about them.

These include:

- **The Smokies Backcountry (Deep Water, Norton Creek, Clingmans Dome)**

- **The Monongahela National Forest**

- **The Daniel Boone National Forest**

- **The George Washington & Jefferson National Forests**

- **North Georgia's Cohutta and Blue Ridge regions**

- **The Linville Gorge Wilderness**

These places are known by SAR teams for:

- fast-moving fog

- sudden weather shifts

- confusing terrain

- magnetic anomalies

- vanishing tracks

- hikers walking in circles despite compasses

But the disappearances go beyond lost-person scenarios.

People vanish:

- without supplies being found

- without scent trails

- in flat areas

- near trails

- next to water

- close to campgrounds

In one case, a boy vanished from a flat, open area near a field where searchers found no footprints except his — and then his tracks simply stopped.

Stopped.
In the middle of a grassy meadow.

No drag marks.
No animal sign.
No disturbance.

It's the kind of detail that matches vanishings in the Yukon and the Rockies almost perfectly.

Different mountains.
Same signature.

The Searchers Who Won't Talk

Every region with these kinds of disappearances has the same type of people — SAR volunteers, rangers, and trackers who know far more than they're willing to put on paper.

In Appalachia, a few themes repeat:

1. "We found patterns we can't explain."

Search teams sometimes find footprints:

- that lead straight up slopes too steep for humans

- that end abruptly on bare rock

- that start *after* a person should have been too lost to walk

2. "Something stalks the searchers."

Rangers talk about:

- footsteps matching their own

- heavy breathing from the trees

- glowing eyes watching

- stone taps trailing them

- a sense of being herded

This is identical to ranger accounts from:

- Rainier

- Algonquin

- Yosemite

- Banff

- Tongass

Wherever these vanishings happen, something follows those looking for the missing.

3. "Sometimes we know they're not coming back."

One ranger in the Virginias said:

"It's not the weather. It's not the animals. There are places in those woods where people don't come back. Period."

And that line — *there are places where people don't come back* — shows up almost word-for-word from rangers in British Columbia, Alaska, and Montana.

Patterns traveling across continents should make you uneasy.

It means it's not random.

Something is consistent.
Something is shared.

The Ones Who Return — Broken Stories, Fragmented Memories

Not everyone who vanishes stays gone.
Some come back — in strange, damaged, confused states.

They describe:

- missing hours or days

- waking up far from where they disappeared

- having no memory of walking that distance

- hearing whispers in the woods

- feeling led by a figure they couldn't see

- bright lights appearing in the trees

- a creature pacing beside them in the dark

A hiker in North Georgia was found five miles from his last known location, uphill, through dense brush no person could cross without being ripped to shreds.

His clothing wasn't damaged.
His boots were unlaced.
And he kept repeating:

"The tall man told me to hide."

A man in West Virginia was found with mud behind his ears, in a spot search teams had swept dozens of times.

He had no idea where he'd been.
No memory at all.

His last clear recollection:
"I heard someone calling my name, but it wasn't anyone I knew."

These aren't isolated cases.
They echo through wilderness vanishings everywhere:

- Yosemite

- the Rockies

- the Gaspé

- central Alaska

- northern Saskatchewan

The same themes appear:
being guided, being watched, being disoriented, being taken—by what, they never say, because they don't know.

Or they won't describe it.

The Creatures Connected to the Missing

One of the uncomfortable truths of Appalachian vanishings is this:

People often see *something* before a disappearance happens nearby.

The sightings include:

1. Ridgewalkers (the giants)

Seen pacing hikers near disappearance zones.
Huge silhouettes crossing fire roads.
Long strides in soft mud.

2. Little People

Chattering sounds.
Small shadows moving fast.
Tiny footprints near search areas.

3. Panthers and Black Cats

Large, silent feline presence.
Eyes above ground level.
Quiet tracking behavior.

4. Wolves That Aren't Wolves

Massive canines escorting people out — or deeper in.
Growls near missing-person sites.

5. Winged Beings

Seen circling certain ridges before storms.
Silent silhouettes above searchers.

6. Lights

Orbs pacing ridges.
Lantern-like glows moving uphill.
White flashes seen just before someone vanishes.

It's never clear which creature is responsible in each case — or if the disappearance is the result of something unseen entirely.

But the correlation is undeniable.

Where the missing appear, the creatures appear.
Or vice versa.

It's an ecosystem.
A system of watchers, predators, guardians, and something else we don't have a name for.

The Cases That Haunt SAR Teams

Most SAR stories remain unofficial, passed quietly at training camps or late-night fires.

A ranger told me about a case where they found a child's boot high in a tree — too high for a child to reach, too strong to be a simple toss. No claw marks. No damage. Just… placed.

Another SAR member found a circle of stones arranged perfectly around a missing person's last known spot. The stones weren't there the day before.

Another searcher in Virginia saw what he described as "a shape the size of a refrigerator" step away from a tree at twilight and then… disappear. Vanish. No retreat. Just gone.

They found the missing person three days later — dazed, dehydrated, confused — with no memory of leaving the trail.

"I followed the tall man," he said again and again. "I thought he was a ranger."

That phrase appears all over North America.
Survivors describing the figure they followed — a guide, a guardian, or something pretending to be one.

It's always tall.
Always man-shaped.
Never fully human.

The Red Zones — Places the Locals Won't Go

Every region has its don't-go-there places.
In the Appalachians, these areas are spoken of quietly:

- certain hollers

- certain cliffs

- certain ridge gaps

- certain abandoned towns

- certain forgotten cemeteries

Locals say:

"People disappear up there."
"Things move in those woods that aren't animals."
"You won't catch me in that hollow after dark."
"They don't like strangers in that part."

The phrasing changes from town to town, but the meaning stays the
same.

There are places in these mountains where the rules shift.
Where something waits.
Where people go missing at a rate too high to ignore.

These places exist around the world —
the Nahanni Valley,
Aokigahara,
the Hoia-Baciu Forest,
Lake Baikal,
parts of the Amazon,
the Australian bush,
coastal Oregon,
interior Alaska.

The Appalachians belong on that list.

Ancient places that keep their own.
Places that breathe.
Places that decide.

Conclusion: The Missing Are a Warning

When you track these vanishings long enough, a hard truth settles in:

People don't vanish from the Appalachian Mountains because the terrain
is dangerous.

People vanish because something in the terrain chooses them.

These disappearances aren't scattered.
They form patterns — geographic, behavioral, seasonal.

They echo other global hotspots where the land seems to have a mind of its own.

Whether it's giants, shadow beings, panthers, little people, underground watchers, or something else entirely — the Appalachians have more vanishings than most mountain ranges for a reason.

The mountains aren't empty.
They aren't passive.
They aren't asleep.

They are selective.

And sometimes, when the wrong person walks the wrong trail on the wrong day, the mountains simply close behind them.

In the next chapter, we go to the people who know this better than anyone — the Search & Rescue teams — and step into the stories they share only when the radios are off, the fire is low, and no one is around to write anything down.

Chapter 22 will take you into the SAR diaries — the things they see, the things they hear, and the cases that keep them awake decades later.

Chapter Twenty-One — The Lights in the Timber

There are nights in the Appalachian Mountains when the forest carries a glow that shouldn't exist. Not moonlight. Not fire. Not the distant sweep of a ranger's truck light drifting across a ridge. This glow moves with intent — drifting, pulsing, weaving between the trees like something alive.

People call them **ghost lights**.
Some call them **lantern men**.
Old-timers call them **wandering lights**.
Scientists call them **atmospheric anomalies**.

Whatever the name, the lights remain one of the most persistent and unsettling mysteries in the Appalachian wilderness.

These lights have been seen for generations — long before electricity, long before roads carved the hollers, long before families settled the steep valleys and ridge tops. They show up where the forest is oldest, where the canopy still knits together into deep shadow, where human voice and flame feel out of place.

And like so many Appalachian mysteries, the phenomenon is not unique to these mountains.
Almost identical lights appear in forests and mountains across the world:

- in the outback deserts of Australia

- in the bogs of Ireland

- above the taiga in Siberia

- in the deep interior of British Columbia

- along river valleys in Alaska

- in the wooded highlands of Scotland

- in the remote Adirondacks

- across Mexico, South America, and Japan

Different hemispheres.
Different cultures.
Same lights.

It's not a local superstition.
It's a global pattern.

And the Appalachian Mountains may be one of the most active regions on Earth.

The First Time You See One

Most people who encounter the lights do so under the same conditions:

- dusk settling in

- a cool drop in temperature

- mist forming in low valleys

- fog drifting across old timber roads

- late-autumn air

- early winter darkness

The first sighting often looks like a single glowing sphere hovering between the trees, usually:

- the size of a fist

- white, yellow, or pale blue

- floating anywhere from waist height to the canopy

- silent

- slow

- purposeful

It's easy to confuse it with a headlamp or another hiker at first. But the lights don't behave like people.

They glide uphill with no effort.
They drift sideways at angles that defy gravity.
They hover in place for minutes.
They extinguish instantly — only to reappear somewhere else.
They weave through dense branches without illuminating them.

A hunter in western North Carolina once described watching a tennis-ball–sized white orb float between oak trees like an insect searching for a landing spot. It moved slowly, deliberately. When he stepped toward it, the orb blinked out.

Seconds later, it reappeared twenty feet behind him.

"I left," he said. "Whatever it was… it wasn't for me."

Even seasoned hunters don't follow lights like that.

The Lantern Men of West Virginia

West Virginia has some of the most famous light sightings in the Appalachians. Deep in the hollers, drifting along forgotten mining roads and abandoned rail cuts, people regularly report glowing orbs that move like swinging lanterns.

These lights:

- sway as though carried by an unseen hand

- follow old trails long erased

- hover over creek beds

- vanish at the sight of a human

- reappear exactly where they were days later

For generations, coal miners told stories of seeing lantern glows deeper inside tunnels than any living worker could have been. No footsteps. No voices. Just a faint light floating between the wooden braces.

One miner wrote in a journal:

"The lantern swung slow, too slow for a man. I shouted, but got no answer. The light drifted to the left wall and dissolved like fog."

Scientists blame methane gas.
Locals blame restless spirits.
But people see the same lights miles from any mine.

Whatever they are, they don't care about folklore.
They move as they please.

The Blue Orbs of the Smokies

The Great Smoky Mountains have their own brand of lights — bright blue or electric white, almost neon in color.

Witnesses describe them as:

- hovering just above the ground

- bobbing like fishing floats

- pulsing in intensity

- zipping between trees

- splitting into multiple orbs

- vanishing silently

One backpacker swore he watched a pale blue orb drift toward him along a ridge. When he raised his flashlight, the orb dimmed. When he lowered it, the orb brightened and moved closer.

He didn't sleep that night.

These blue orbs match global patterns:

- the Min Min Lights of Australia

- the Paasselkä Lights of Finland

- the Marfa Lights of Texas

- the Chaneques lights of Mexico

- the murrain glows of Scotland

Same movement.
Same size.
Same intelligence.

The Smokies simply seem to have more of them.

Lights That Lead You Off the Trail

Among the eeriest Appalachian encounters are lights that appear to *guide* hikers — or mislead them.

These lights don't stay still. They play a strange form of distance control:

- gliding ahead on the trail

- stopping when the hiker stops

- blinking out if approached too fast

- reappearing off the trail, deeper in the timber

- luring hikers into unstable or dangerous ground

A hiker near Black Balsam Knob followed what he assumed was a lost camper's headlamp. The glow moved steadily down an overgrown track. Each time he paused, the light also paused.

Finally, the trail beneath him gave way. He slid down a steep slope into dense brush. When he looked back up, the light hovered above him — calmly drifting.

He realized the truth much too late:

"It wasn't trying to help me. It was trying to lead me somewhere."

Similar stories come from:

- Ireland (will-o'-the-wisp)

- Nepal (mountain spirits)

- Scandinavia (huldra lights)

- rural Japan (ghost lanterns)

- the Ozarks (spooklights)

- Western Canada (valley orbs)

Wherever the phenomenon appears, people learn quickly:

You don't follow the lights.
They're not guides.
They're invitations.
And you don't want to know where they lead.

The Brown Mountain Connection

North Carolina's Brown Mountain Lights are the backbone of the entire Appalachian orb tradition. For over a century, thousands of witnesses — rangers, hunters, tourists, locals — have reported glowing orbs rising from the treetops, drifting along the ridges, pulsing in the night.

The lights:

- float above the canopy

- glide horizontally for long distances

- split into multiple spheres

- rise vertically like sparks

- vanish without fading

- appear on perfectly clear nights

Multiple scientific expeditions attempted to explain them. None succeeded. The lights show up before cameras and after cameras. Before electricity. Before modern roads.

Whatever the Brown Mountain lights are, they behave nearly identically to the ghost lights witnessed across the Appalachian chain.

It's one system — a web that spans states and generations.

Something in these mountains glows.

And the glow is alive.

The Lights That Enter Camps

Most encounters happen at a distance — a flicker in the trees, a pulse near the ridge. But some lights cross an unspoken boundary and drift directly into human camps.

These stories unsettle even lifelong woodsmen.

A backpacker in the Monongahela woke to a soft glow on the inside of his tent. At first he thought it was moonlight, until he realized the glow moved — brightening and dimming like slow breath.

He unzipped the door and stepped out.

The glow retreated instantly, stopping at the edge of camp, hovering at knee height. It stayed there for nearly thirty seconds before fading like an ember falling into ash.

He didn't wait for it to return.
He packed and left in the dark.

Similar events occur in:

- the Adirondack backcountry

- BC's interior forests

- Alaska's river valleys

- Scotland's lonely stone ruins

- deep Australian bush camps

Some lights approach tents as if examining them.
Others drift around campfires like cautious animals.
Some hover near sleeping bags.
Others appear behind logs or stumps, pulsing slowly.

Nothing in nature behaves this way.
These lights are curious — but curiosity is not safety.

Lights Inside Abandoned Cabins

Appalachian hikers often explore old cabins — remnants of settlers, moonshiners, trappers, or families who left generations ago. Many of these structures are half-collapsed, roofs sagging, windows broken, floors soft with rot.

And yet hikers report seeing faint lights glowing *inside* these ruins at night.

The glows are often:

- pale blue or white

- the size of a fist

- floating about chest level

- drifting from room to room

- extinguishing instantly when approached

A pair of hikers near an old hunting cabin in Virginia described seeing light moving behind the window glass — long after they'd confirmed the cabin was empty.

When they entered:

- no footprints

- no lanterns

- no candles

- no wildlife

- no gear

Only the faint smell of ozone, like the aftermath of lightning.

Cabin lights are among the oldest Appalachian ghost reports — predating electricity by centuries. Yet they match modern sightings in:

- Alberta

- Norway

- Finland

- Tasmania

Lights that explore abandoned places almost like keepers checking on their territory.

Campfire Visitors

If there is one location the lights seem consistently drawn to, it's the soft flicker of a campfire.

Campers across the Appalachians report small, bright orbs drifting toward fires, hovering at the outer edge of the light, then circling the camp as if taking stock of the people gathered.

A man camping alone on the Tennessee side of the Blue Ridge watched a white orb drift to within six feet of his fire, hover for ten seconds, then slide silently behind his tent.

He listened to it move — though it made no sound — feeling every instinct tighten.

When he finally shone his flashlight, nothing was there.

Another family camping in Shenandoah reported three pale orbs that weaved around each other above the firepit at dusk like synchronized swimmers.

The moment the fire cracked loudly, the orbs vanished.

Just gone.
As if absorbed by the dark.

Lights That Pass Through Solid Objects

One of the most disturbing categories of encounters involves lights that ignore physical boundaries entirely.

A hunter sleeping in a canvas wall tent in Tennessee woke to find a white light hovering just below the roof peak. Before he could sit up, the orb drifted downward — and passed directly through the tent floor.

No rip.
No burn.
No trace.

When he stepped outside, the forest was silent.
Not dead — but waiting.
As though something had been there moments before.

This phenomenon appears globally:

- lights drifting through stone huts in Scotland

- orbs entering Alaskan trapper cabins

- lights passing through trees in Finland

- glowing spheres sinking into the ground in Australia

Nothing in known physics moves like this.

The Lights That Watch Campers Sleep

Perhaps the most intimate and unnerving encounters involve lights hovering near tents at night — sometimes inches away from the thin mesh windows.

Campers describe:

- white or blue glows hovering at eye level

- soft pulsing light like breathing

- orbs rising and falling slowly

- lights drifting around the tent in slow circles

A couple sleeping in North Carolina woke to a white glow hovering outside their tent vestibule, floating three feet off the ground.

When the man whispered to his wife, the orb brightened — as if reacting.

It then drifted backward into the timber, maintaining perfect height, before blinking out.

Some lights behave almost like animals.
Others behave like observers.
None behave naturally.

Historical Accounts: The Lantern Walkers

Hundreds of years before LED lights or flashlights, early settlers described "lantern walkers" — glowing spheres drifting along old wagon paths.

They wrote about:

- lights pacing horses at night

- glows seen through fog long before a ridge appeared

- lights ascending hillsides silently

- beams swinging like a lantern in dead wind

Cherokee and older Indigenous traditions also reference wandering spirit-lights — not malicious, but boundary-keepers between worlds.

Scots-Irish settlers had already seen them in the Highlands. They recognized the lights instantly.

They were older than Appalachia.
Older than the trees themselves.

Attempts to Explain the Lights

Dozens of theories exist:

- methane ignition

- glowing insects

- swamp gas

- bioluminescent fungus

- ball lightning

- reflections off moisture

But none of these fit the observed behaviors:

- directional movement

- intelligent adjustment

- ability to stop and wait

- entering shelters

- passing through objects

- returning to the same sites for centuries

There is no known natural phenomenon that behaves like a curious, mobile, reactive sphere of light.

Which leaves the same two possibilities researchers quietly acknowledge:

1. **A physical phenomenon science has not yet identified.**

2. **A nonphysical phenomenon that interacts with the physical world.**

Neither is encouraging.

Conclusion: The Lights Know You're There

The ghost lights of the Appalachian Mountains are not imagination, nor cultural artifact, nor old miner superstition. They exist independent of witness background, age, location, or expectation.

Children see them.
Hunters see them.
Rangers see them.
Campers see them.
People from countries with their own light lore instantly recognize them.

The lights behave like observers.
Careful.
Curious.
Intelligent.
And aware of the people near them.

They watch camps.
They approach fires.
They hover outside tents.
They enter cabins.
They inspect.
They linger.
And then they vanish, leaving nothing but an electric feeling in the air.

Whatever these lights are, they are not passive.

In the next chapter, we step away from the orbs and into the places where
the mountains themselves seem to breathe — the haunted hollers,
abandoned mining towns, silent ghost settlements, and forgotten valleys
where the land keeps its own dark memory.

Chapter Twenty-Two — The Hollers That Don't Let Go

There are places in the Appalachian Mountains where the past never really dies. Towns that existed for a time — a few decades, a generation or two — before the mines shut down, the timber companies pulled out, the rail lines rusted, or the families simply vanished into deeper valleys.

Some of these places are still on maps.
Most of them aren't.

In the Appalachians, they're called **lost hollers**, **dead hollers**, or **forgotten valleys** — places where entire communities once lived, prayed, worked, buried their dead, and then walked away without looking back.

The forest reclaimed the houses.
The kudzu swallowed the porches.
The wells collapsed.
The cemeteries tilted.
The roads dissolved.
And nature filled in the silence with something else entirely.

Even now, hikers stumble into these hollers and describe the same sensation:

You're being watched.

Not from a distance.
Not from deep ridgelines.
But from inside the hollow itself — as though the very bones of the land remember the people who lived there and haven't decided whether you belong.

This phenomenon isn't unique to Appalachia. Forgotten settlements in:

- northern Ontario

- the Adirondacks

- British Columbia mining camps

- the Yukon's Klondike trails

- ghost towns in Nevada

- Scotland's abandoned glens

- Siberian timber villages

- Patagonia's old sheep stations

all share the same unsettling atmosphere.

But Appalachia does it differently.

Here, the hollers aren't empty.
They feel occupied.

And the deeper you go, the more the land feels like it's waiting.

The Places Time Forgot

Walk long enough in these mountains and you'll eventually find them:

- collapsed porches half-swallowed by earth

- chimneys standing like grave markers

- rusted bed frames among oak roots

- hand-dug wells choked with leaves

- stone steps leading nowhere

- barns folded inward like broken ribs

- abandoned churches where the windows stare like empty eyes

Some hollers sank because the mines dried up.
Others drowned when rivers were dammed.
Some were abandoned after floods or landslides.
Others faded one family at a time until nothing remained but silence.

A hiker in West Virginia told me about finding a schoolhouse foundation deep in a valley, the only sign it ever existed being a fallen bell and a cracked slab of concrete.

"There was no trail," he said. "No road, no markings. It felt like the forest had put the whole place under a spell."

He didn't stay long.
Most people don't.

Something about abandoned hollers urges you to keep walking — not because you're unwelcome, but because the place is holding its breath around you.

Ghost Towns the Forest Refuses to Give Back

Unlike the ghost towns out West — sun-bleached boards, clapboard structures, wide views — Appalachian ghost towns are swallowed by forest so thoroughly that you can walk within twenty feet of a house and never know it's there.

The wilderness devours things quickly here.

But some structures fight back.

In eastern Kentucky, hikers find old mining houses still locked tight after seventy years, windows intact, curtains crumbling behind the glass.

Some of these houses have strange details:

- doorframes nailed shut from *inside*

- chairs propped under knobs

- pantry doors left wide open

- old clothes hung neatly on nails

- children's toys stacked in corners

- dishes on tables, fused with dust and time

One hiker found a set of muddy footprints inside a house — not human, not animal — long after the last resident had died.

Another reported hearing footsteps on the floorboards of a church that had partially collapsed, even though the roof and half the walls were gone.

You don't get that in western ghost towns.
You get that in places where the land has soaked up generations of life — and refuses to let it go.

Hollers Locals Avoid After Dark

Ask locals where not to go after sunset and they'll lower their voices, glance around, and tell you about places that never felt right:

- hollers with no birds

- roads that eat headlights

- cemeteries that "breathe cold"

- creek beds that glow faintly at night

- valleys that echo footsteps

- ridges where voices drift long after dark

They'll tell you about houses where no animal will enter — dogs stop at the threshold, tails tucked, refusing to cross the line.

They'll tell you about places where the air feels thick, where the wind doesn't pass through, where sound doesn't carry.

One old man in north Georgia told me:

"My granddaddy said there's hollers you can walk into just fine, but they won't let you walk out the same."

He meant it metaphorically.

I'm not entirely sure he meant it *only* metaphorically.

The Cold Spots in Warm Valleys

Some hollers hold strange temperature pockets — places where warm summer air becomes refrigerator-cold in seconds.

Hikers describe:

- fog forming instantly

- breath turning visible

- chills running down their backs

- sudden goosebumps

- the feeling of a presence behind them

One man exploring an abandoned homestead in Virginia said he entered a cellar where the temperature dropped thirty degrees. His camera battery died instantly. His flashlight dimmed. When he stepped back out, the world returned to normal.

Cold spots like this appear in:

- abandoned mining camps in BC

- ghost towns in Colorado

- ancient valleys in Scotland

- WWII bunkers in the Aleutians

- Sami reindeer pastures in Norway

Places heavy with history.
Places where memory lingers.

But in Appalachia, the cold isn't just atmospheric.

It feels personal.
Deliberate.

Like something is reaching through the air to touch you.

The Cemeteries No One Visits

Deep in the backcountry lie old graveyards — family plots dating back a century or more, hidden beneath tangled vine and fallen trees.

Some are marked by carved stones.
Others by simple field rocks.
Some by nothing at all.

People who stumble on these graveyards often describe the same sensations:

- a sudden heaviness in the chest

- a shift in air pressure

- the feeling of trespassing

- faint whispers in windless air

- the sense of eyes on them

- dread with no visible source

One backpacker found an old cemetery on a slope above an abandoned church. Every stone leaned in the same direction — as though pulled toward something.

He felt watched by the ground itself.

When he stepped away, the forest sounds resumed.
When he stepped back in, the silence fell again.

He didn't stay to investigate.

Some places aren't meant for visitors.

The Sound of Voices Where No Houses Stand

One of the strangest Appalachian holler phenomena is the sound of voices in places where no settlement remains — not even traces of foundations.

Hikers report:

- muffled conversation

- distant laughter

- a baby crying

- a woman humming

- a man calling out

- whispers from behind trees

- the sound of footsteps on nonexistent floorboards

A woman hiking alone in Tennessee heard a dinner bell ringing in the forest — clear, metallic, echoing down a valley with no houses, no old farms, no structures of any kind.

She turned back immediately.

Another hiker heard what sounded like a fiddle tune drifting down a ridge at dusk. When he checked his GPS, he realized no trail or cabin was within two miles.

These phantom sounds appear worldwide in old settlement sites:

- Irish famine villages

- Siberian mining camps

- abandoned Japanese mountain towns

- Andean shepherd settlements

But in Appalachia, the sounds often accompany a sensation far stranger:

A feeling that someone is standing right behind you, just outside your peripheral vision.

The Hollers That Make You Walk Faster

There are valleys in these mountains where people move quicker than they intend to — not out of fear exactly, but instinct.

Something feels off.
Something feels wrong.

Hikers describe:

- the sensation of being followed

- footsteps matching their pace

- a heavy pressure on the back of their neck

- the instinct to *leave now*

- a cold breeze when the air is still

- the sense that the land itself is aware of them

One hunter said:

"It felt like the hollow was watching me. Like it was deciding what to do with me."

The feeling lifted the moment he climbed out of the valley.

I've heard nearly identical stories from:

- deep Temagami

- northern California redwoods

- BC's interior plateau

- the Adirondacks

- the New Mexico mesas

- near the Nahanni Valley

Places where the land is ancient enough to develop a personality — or an attitude.

Appalachian hollers are some of the oldest pieces of land in North America.

Old enough to remember.
Old enough to judge.
Old enough to keep secrets.

The Settlements That Shift in Memory

Some of the eeriest accounts come from people who swear they've seen buildings that weren't there when they returned.

A father and son hiking in Kentucky claimed they found a small shack along a creek — intact, with a metal roof and glass windows. They saw nothing strange except that it looked lived in, though abandoned.

Two weeks later, they returned to the spot.

Nothing.
No shack.
No foundation.
No metal scraps.
No clearing.
Just forest.

Another man in North Carolina described seeing an old cabin one autumn, only to return in spring and find a collapsed ruin — decades worth of decay that shouldn't have happened in a few months.

And some see houses that look whole, only to approach and find they were never full houses — just two walls, a collapsed chimney, and the memory of something that once existed.

It would be tempting to chalk this up to misremembered trails, shadows, or tricks of light.

But the same phenomenon appears around the world:

- phantom lodges in the Yukon

- "shifting huts" in Norway

- cabins that appear and disappear in the Alps

- ghost towns in the Amazon that move between sightings

Settlements with memory.
Structures that cling to existence the way a half-forgotten dream clings to the edge of waking.

Conclusion: The Hollers That Never Forgot Their Dead

Appalachian hollers are not empty places. They carry generations of human history — the triumphs, the hard years, the laughter, the grief, the tragedies, the unmarked graves.

When people leave, those stories don't vanish. The forest absorbs them.

And something remains.

Call it energy.
Call it memory.
Call it spirits.
Call it the land itself refusing to forget.

But when you stand in an abandoned valley and feel a pressure behind your ribs, a weight on your shoulders, the sense of being watched by a presence you can't name... it's not your imagination.

The holler remembers.
And for brief moments, it remembers *you*, too.

In the next chapter, we step into another Appalachian mystery — one that blurs the line between folklore and physical reality: **the shadow people and watchers seen along ridgelines, roads, and abandoned trails**.

Dark silhouettes.
Human shapes.
Silent observers.

The Appalachians are full of eyes.

Chapter Twenty-Three — The Phantom Travelers

There are roads in the Appalachian Mountains that don't feel like roads at all. They feel like scars — narrow ribbons of gravel and broken asphalt cut through forests older than memory. Some of these roads follow ancient animal paths. Others sit on top of forgotten wagon routes. A few were once the main arteries for towns that no longer exist.

Drive these roads long enough, especially at dusk or under fog, and you might see someone walking the shoulder — a lone figure, a silhouette carrying something, a traveler heading somewhere they no longer belong.

Except when you slow down, the figure disappears.
And when you check the rearview mirror, there's no one behind you.

The Appalachians have always been full of **phantom travelers** — people who died on the roads, or lived and left, or simply walked off history's edge. Ghosts without homes. Wanderers between worlds.

They appear to:

- hunters returning home after dark

- truckers crossing mountain gaps

- hikers on old ridge paths

- night drivers cutting through fog

- locals who know better than to stop

- tourists who don't

These travelers don't always look ghostly.
They don't float.
They don't glow.
They look real — until they don't.

And while the Appalachians may be one of the most famous regions for roadside apparitions, identical figures appear across the world:

- Scotland's mountain passes

- the Yukon's Klondike roads

- Ireland's famine paths

- Japan's wooded highways

- rural Alaska

- old European carriage routes

- desert roads in Nevada and Utah

Different landscapes.
Different histories.
Same lonely travelers.

But nowhere do they feel quite as close — or as uncomfortably alive — as in the Appalachian Mountains.

The Woman in the White Shawl

The most well-known phantom traveler in the Appalachians is not a threat but a mystery — a woman described as wearing a simple white shawl, seen walking barefoot along old mountain roads in North Carolina, Tennessee, and Virginia.

She doesn't look frightening.
She doesn't lunge at cars.
She doesn't scream or vanish dramatically.

She simply walks.

One witness, a truck driver delivering lumber through a remote stretch near Unicoi Gap, described slowing down when he saw her on the shoulder. He thought she was lost or injured.

"It was cold," he said. "Cold enough breath hung in the air. She didn't have shoes. No bag. No coat. Just a white shawl pulled around her shoulders like she didn't feel the cold at all."

When he pulled alongside her to ask if she needed help, she continued walking — her face obscured by the shawl.

He drove ahead a few hundred yards, found a place to turn around, and came back.

The road was empty.

She had vanished into thin air.
No footprints.
No movement in the brush.
No sound.

People have seen her for decades — always alone, always barefoot, always with the same slow, deliberate pace.

Some say she was a woman searching for a child lost in the mountains.
Others say she died fleeing something.
Others believe she never lived in this time at all.

But everyone agrees:
You don't stop.
You don't speak.
You drive on.

The Lantern Man of Black Hollow Road

In West Virginia, locals whisper about a man seen carrying a lantern along Black Hollow Road — a narrow, twisting route that barely fits a single car.

Witnesses describe him as:

- tall

- wearing a coat or long shirt

- carrying a dim, amber lantern

- walking slowly with his head down

Drivers say his lantern casts no light on the surrounding road.
It illuminates only himself.

An older man told me he saw the Lantern Man five times in his life. The
figure never reacted to cars, never lifted his head, never changed
direction.

"He's walking somewhere he used to go," he said. "And he ain't got
there yet."

Several drivers report the same impossible detail: when they pass him,
their engines sputter — just for a moment, like the air thickens around
them.

Locals warn newcomers:
"If you see the lantern, drive slow but don't stop. He isn't for this world
anymore."

The Man on the Switchback

Hikers on old trails in the Smokies tell stories of a man seen standing at
long-forgotten switchbacks — not interacting, not calling out, just
watching hikers approach before stepping off the trail and disappearing
into solid rock.

One hiker recounted:

"At first I thought he was another hiker waiting for me to pass. He was
standing perfectly still. Too still. I said hello. He didn't answer. When I
got within ten feet, he turned and walked straight into the mountainside.
Like he melted into it."

Reports from as far back as the 1930s reference the same figure on the
same trail.

He has no pack.
No gear.
No hat.
No hiking clothes.

Just a tall silhouette that appears where the old trail once bent sharply to avoid a deadly cliff.

Some say he's a warning.
Others say he's a memory.

Whatever he is, people avoid that trail after dark.

The Appalachian Coachman

One of the rarest phantom traveler sightings is the **Appalachian Coachman** — the ghost of a man driving a horse-drawn wagon along routes where the last stages and mail coaches ran over a century and a half ago.

Drivers describe hearing:

- hoofbeats behind them

- the rattle of old wagon wheels

- chains clinking

- the snap of reins

- a muffled male voice shouting a command

All this on empty night roads miles from any farm.

Some see the wagon.
Most don't.

A few have reported a dark silhouette of a man wearing an old coat and wide-brimmed hat, riding just behind their car for several seconds before vanishing.

Truckers say he appears in the fog.
Locals say he appears when storms roll in.

Nothing about these encounters feels threatening, but they do feel heavy — like passing briefly through someone else's history and then back into your own.

The Miner on the Ridge Road

Near old coal towns in southern West Virginia and eastern Kentucky, drivers frequently report seeing a man in a soot-blackened shirt walking the ridge roads at night.

He is always:

- alone

- limping

- covered in coal dust

- holding a metal lunch pail

- staring straight ahead

Drivers slow down to avoid hitting him.
Some honk.
Some flash headlights.

None get a response.

When they pass him, the figure dissolves instantly — not into mist, not into the trees, but into nothing at all.

Men who worked the mines swear the apparition is a miner who never made it home after a cave-in. His body was never recovered. His spirit still follows the road he walked every night of his life.

Apparitions like this appear in mining regions around the world:

- British Columbia's silver camps

- California's gold country

- Colorado's ghost towns

- Cornwall's tin mines

- the Yukon's Klondike trails

Wherever hard men once worked dangerous ground, the land seems to keep one of them.

The Appalachians are full of these men.

The Children on the Old School Route

This one is harder to talk about — but locals in Tennessee, North Carolina, and Virginia mention it quietly.

Drivers on old mountain roads that once served schoolhouse routes sometimes report seeing children standing near bends in the road at dusk.

Not moving.
Not waving.
Just standing.

Some say they're wearing outdated clothing — wool coats, small dresses, knickers, suspenders, worn-out shoes.

Others say the children vanish the moment a driver blinks.

Few talk about it publicly.
No one stops.
No one gets out of the car.

One woman who saw them said:

"They weren't alive. I knew that as soon as I saw them. It wasn't fear. It was sadness. Like they were waiting for something that would never come."

Across North America, old school routes from the late 1800s and early 1900s have similar sightings — children seen where schools once stood before being reclaimed by the forest.

Ghosts of a generation the world forgot.

The Phantom Hitchhiker of Route 129

On the Dragon — the famous 318-curve stretch of Route 129 between North Carolina and Tennessee — motorcyclists and sports car drivers talk about a hitchhiker who appears on foggy nights.

He's described as:

- tall

- wearing a dark coat

- carrying a bag

- standing perfectly still

Riders who pass him say he never lifts his head.
Some claim he vanishes a second after they go by.
A few swear he appears in their mirrors as a dark figure sitting upright on the double yellow line before fading out.

Truckers call him "the ghost of the Dragon."
Locals say he died in an accident decades ago.
Others believe he's older than the road itself.

The strangest detail:
People report seeing him walking downhill — but never uphill.

Ghosts stuck in loops often follow the same path forever.

Phantom Travelers Inside the Forest

Not all travelers are roadside apparitions. Some appear deep within the forest, walking old trails long forgotten.

Hunters describe seeing:

- a man crossing a creek with no sound

- a woman with long hair drifting between trees

- a figure standing at the base of an abandoned cemetery

- footsteps on wooden planks that no longer exist

- silhouettes near old homesteads

One hunter in Kentucky watched a figure walk into the timber at dawn. He followed the trail and found a clearing with a collapsed cabin.

The figure was gone, but the clearing smelled faintly of wood smoke — though no fire burned, and no ashes remained.

It's not unusual for phantom travelers to appear near structures where life once flourished.

What's unusual is how *alive* they often look.

These aren't pale, translucent figures.
They're solid.
Heavy.
Human-shaped.
Fully realized.

Until they're not.

Why Phantom Travelers Linger

Ghosts in cities haunt rooms.
Ghosts in cemeteries haunt graves.

But ghosts in the mountains?
They haunt the routes they walked in life.

The Appalachian phantom traveler tradition likely exists because:

- people walked everywhere

- roads were lifelines

- paths were passed down generations

- hollers held history like a living book

- communities rose and fell with the land

- tragedies happened far from help

- the mountains isolated lives as much as they protected them

And when someone died suddenly — or violently — the land absorbed that moment.

In Alaska, phantom travelers follow sled trails.
In Scotland, they walk the moors.
In Quebec, they drift along river routes.
In Japan, they walk forest roads where suicides occurred.
In Norway, they haunt mountain passes used for centuries.

The Appalachians are no different — except for one thing:

The travelers here feel close.

Like they could speak if they wanted to.
Like they could reach out.
Like they haven't fully let go of the world.

Conclusion: Roads the Dead Still Travel

The Appalachian Mountains are full of ghost towns, forgotten trails, and abandoned homesteads. But the roads — even when they're nothing more than faint lines beneath leaf litter — remain pathways for something older than memory.

Phantom travelers move along these routes as if the world never changed.
As if their journey never ended.
As if they still have somewhere to be.

They appear solid.
They appear human.
They appear alive.

And then they vanish, leaving behind only the unsettling certainty that the mountains remember every step ever taken upon them.

These travelers aren't haunting the land.

They're part of it.

In the next chapter, we shift from phantom travelers to something far stranger — the **Disappearing Doors and Vanishing Houses** of the Appalachians. Structures that appear one moment and are gone the next, places hikers see once and never again, and locations that seem to slip in and out of the physical world.

The mountains hide many things.

Some of them only appear when they want to be seen.

Chapter Twenty-Four — The Disappearing Doors

There are stories in the Appalachian Mountains that don't fit anywhere else in the paranormal catalogue. They aren't ghosts, exactly. They aren't creatures. They aren't lights or vanishings or classic hauntings. They belong to something stranger — moments where the landscape itself seems to shift, revealing structures that shouldn't exist and then swallowing them back into the earth.

These stories usually begin the same way:

A hiker sees a house — or a cabin — or a doorway — in a place where there should be nothing but trees.
They blink.
They turn away for a moment.
And when they look back… it's gone.

The Appalachians have countless accounts like this:

- a cabin seen between two pines that vanishes seconds later

- a house on a ridge where no house has stood in a century

- a doorframe in the middle of the forest with no walls

- a porch with steps but no house

- a barn that looks whole from a distance but dissolves when approached

- a building that appears fully intact but is nothing but ruin up close

People think these are stories from fantasy novels or urban legends, but the accounts appear consistently in Appalachian oral history — and in modern hikers' reports.

They also appear across the world:

- phantom cottages in Ireland

- disappearing huts in Norway

- vanishing shacks in Alaska

- ghost lodges in the Yukon

- stone ruins in Scotland that appear intact only at dusk

- Amazonian phantom villages

- Mongolian steppe "mirage huts"

Different cultures.
Different terrain.
Same phenomenon.

The mountains reveal things only for moments — and only to certain people.

The Cabin That Only Exists Once

One of the most common Appalachian stories involves hikers who see a cabin once — fully intact — and never see it again, even when they return to the exact spot.

One witness, a seasoned backpacker from Virginia, described finding a cabin on a ridgeline during late afternoon. He saw:

- a metal roof

- an intact door

- the outline of curtains in the window

- a woodpile stacked neatly outside

- a rusted horseshoe nailed above the doorway

He didn't approach, because the place felt "wrong," as he put it — not threatening, just *out of place*, like seeing a house inside a dream.

Two weeks later he hiked the same trail with a friend.
He looked for the cabin.

There was nothing but forest.

No foundation.
No clearing.
No trace a building had ever existed.

He said the strange part wasn't the absence of the cabin.
It was that the forest where it should have been looked undisturbed —
like a place untouched by human presence for decades.

"I felt like I had glimpsed something from the past," he told me, "or
something that didn't want to be seen twice."

Doors Standing Alone

One of the eeriest Appalachian phenomena is the **solitary door** — a
wooden or metal doorframe standing upright in the forest with no walls,
no foundation, no evidence of a structure around it.

Hikers describe seeing:

- a single door in the middle of dense timber

- an old frame leaning slightly, but upright

- vines climbing the edges

- no flooring

- no footprints

- nothing that explains why it's there

Some claim the door vanishes when approached.
Others say the door remains, but the space around it feels like stepping
into colder air, as if crossing an invisible threshold.

One man in western North Carolina saw a faded blue door standing alone in a clearing at dawn. He circled it once, confused, thinking it must be the remains of an old shack.

When he reached out and touched the handle, he heard footsteps behind him.

Not human.
Not animal.
Something heavy.

He turned — nothing.
He looked back at the door.

It was gone.

In its place stood only an ordinary patch of ferns.

Structures That Shift When You Blink

Several hikers report seeing buildings that seem to change shape or position as they approach.

A woman in Tennessee described seeing a barn from twenty yards away — a full, standing structure with walls and a roof. But every few steps, the barn looked slightly different:

- smaller

- older

- leaning more

- missing boards

- collapsing

When she finally reached the clearing, the barn was nothing but a pile of rotted wood.

She walked away quickly, saying:

"It felt like the barn was showing me its death in real time."

This "shifting structure" effect appears in:

- old Scots-Irish folklore

- Algonquin legends

- Norse ghost stories

- Shinto tales of mountain spirits

- Alaskan First Nations accounts

Some cultures interpret it as the land testing travelers.
Others say it's the memory of the building, not the building itself.

The House That Watched Back

One Appalachian hiker recounted a disturbing encounter while exploring an old homestead foundation.

He saw a full house in the woods — perfectly intact:

- roof straight

- porch standing

- windows unbroken

- curtains drawn

- chimney without collapse

But something about it felt wrong — too clean, too new.

He approached slowly.
Halfway to the porch, he saw something move behind the curtain.
A shadow.
Human-sized.

He froze.

The curtain fell still.

He stepped backward, heart pounding.

The shadow moved again — this time closer to the window.

He turned and ran.

When he brought two friends back the next day, the clearing was empty aside from a stone foundation and a few decaying boards buried under moss.

No windows.
No curtains.
No chimney.
No standing structure at all.

Buildings shouldn't vanish overnight.
Shadows shouldn't watch from windows that don't exist.

The Vanishing Porch

In a remote part of West Virginia, hikers and hunters repeatedly report seeing a porch — nothing more — standing in the woods like a stage waiting for actors.

The porch is described as:

- wooden

- weathered but intact

- with two or three steps

- no house attached

- no supports

- no foundation

One hunter told me he sat on the porch once, curiosity overwhelming his fear. He said the boards felt solid beneath him, real as any porch he'd ever sat on.

He got up, walked a few yards to check something in the brush, and when he turned back, the porch was gone.

Gone without sound.
Gone without trace.
Gone without disturbance of leaves.

He swore he could still feel the pressure of the boards under him hours later — as if the memory of sitting was more real than the porch itself.

Doors That Lead Nowhere — And Everywhere

Some Appalachian folklore describes doorways that act as portals — thresholds between worlds.

Hikers describe:

- stepping through an old doorframe

- feeling a sudden chill

- hearing voices on the other side

- seeing fog thicken instantly

- sensing a presence behind them

- stepping back through and finding the air warmer

In some cases, people say the forest *looked different* on the other side of the doorframe — the trees thicker, the light dimmer, the air heavier.

One man walked through a lone doorframe in Kentucky and found himself in a foggy clearing he didn't recognize. When he stepped back through, the fog cleared instantly — and the clearing behind the door was gone.

Some of these accounts sound supernatural.
Some sound psychological.
But they all share one theme:

Thresholds.

The Appalachians are full of thresholds — both physical and invisible.

Mirage Houses of the Ridge Trails

Long-distance hikers on the Appalachian Trail occasionally report seeing houses perched on ridges where no such buildings exist.

They describe:

- lights glowing faintly

- a porch with a rocking chair

- a small window illuminated

- a chimney silhouette against dusk

But when they look again, nothing is there.

One hiker near Roan Mountain saw what she thought was a thru-hiker shelter — a full cabin with a slanted roof — only to discover the next morning that there was no shelter in that section of the trail.

The outline she saw the night before had been perfect.
The structure simply wasn't real.

Or it wasn't *physically* real.

What These Structures Really Are

No one has a definitive explanation, but there are theories.

1. Time Slip Phenomena

Some believe certain Appalachian valleys allow glimpses of the past —
visual echoes of buildings long gone.

2. Residual Hauntings

Energy from traumatic or meaningful events embedded in a location
replaying itself like a loop.

3. Spirit Architecture

Structures built by entities that are not bound by physical laws — a
common theme in Indigenous lore.

4. Liminal Zones

Places where the veil between worlds thins, allowing partial overlap.

5. Wilderness Memory

The land itself storing impressions of history, the way stone absorbs heat.

Each explanation is unsettling in its own way.

Conclusion: The Mountains Show You What They Want

The vanishing houses and disappearing doors of the Appalachian
Mountains aren't hallucinations or tricks of fog.

They're selective.

People don't find them by accident.
They see them because the mountains allow it — for a moment.

A cabin appears for one hiker but not for another.
A door stands for ten minutes and then dissolves.
A porch exists long enough to sit on but not long enough to doubt.
A window reveals a shadow in a house that hasn't stood in seventy years.

These are not just ghost sightings.
They are glimpses into another layer of reality — a place the mountains keep hidden most of the time.

In the next chapter, we step into one of the strangest aspects of Appalachian mystery: **The Woods That Rearrange Themselves** — trails that loop, landmarks that shift, lost time, and the disorienting sense that the forest itself is moving around you.

The mountains here are alive.

And sometimes, they move.

Chapter Twenty-Five — Appalachian Guardian Spirits

There are moments in the Appalachian Mountains when the forest feels strangely gentle — not quiet, exactly, and not safe, but watched in a way that doesn't feel hostile. A rustle behind you that makes you turn but doesn't make your heart pound. A sense of direction when the trail seems lost. A presence in the trees that feels more like guidance than threat.

Local people have always spoken about **guardian spirits** in these mountains. The Cherokee called some of them **Nunnehi** — beings who lived alongside humans, sometimes visible, sometimes not, protectors who guided lost travelers and helped people return home.

These weren't ghosts.
These weren't monsters.
And they weren't the spirits that chased people out of hollers.

They were something older, gentler, and deeply tied to the land.

Even now, hikers and locals describe moments in the mountains where something unseen seems to intervene — a sudden shift, a voice when there shouldn't be one, or a feeling of being accompanied out of danger.

The Appalachians may have more terrifying presences, but this chapter is about the rare ones that seem to help.

The Ancient Guides of the Ridge Tops

Long before Europeans arrived, the Cherokee believed that certain ridges were home to beings who existed entirely between the physical and spiritual worlds. They weren't gods or deities — they were more like protectors of specific places.

These guardian presences were said to:

- guide hunters back to camp

- protect children who wandered too far

- warn travelers of storms

- lead people around danger

- appear during illness or loss

- stand watch at high mountain passes

They were described not as monsters or beasts, but as tall, humanlike figures with a calm presence — sometimes seen walking just ahead, sometimes only sensed.

Settlers who later came into these mountains reported similar experiences, often without knowing the old lore. They spoke of:

- a "figure" walking in front of them on lost trails

- a "man in the mist" pointing toward safer ground

- a "shadow" that moved with them until they reached a ridge

- footsteps behind them that vanished when they reached a clearing

These helpers didn't speak, didn't show faces, and didn't linger once a traveler found safety.

One man in western North Carolina wrote in his 1890 journal:

"The woods were darker than I'd expected, but I felt someone just ahead of me. Not a man made of flesh, but something that carried me along, step by step, until the dawn showed me the right path."

No footprints were found.
No lanterns.
No horses.
Nothing but a sense of calm following him down the mountain.

The Voices That Lead You Out

There's a kind of Appalachian story that almost no one admits to publicly — because it sounds too strange, too mystical, too close to fiction — but it shows up again and again if you talk privately with the right people.

Someone is lost.
Panic sets in.
The forest presses close.
Shadows deepen.
Orientation scatters.

And then a voice calls out.

It's not the voice of a loved one.
It's not a mimic — those voices sound wrong, out of place, predatory.

This voice is calm.
Soft.
Reassuring.
Simple.

"Over here."
"This way."
"Come on."
"You're safe."

Hikers describe the voice leading them toward:

- an unexpected clearing

- a trail junction

- the glow of a ranger cabin

- the sound of a road

- the safety of running water

One hiker in Virginia told me:

"I'd gone off trail without realizing it. I was climbing and descending little ridges that all looked the same. I don't know what happened, but the next thing I remember was hearing someone call my name — not loudly, but close. Calm. Familiar, even though it wasn't anyone I knew."

He followed the voice.

It led him onto the Appalachian Trail.

He'd been drifting away from it for over two hours.

"There was nobody there," he said. "I looked everywhere. There were no footprints behind me. Nothing. But something helped me."

The Light That Only Moves When You Need It

Unlike the malevolent lights that drift into camps or creep through hollers, the guardian lights of Appalachia behave differently.

They:

- stay at a distance

- move slowly

- appear only briefly

- never approach directly

- always guide toward safer terrain

People describe them as faint orbs — white or pale amber — drifting along ridges or old paths. Hunters say they've followed these lights unknowingly, only to realize later that the light had disappeared just as they found their own trail again.

A man in Tennessee told a story passed down from his grandfather:

"When he was a boy, he went out looking for a lost cow. Fog came in heavy. He lost the ridge and didn't know which direction led home. That's when he saw a light. It wasn't a lantern, too steady and too white.

It moved slow. When he followed it, it took him right to the edge of his family's pasture."

The light vanished the moment he stepped onto familiar ground.

These lights aren't common.
They aren't dramatic.
They don't perform.

They appear when needed, then disappear without a trace.

The Feeling of a Hand on Your Back

This is one of the most unsettling types of guardian encounters — not frightening in intent, but unsettling because it is undeniably physical.

Hikers describe the sensation of:

- a hand between their shoulder blades

- a gentle push forward

- a steadying grip

- a presence just behind their left shoulder

Some feel guided around deadfall.
Others say the sensation pulled them away from a cliff edge they didn't realize was there.

One woman hiking alone in Virginia said she slipped on wet leaves, sliding toward a steep drop. Just before she went over, she felt something grab the back of her jacket with tremendous force.

She jerked backward onto the trail.
When she turned around, no one was there.

No footprints.
No sound.
No movement in the trees.

She said it felt like someone saving her life.

The Nunnehi Stories — Benevolent but Distant

Cherokee tradition describes the **Nunnehi** as a race of immortal, spirit-like people who helped humans but never interfered too much. They lived in hidden places — mounds, hills, caves, and deep forest.

Stories say the Nunnehi:

- assisted hunters

- rescued lost children

- escorted the wounded

- helped travelers cross dangerous land

- appeared before storms

- guided escape from enemies

- vanished as soon as safety was reached

Cherokee elders told stories of people invited into great halls beneath the earth — places filled with warm firelight and music. These stories are symbolic, but they speak to a larger truth:

There are presences in these mountains that aren't here to harm.

Settlers who arrived later echoed these experiences, though they didn't know the ancient names.

They simply called them:

- the helpers

- the watchers

- the guides

- the ones who keep you safe

A miner in the 1920s wrote of a glowing figure helping him cross a swollen river after a cave collapse left him disoriented. He crossed where no crossing should have been possible.

When he looked back, the figure was gone.

Moments of Impossible Luck

Many Appalachian locals speak about bizarre strokes of fortune while in dangerous terrain — moments where something seems to intervene.

Stories include:

- a tree falling in a direction that saved a logger

- a sudden break in weather allowing safe passage

- a lost hunter spotting an impossible landmark

- a child wandering out of the woods unharmed

- a misfired gun that should have killed someone but didn't

- a misstep corrected by "invisible force"

People chalk these moments up to luck.
But the frequency with which they occur in the mountains is noteworthy.

Some say the Appalachians themselves have a way of nudging fate.
Others believe the old spirits never left.

The Guardian That Walks Beside You

One of the strangest — and most comforting — Appalachian accounts involves people feeling a presence walking alongside them during difficult hikes.

The presence keeps perfect pace.
Never too close.
Never too far.
Soft steps, steady rhythm.

Not threatening.
Not watching.
Just accompanying.

One AT thru-hiker described it perfectly:

"I was having a horrible day — the kind where you question why you're out there. I remember feeling like someone was walking beside me for two hours. I never saw anything, but the feeling was so strong it calmed me down. I got to camp safely and then the feeling just… left."

These encounters happen most often:

- near ancient mounds

- on long ridges

- near waterfalls

- on old Cherokee routes

Places deep with history, deep with sorrow, deep with memory.

Why Some Presences Help

If the darker spirits in the Appalachians guard territory, then the guardian spirits seem to guard people — or at least certain people at certain times.

Why?

Theories range from:

1. Echoes of Ancient Traditions

The Cherokee believed the mountains themselves were alive — and that some spirits served as intermediaries.

2. Ancestral Memory

Guardian encounters might be tied to lineage, family, or unspoken history.

3. Spirits Bound to the Land

Some presences may simply be protectors of certain places — forest guardians who keep balance.

4. Unseen Intelligence

Not ghosts, not gods — something in-between: aware, benevolent, and invested in human survival.

5. Residual Compassion

A place shaped by generations of hardship might hold onto the urge to help the living.

Every theory is unsettling in its own way.

Conclusion: The Mountains Do Not Always Wish You Harm

For all their darkness, the Appalachian Mountains have moments where they feel strangely kind — where the forest seems to steady your hand, guide your steps, or whisper the right path out of danger.

These guardian spirits are not tame, not predictable, and not friendly in the human sense. They don't form bonds. They don't linger once the crisis passes. They don't offer comfort beyond survival.

They simply appear when needed — and disappear when the danger is gone.

The mountains hold many terrors, but they also hold old protectors. And sometimes, in the loneliest stretches of forest, when the night presses in and the trail vanishes beneath your feet, you may feel something stand beside you — not to harm, but to guide.

In the next chapter, we step into the darker side — the **territorial spirits** of the deep hollers, the presences that do not lead you out, but push you away. The ones that watch with hostility, not compassion.

Not all spirits in Appalachia are guardians.

Some want you gone.

Chapter Twenty-Six — The Darker Spirits of the Deep Hollers

If the Appalachian guardian spirits are gentle hands guiding travelers out of danger, then the deeper hollers hold something entirely different — presences that do not protect, but repel. Forces that do not lead you home, but drive you away with a cold, territorial warning woven into every step you take.

These are the spirits that locals refuse to talk about.
The ones early settlers wrote about only in brief, fearful notes.
The ones that don't follow or shepherd or guide.

They simply don't want you there.

People describe these presences with words like:

- **hostile**

- **old**

- **ancient**

- **angry**

- **territorial**

- **watchful**

- **wrong**

These spirits don't stalk.
They don't whisper.
They don't lure.

They push.

And if you don't leave, the forest stops being a forest — it becomes an environment that actively resists your presence.

This chapter explores the entities that make the most hardened outdoorsmen turn around without hesitation.

Where the Hollers Go Dark

There are valleys in these mountains where the air feels heavier, thicker — not oppressive like bad weather, but charged with something that makes your instincts tighten.

Locals call them:

- **bad hollers**

- **dead hollers**

- **holler of the old ones**

- **no-sound valleys**

- **never-go hollers**

When people say a holler "goes dark," they don't mean sunset.

They mean:

- birds go silent

- wind stops

- crickets freeze mid-song

- leaves hang motionless

- footsteps echo strangely

- air feels colder

- shadows deepen unnaturally

- time seems to slow

You can feel it in your teeth, in your chest, in the small hairs on your arms.

Something aware is nearby — something that doesn't want you staying long.

One hunter in eastern Kentucky said:

"The woods didn't just get quiet. They got watchful."

He left without taking a shot.
He refused to hunt that valley again.

The Presence That Follows Behind

Unlike the guardians, who may walk beside or ahead, these darker spirits stay behind — close enough to hear, close enough to feel, but never close enough to see.

People describe:

- footsteps matching their pace

- the sensation of breath on the back of the neck

- branches cracking in perfect sync with their steps

- heavy pressure behind them

- pacing that stops when they stop

- a coldness at their back like a shadow with weight

One man hiking alone in Tennessee said:

"It felt like someone was standing just out of reach — not following me, not stalking me, but pushing me out."

He left the trail and never returned.

Settlers in the 1800s described the same sensation:

"Something large behind me, without body nor breath, urging me up the ridge."

This wasn't fear of animals.
It wasn't instinct.
It was presence.

Something that knew they were there — and wanted them gone.

The Holler That Doesn't Want You In

Several Appalachian hollers are infamous for ejecting hikers — not violently, not physically, but through a growing sense of dread so intense that even seasoned outdoorsmen retreat.

They describe:

- sudden panic

- the urge to turn around

- nausea

- dizziness

- overwhelming dread

- a sense of trespass

- feeling "pushed uphill"

One hunter told me:

"I walked into the hollow like it didn't want to let me breathe. Every step forward felt like pushing against warm water. Then something snapped a stick behind me — not an animal, not wind. It was directed at me. I got the hell out."

These sensations appear in:

- deep Tennessee hollers

- North Georgia valleys

- isolated West Virginia ravines

- abandoned Virginia logging draws

The pattern is consistent:
People feel unwelcome long before anything visual happens.

The danger is in the air, not the trees.

The Territory Line

Locals speak — always in hushed tones — about invisible boundaries in certain hollers. Cross them, and the air chills instantly.

Hunters report:

- goosebumps

- sudden silence

- thick air

- a smell of earth or rot

- the sense of a presence standing directly behind them

A man in North Carolina described a boundary so sharp he felt it physically:

"One step was normal. The next step felt like stepping into cold mud — the air changed, the pressure changed, everything changed. It wasn't natural."

He turned around immediately.

These territorial zones appear to be fixed — generation after generation, the same valleys, the same bends, the same ridges carry the same oppressive presence.

Almost as if something ancient claimed the land and never let go.

The Shadow at the Tree Line

While this chapter does **not** overlap with the shadow entities seen on
ridges or roads, deeper hollers have their own type of visual presence —
something more rooted, older, and less humanoid.

Witnesses describe:

- a tall mass

- dark, but not shaped like a person

- standing at the edge of the trees

- not moving

- not blinking

- not reacting

- observing

Settlers described this presence as "a shape the forest wore" — not a
creature, but a darkness given form.

Hikers say:

"Something was standing there. Not a man, not an animal, but the
absence of light. A hole in the shape of a body."

These sightings don't usually involve movement.
The presence simply watches.
Its stillness is colder than motion.

The Wind That Pushes You Out

Another consistent hallmark of hostile hollers is the sudden appearance
of wind — not gentle wind, not natural gusts, but wind that feels
directed.

Hikers describe:

- wind pushing their backs

- wind hitting them in pulses

- wind blowing only on the trail rather than the trees

- wind increasing the deeper they go

- wind ceasing instantly when they turn to leave

One man in Georgia said:

"I turned around, and it felt like the woods exhaled relief."

This is not meteorological.
It is behavioral.

Almost purposeful.

The Crashing in the Underbrush

Many hostile holler encounters involve loud crashing — deliberate, forceful, and often close.

What's strange is what's missing:

- no animal ever appears

- no tracks are found

- no broken trees remain

- no bushes stay disturbed

- no sound continues once the person leaves

One hunter said:

"It sounded like something big running at me, but nothing came out of the brush. Nothing ever showed itself. The crashing stopped the second I stepped out of the hollow."

This is not bluff-charge animal behavior.
This is designed to intimidate.

To drive you out.
To warn you.

The Feeling of Being Rejected

Some people describe not fear — but rejection.

Not terror — but the sense they are intruding on something sacred, ancient, or territorial.

A hiker in Virginia described it as:

"The feeling you get walking into a room where an argument just happened. Except the argument wasn't human."

Another hunter said:

"The forest didn't want me there. Not scared. Just... unwelcome."

This rejection runs deeper than instinct.

It feels purposeful.
Direct.
Intelligent in a way that animals are not.

And older than people can understand.

What These Spirits Might Be

No one knows what these presences truly are, but theories include:

1. Ancient Territorial Spirits

Rooted in Cherokee and Shawnee belief — not evil, just protective of certain places.

2. Land Memory

Residual energy from centuries of tragedy, violence, or ceremony.

3. Guardians of Specific Valleys

Not guardians of people — guardians of land itself, keeping outsiders away.

4. Natural Sentience

The oldest forests on the continent holding an awareness that reacts to intrusion.

5. Unseen Entities Older Than Any Culture

Not ghosts.
Not spirits of the dead.
Something primordial.

Each theory explains part of the phenomenon — but none fully account for the force and intent behind the encounters.

Conclusion: Not All Spirits Are Friendly

The Appalachians are deep, ancient, and full of stories. For every account of a guardian spirit leading someone home, there is another of something dark pushing a traveler out.

These presences are not malevolent in the way monsters are.
They don't stalk.
They don't hunt.
They don't lure.

Their hostility is territorial — the mountain equivalent of a warning growl.

These hollers don't want you.
These valleys don't welcome you.
These presences don't negotiate.

You enter at your own risk.
You leave quickly — if you're wise.

In the next chapter, we step into the mysterious spaces known as **thin places** — areas where the veil between worlds feels weak, where the landscape doesn't fully hold itself together, and where people glimpse things that don't belong to this world at all.

Some places reject you.
Others reveal too much.

Chapter Twenty-Seven — Rangers & Locals Speak Out (Off the Record)

Official reports from Appalachian park rangers often read like weather logs:
clear skies, minor search effort, hiker found safe, animal activity normal, trail maintenance required.

Those are the public files — the safe ones.

But talk to rangers long enough, in the right setting, and you'll hear a second, hidden layer of the mountains. Things that never get written down. Things that don't fit into law enforcement forms or SAR summaries. Things that don't belong to accepted wilderness science.

This chapter isn't made of legends or folklore.
It isn't about old miners or Civil War stories.

These are **modern voices** — rangers, wardens, firefighters, retired hikers, lifelong mountain locals — telling what they've experienced in the last five, ten, twenty years.

No embellishment.
No dramatic flair.

Just the disturbing truth of what people see, hear, and feel in the deepest parts of the Appalachian Mountains.

And all of it off the record.

"We Hear Screams, but They're Not Animals." — Ranger, North Carolina

A ranger in western North Carolina spoke quietly over a late summer campfire, eyes fixed on the flames.

"We get screaming calls," he said. "Hikers report someone shouting for help. Screams echoing through the ridges. High, low, panicked… you name it."

"Do you find them?" I asked.

He shook his head slowly.

"Always the same thing. We gear up, we head out… but the sound keeps moving. Every time we close in, it jumps a ridge. Then another. Then another. No footprints. No disturbed brush. No sign of a person."

He paused.

"It's not a cougar. It's not a bobcat. It's not any animal I've heard. It sounds human — until it doesn't."

He never filed a sound report again.
Not after the third time.

"Something Walked Around My Fire Tower All Night." — Fire Lookout, Tennessee

A retired fire lookout from Tennessee told me a story that never made it into official logs.

"One night, something walked around the base of the tower. Slow steps. Heavy. Like a man circling the legs of the tower, thinking about climbing up."

He shone his light down.
Saw nothing.

The steps continued — one full circle every five or six minutes.

"I went down at dawn," he said. "No tracks. No mud. No sign anything had been there."

He took a week off.
Then he left the job.

"I wasn't scared," he said. "It was worse. I felt observed."

"We Found His Gear. We Never Found Him." — Backwoods Warden, Virginia

A backwoods warden from Virginia told me about a missing hiker.

"His pack was next to a fallen log. Food untouched. Water full. Boots neatly placed by the fire ring like he took them off to rest."

He shook his head.

"No prints leading away. No slide marks. No signs he fell. No animal drag. Nothing."

The man was never found.

The warden's voice grew quieter.

"The forest felt wrong that day. Heavy. Like something was closed around us. I've never felt that again. Not anywhere else."

He admitted he never returned to that holler except when absolutely required.

"Some Trails Go Silent When You Step On Them." — Ranger, West Virginia

A ranger in the Monongahela National Forest mentioned a phenomenon I'd heard whispers about before — but never this directly.

"There are trails that go dead. You step onto the first fifty feet, and every sound cuts off. No birds. No insects. Not even wind in the leaves."

I asked him how often it happened.

"Couple times a year," he said. "Always the same trails. Always the same sections."

He leaned back and exhaled.

"It feels like stepping into someone else's house uninvited."

"We Don't Go Into That Hollow After Sunset." — Local Hunter, Kentucky

A Kentucky hunter gave me a warning that came without any theatrics — just plain, matter-of-fact Appalachian honesty.

"There's a hollow down by the old logging road. You don't go there after dark."

"Why?"

He shrugged lightly.

"The trees feel wrong. Like they're leaning in. Like something's behind you every step."

He paused.

"I don't carry fear in the woods. I grew up in these mountains. But that hollow... there's something in it that doesn't like people."

I asked if it was dangerous.

"Dangerous?" He shook his head. "No. Not like that. It just... wants you gone."

"I Saw Lights Moving Like They Were Searching for Someone." — Ranger, Georgia

A ranger in northern Georgia described a night patrol unlike anything in his career.

"I saw three lights moving in the trees. Not flashlights — no beam, no sway, no bounce. They moved slow, like someone floating lanterns through the woods."

He radioed HQ.
No one else reported lights in the area.

"When I reached the ridge they'd been moving toward, everything went dark. Instantly. Like someone flipped a switch."

He didn't file a report.

"Nobody wants to be the ranger who files ghosts."

"Something Took the Dogs Off-Leash." — Search Dog Handler, Tennessee

A canine SAR handler shared one of the most unsettling stories I've heard.

"We were tracking a missing woman. Clear scent. Dogs solid on the lead."

She paused.

"Then both dogs stopped dead. Ears up. Whining. Not afraid. Alert. Like someone else had stepped onto the trail ahead."

Then the impossible happened:

"...their leashes unclipped."

She said it wasn't possible.
The clips were secure.
The dogs hadn't pulled.
Nothing brushed them.

The dogs looked into the trees — tails low, ears locked — and refused to go forward.

"We turned back," she said. "Not because of the dogs. Because the forest felt like it was... watching."

She still remembers the exact moment.

"It felt like we weren't supposed to be there."

"We Heard Footsteps on the Roof." — Camp Host, North Carolina

A camp host in the Nantahala Forest described nighttime footsteps on the metal roof of the ranger outpost cabin.

"Not branches. Not animals. Not wind. Footsteps. Slow. Heavy. One at a time."

Inside the cabin, dust shook loose from the rafters.

"When I went outside — nothing. The roof is steep. Nothing could walk up there without slipping."

The next night, the footsteps returned.

He left early the following morning and asked to be reassigned.

"I've worked forests in five states," he said. "Only the Appalachians give me that feeling."

"We Get Calls About Singing." — Dispatcher, Smokies

A ranger dispatcher in the Smoky Mountains gave me a detail that stuck with me long after the conversation ended.

"Every now and then, we get calls about singing in the woods. A woman's voice. Soft. Clear. Sometimes humming. Sometimes full songs."

Are the callers mistaken?
He doesn't think so.

"It's always the same stretch of trail. Always just before dawn. And there's no one out there at that hour."

He leaned in slightly.

"The weird part? Most callers say the same thing... 'It sounded like she was singing to someone else.'"

"Not Everything in These Mountains Wants You Dead." — Retired Ranger, Virginia

A retired ranger from Shenandoah summarized it in a way I'll never forget.

"These mountains aren't evil. People like to make them sound that way. They're not haunted in the Hollywood sense. It's older than that. Smarter than that. Alive in a way we don't understand."

He tapped the table gently.

"Some places protect you. Some places push you out. Some places just watch."

He took a slow breath.

"And then there are things that don't fit any category."

He smiled — the tired kind, the kind that carries decades of unspoken stories.

"I'm too old to pretend I know what walks in these woods. I just know it's not just deer and bears."

Conclusion: The Unwritten Stories

Rangers won't put these things in reports.
Locals won't mention them to strangers.
Hikers don't post them online.
Wardens keep them to themselves.

But the truth is simple:

There are things in these mountains that don't behave like animals.
There are sounds that move with intention.
There are places that watch, warn, and sometimes help.
There are moments that never make it onto paper.

And the people who spend their lives in the Appalachians know it.

Some talk.
Most don't.
But all of them — every ranger, every warden, every lifelong local —
carries one story they will never forget.

The mountains see us.
And some nights, they speak.

Chapter Twenty-Eight — AT Hikers & Backwoods Campers: The Stories They Don't Tell Online

There's a code among Appalachian Trail hikers — a silent agreement that some things simply aren't talked about online. Trail journals are filled with stories about weather, injuries, bears, blisters, kindness, and the simple joys of a long walk. But the darker experiences? The ones that happen deep in the trees, far from roads and shelters, in stretches of forest so silent it feels like the world forgot you exist?

Those stories stay inside whispered conversations:

- on rainy nights in shelters

- during zero-day rest stops

- around campfires where trust has formed

- or between two hikers sitting on opposite bunks, unable to sleep

The AT runs 2,190 miles through some of the oldest forests on earth. And for many thru-hikers, the scariest moments aren't from wildlife or weather.

They're from the feeling that they are not alone.

This chapter isn't about lore.
It's about firsthand accounts — the ones hikers share only with each other.

"Something Walked Around My Tent for Three Hours." — North Carolina Section

A hiker from Ohio told me a story he never posted in his online trail journal. He was camping alone between shelters, far from any road.

"It started at midnight — soft footsteps circling my tent."

He stayed still, listening.
The steps were slow, deliberate.

"Not a deer. Deer move fast, unpredictable. This was walking. Heavy. Purposeful."

He called out, thinking it might be another hiker.

No response.

The steps continued.
Circling.
Pausing.
Circling again.

At one point, he said the steps came so close he could feel the ground compress beside him.

"I thought about unzipping the flap," he said. "But something in my gut told me not to. Whatever it was… it wanted me to look."

The steps continued until just before dawn.
Then everything went silent.

He packed up in less than five minutes and didn't stop hiking until he reached the next shelter.

"I never camped alone again on the AT," he said quietly.

"Someone Knocked on My Shelter in the Middle of the Night." — Tennessee

A woman hiking solo through Tennessee stayed in an AT shelter late in the season — no one else for miles.

At 2 a.m., she woke to the sound of someone **knocking** on the wooden wall of the shelter.

Three slow knocks.
Then nothing.
Then three more.

She sat up instantly, heart pounding.

"I thought maybe it was a bear," she said, "but bears don't knock politely."

She turned on her headlamp.
The forest was dead silent.

Another three knocks — this time from the back wall.

She scrambled out of her sleeping bag and grabbed her trekking poles, bracing for anything.

When she shone her light on the back of the shelter from outside, there was nothing there. No tracks. No movement.

The knocks stopped.

The next morning, she found a single handprint on the back wall — small, but too high for a child.

She didn't take a picture.
She didn't tell anyone on trail.

She just kept moving north.

"We heard laughing in the woods. But it wasn't human." — Smoky Mountains

Three thru-hikers were camped together in the Great Smokies. They'd spent enough nights out that fear didn't come easy.

Around midnight, they heard **laughter**.

Not close.
Not far.
Somewhere in the middle.

"It sounded like a person laughing," one hiker said. "Except it wasn't right. It was slow. Drawn out. Like someone mocking the idea of laughter."

The sound drifted around them, moving between trees.

They checked for headlamps.
Nothing.
They called out.

The laughter stopped instantly.

Then a few minutes later, it started again — this time from behind them.

None of them slept that night.

One hiker told me later:

"It didn't sound like a joke. It sounded like something pretending to laugh."

"My compass spun in circles." — Virginia Creeper Trail Intersection

A veteran hiker told me about a strange moment in Virginia, near a quiet intersection where the AT crosses the old Creeper Trail.

"I pulled out my compass. The needle was spinning. Full rotation. Constantly."

He checked his phone.
Dead.
Battery full an hour earlier.

Something in that patch of woods felt off — heavy, electric.

"I felt sick," he said. "Like the forest was pressing on my chest."

He walked fifty yards away. The compass stabilized.

He walked back. It spun again.

He marked the location on his map but never reported it.

"Who's going to believe that?" he asked.

"It wasn't an animal. It crawled across the trail like a person." — Shenandoah

A hiker in Shenandoah told me about a foggy morning when visibility dropped to ten feet. As he rounded a bend, something moved across the trail.

"It wasn't upright," he said. "It was crawling. Fast. Like a person, but wrong. Too quick. Too low."

He froze, waiting for the shape to emerge from the fog on the other side.

It didn't.

No sound.
No breathing.
Nothing.

He waited ten minutes before moving again.

"I tell myself it was a deer," he said. "But it wasn't a deer."

He never camped alone again.

"There were footsteps on the shelter roof." — Georgia

At a lean-to in northern Georgia, two hikers shared a story almost identical to one I heard from a ranger days later.

"We were settling down for the night," one said, "when heavy footsteps crossed the shelter roof."

No tree branches overhead.
No wind.
No falling debris.

Actual footsteps.
Deliberate.
Pacing.

They shone lights in every direction.
Nothing moved on the roof.
Nothing moved in the woods.

But the pacing continued for more than thirty minutes.

The next day, a ridge runner told them:

"You're not the first to hear that."

"Something whispered my trail name." — Pennsylvania

Trail names are sacred on the AT — earned, not chosen. They carry personality, history, and identity.

So when a Pennsylvania hiker heard **his** trail name whispered just outside his tent at 3 a.m., it froze him in place.

"It whispered twice," he said. "Soft. Like it was right beside the tent wall."

He unzipped the flap.
No one there.

He called out, thinking a buddy was messing with him.

No answer.

He checked for footprints.
Nothing.

He told no one until months later, around a fire in Maine.

The other hikers didn't laugh.

One of them had the same experience in Vermont.

The Silent Campsites

Several hikers talked about campsites where the woods simply… shut off.

They described:

- no birds in the morning

- no wind

- no bugs

- no forest noise

- a feeling of being watched by multiple unseen eyes

These silent camps all shared something in common:

They were off-trail sites where older shelters once stood.

One hiker said:

"It felt like I was sleeping in a place the forest hadn't forgiven."

He left before sunrise.

"I woke up with footprints around my hammock." — West Virginia

Hammock campers on the AT are used to strange sounds at night. But a hiker in West Virginia woke to something far worse.

Footprints.
Large ones.
Circling his hammock.

"When I dropped down in the morning, I saw prints in the leaf litter," he said. "Deep. Human-shaped. Barefoot."

He took a photo but deleted it days later.

"I didn't want people asking questions," he said. "I didn't want to think about it."

"Sometimes you feel accompanied for miles."

A surprising number of hikers describe the same phenomenon — not threatening, not dangerous, but unnerving:

The sense of being accompanied.

Not followed.
Not stalked.

Accompanied.

One hiker described it perfectly:

"It felt like someone walked beside me for ten or fifteen miles. Never close. Never far. Just... there."

When he reached a trail crossing near a road, the sensation disappeared instantly.

Another hiker said:

"It felt almost protective. But the whole time, I knew it wasn't a person."

"I saw someone sitting on the shelter roof." — Vermont

One of the most chilling stories came from a hiker in Vermont.

"I came into the shelter just before dark. Someone was sitting on the roof. Legs dangling."

He waved.
The figure didn't move.

He called out.
No response.

Then a cloud passed over the moon, dimming the clearing.

When the light returned — the figure was gone.

No sound.
No movement.
Nothing on the roof or in the woods.

He slept with his knife in his hand that night.

Conclusion: The Stories That Stay on Trail

The Appalachian Trail is full of beauty: sunrise on ridges, summer storms, sweeping views, friendships born in exhaustion and mud.

But beneath that beauty is something older — something that watches hikers pass through its world, one step at a time.

These stories aren't told online because they don't fit the image of the trail.
They don't fit the planned photos, the gear lists, the motivational posts.

They're shared quietly:
at shelters, around fires, in whispers.

The AT is more than a trail.

It is a living thing.
And sometimes, it lets you know you're not alone.

Chapter Twenty-Nine — The Places You Should Never Go Alone

There are places in the Appalachian Mountains that even the bravest hikers and seasoned locals avoid after dark — some avoid them altogether. These locations aren't haunted houses or tourist traps or spots marked with warning signs. Many don't appear on maps anymore. Some never did.

These places share a few unsettling traits:

- the forest grows too quiet

- the air feels heavier

- time feels slower

- the trail seems to resist your steps

- you sense a presence you can't see

- you feel watched from the moment you arrive

These aren't destinations. They're warnings buried in the landscape.

You can walk through most Appalachian forests without trouble. But go deep enough into the mountains — far past towns, trailheads, shelters, and well-beaten paths — and you eventually encounter pockets of land that feel different.

Older.
Darker.
Less forgiving.

Locals don't claim to understand what lives or lingers in these places. They just know better than to visit alone.

This chapter is about those locations — the ones hikers mention quietly, the places rangers refuse to enter at night, the hollers that repel even the hardened mountain folk.

The places you should never go alone.

1. The Dead-Silent Hollers

These are valleys where all noise dies the moment you step inside.

Birds stop.
Wind quits.
Insects freeze.
The forest holds its breath.

Rangers call them **acoustic voids**.
Locals call them **hollers of the old ones**.

A man in southern West Virginia described it perfectly:

"The sound died between one step and the next. No warning. No fade. Just gone. I swear I could feel something behind me... like the woods were waiting."

These hollers often have:

- moss that grows thicker than elsewhere

- trees leaning inward, as if bending toward a center

- unusual pockets of cold air

- a distinct smell of earth, old and damp

- an oppressive atmosphere

People who linger too long report:

- dizziness

- nausea

- panic

- the sense that something is standing inches behind them

The silence is a warning.
And if you don't listen, the forest feels increasingly hostile.

You can walk through once.
You don't return alone.

2. The Abandoned Mining Villages That Still Feel Occupied

Scattered across Kentucky, Virginia, Tennessee, and West Virginia are ghost towns swallowed by the forest — places where coal camps once thrived, then died, leaving only:

- foundations

- collapsed porches

- rusted pipes

- staircases leading nowhere

- cemeteries tilting into the earth

Yet hikers often describe feeling watched in these places, even when no structure remains.

One hunter told me:

"There's a holler with an old mining home, roof gone but walls still standing. Every time I pass it, I feel eyes on me. Not from the house. From the land around it."

Another said he heard:

- footsteps

- faint speaking

- coughing

- the sound of shovels

- metallic clanks

…despite being the only living human for miles.

Ghost towns elsewhere feel empty.
These feel occupied.

Like the people never left — or something else moved in.

Don't go alone.

3. The Ridge Tunnels

Certain ridge trails curve through natural hallways formed by overgrown rhododendron and laurel. Most are harmless.

A few aren't.

These tunnel-like sections of trail sometimes produce:

- whispers with no speaker

- shadow movement

- sudden wind

- the sensation of being touched

- rushing footsteps behind you

- pressure in the chest

- vertigo

Two thru-hikers told me separately about a ridge tunnel in North Carolina where they refused to stop no matter how exhausted they were.

"It felt like something waited for you to pause," one said.

These ridge tunnels often correlate with:

- old Cherokee pathways

- former burial routes

- long-abandoned settlements

No one knows why certain tunnels feel alive.
They just do.

Never rest inside one.

4. The Fog Corridors

Fog in the Appalachians is normal.
But **fog corridors** are something else entirely.

These are narrow sections of trail or hollow where fog appears:

- instantly

- unnaturally thick

- unnaturally cold

- without weather shifts

Visibility drops to inches.
Sound becomes distorted.
Compass needles spin.
Lights dim.

Hikers report:

- footsteps behind them

- something brushing against their pack

- the feeling of being pulled off trail

- voices mumbling in the fog

- shapes moving inside the whiteout

A ranger in Georgia told me:

"In some fog corridors, we've had search teams walk twenty feet apart and miss each other completely. The fog swallows distance."

Locals say the fog is alive.
Rangers say nothing at all.

Don't enter a fog corridor alone.
If you must, keep walking — never stop inside one.

5. The Stone Circles Deep in the Forest

You won't find these marked on maps.
You won't stumble on them near trails.

They exist in the deepest woods — circles of ancient stones arranged in near-perfect rings, usually ten to thirty feet across.

Cherokee elders say these are **old places**, sacred and dangerous.
Settlers called them **devil rings**.
Hikers who stumble upon them say the air feels wrong.

People report:

- disorientation

- ringing in their ears

- static in the air

- movement in peripheral vision

- the feeling of being surrounded

One man said:

"I walked into the circle without thinking. The moment I did, the forest tilted. Like I'd stepped inside someone else's memory."

He left immediately.

Some believe these circles are:

- pre-Colonial ceremonial sites

- ancient boundary markers

- spiritual thresholds

- retained memories of the land itself

Whatever they are, they demand respect.

Never enter one alone.
Never cross the center.

6. The "Thin Ridge" Overlooks

These are narrow ridges — sometimes no wider than the trail itself — with sudden elevation drops on both sides. They offer stunning views, but something unsettling lingers on many of them.

Hikers report:

- sudden fear

- a feeling of being pushed

- dizziness

- seeing figures at the far ends of the ridge

- footsteps behind them

- phantom whispers carried by the wind

A woman who hiked alone near Max Patch told me:

"I felt hands on my back. Not pushing. Just… resting. Like someone was standing behind me."

She didn't look back.
She walked forward until the ridge widened.

These ridges aren't haunted — not in the traditional sense.

They're thin places.
Places where the world feels fragile.

Don't stop on them.
Don't linger.
And never go alone.

7. The Old Church Grounds Hidden in the Trees

Remnants of old mountain churches dot the Appalachians — but the ones hikers warn about most are the abandoned ones deep in the backcountry.

The buildings are usually gone, but:

- stone steps

- sections of foundation

- overgrown graveyards

- rusted wrought-iron fences

…remain.

These places are charged with emotion, age, and something else — something never spoken aloud.

People report:

- hearing hymns with no source

- seeing flickers of candlelight

- experiencing sudden grief or fear

- feeling unwelcome the moment they enter

- shadow movement among gravestones

A ranger once told me:

"Some of those cemeteries don't like visitors. You walk in and the whole air shifts."

Don't go alone.
Even with company, don't stay long.

8. The Lakes That Shouldn't Be Still

In certain valleys, you'll find lakes and ponds tucked under steep slopes. Most are calm. Some are eerie.

But a few are **too still** — unnaturally glasslike, without ripples even in wind.

Campers hear:

- splashes with no cause

- footsteps in shallow water

- something swimming slowly but unseen

- faint voices carrying across still surfaces

These lakes feel like mirrors — not of the sky, but of something hidden beneath.

Longtime anglers say:

"You don't cast into those lakes. Leave them to whatever's living down there."

Never camp alone at one of these lakes.
And never stare at the water for too long.

9. The Places Where the Trail Vanishes for a Few Steps

This is a rare but striking phenomenon: sections of trail where the path disappears and the forest seems to rearrange itself.

Not dramatically.
Not supernaturally.
Just enough that you freeze.

People report:

- the trail dissolving into undergrowth

- landmarks shifting

- a feeling of being "misplaced"

- sudden panic or confusion

- the sense of someone watching your reaction

These spots almost always appear in areas sacred to Indigenous peoples.

One hiker said:

"It wasn't that the trail vanished. It was that the forest stopped pretending to be a forest."

Don't go alone where the path has a mind of its own.

10. The Crossroads of Old Logging Roads

Finally, the most dangerous place to be alone:
old three-way or four-way logging road intersections deep in the woods.

People report:

- hearing footsteps from multiple directions

- visuals of a person stepping into one road then disappearing

- mimic voices

- oppressive silence

- a sense of being watched from all angles

- lights moving between trees

Loggers used to avoid these intersections after sunset.

They said these places collect movement.
Energy.
Memory.
Presence.

Everyone agrees:
If you hit an old crossroads deep in the Appalachians, don't linger.

And never — ever — camp there.

Conclusion: Some Places Don't Want You Alone

Most of the Appalachian Mountains are safe, peaceful, breathtakingly beautiful. But scattered across the range are pockets of land that feel wrong — ancient, sentient, territorial.

These places don't just hold stories.
They create them.

Some protect you.
Some watch you.
Some push you away.
Some only exist to remind you that the wilderness is older than any language humans have ever spoken.

And these places, above all others, are not meant to be visited alone.

In the next chapter, we'll pull back the lens and examine how Appalachia compares to the world's most haunted, mysterious wilderness regions — and why the same patterns appear across continents and cultures.

Final Chapter — Why Wilderness Needs Its Mysteries

There are places in the Appalachian Mountains where the world still feels wild — the kind of wild that doesn't fit into guidebooks or trail maps or online forums. A wildness older than stories, older than names, older than whatever humans have tried to carve into these ridges over the centuries.

You feel it the moment you step away from the road.
The air shifts.
The trees press closer.
The forest becomes something deeper, older, more knowing.

Most hikers don't put it into words.
Most rangers don't mention it at all.
Most locals speak about it only once, and only to someone who listens the right way.

But everyone who's spent time in these mountains knows the same silent truth:

The wilderness is not just a place.
It is a presence.

And presence demands mystery.

Modern life tries to explain everything — categorize it, diagnose it, reduce it to logic and data and predictions. But the wilderness rejects that. It always has. The Appalachian Mountains especially.

Here, the unknown isn't an oversight.
It's part of the design.

The Value of Not Knowing

Every chapter in this book has circled a simple idea: we don't understand everything that moves, breathes, watches, whispers, or lingers in these forests.

We aren't supposed to.

Mystery is not a flaw.
It is a requirement.

Think about what happens when the unknown disappears:

- wonder dries up

- awe turns into routine

- fear turns into arrogance

- respect fades

- the wilderness becomes a theme park

- and human beings start believing they're alone at the top

But the Appalachians don't let that illusion last.

Spend a night in these trees and you will hear something you cannot explain.
Spend a week here and you will feel a presence you cannot see.
Spend a lifetime here and you will realize how small, how temporary, how beautifully fragile human understanding really is.

The unknown keeps us humble.
Humility keeps us alive.

That is the bargain the mountains insist on.

Mystery Protects the Land

It sounds strange — maybe even backwards — but the mysteries of these mountains protect the wilderness more effectively than any law or regulation.

Ask the locals why certain places remain untouched, and they won't talk about conservation policy or ecological plans.

They'll say:

"That holler ain't safe."
"Don't go past that ridge."
"Things ain't right there."
"You don't stay after dark."
"That place watches you."

Fear keeps people away.
Awe keeps them careful.
Respect keeps them from turning the land into something tame.

Without mystery, these mountains would already have been carved into roads and resorts and developments. The unknown protects what we cannot replace.

The wilderness stays wild because people know, deep down, that some places don't belong to us.

And they never have.

Mystery Teaches Us to Pay Attention

When you're deep in the Appalachians, you don't sleep deeply.
You don't walk blindly.
You don't tune out the world around you.

You listen.

Because you have to.

Mystery sharpens the senses.
It trains you to read the trail like a language:

- the way wind shifts

- the direction of bird calls

- the absence of insects

- the feeling of being watched

- the weight of silence

- the subtle difference between natural and not

People who live or hike here learn the forest the way their ancestors did — not through maps, but through instinct.

Mystery keeps that instinct alive.

It keeps us connected to the land in a way modern life tries to erase.

Mystery Reminds Us We Are Not Alone

This is the truth that unsettles most people:
we are not the only things moving through these forests.

But that truth has its own kind of comfort.

Because there is more out there than us.
More history.
More intelligence.
More presence.

Some things guide.
Some things protect.
Some things warn.
Some things threaten.
Some things simply exist beyond our understanding.

But all of them remind us we share this world — not own it.

A wilderness without mystery is just scenery.
A wilderness with mystery is alive.

And something alive can teach us.
Challenge us.
Change us.

Mystery Is the Last Honest Thing We Have

In a world of explanations and algorithms and endless information, the unknown is one of the few things left that feels pure. Untouched. Untamed.

People come to the Appalachians for:

- adventure

- peace

- escape

- challenge

- solitude

But the thing they remember most is the feeling that the mountains are aware of them. That something ancient stirs in the wind, something that doesn't care about technology or certainty or human theories.

Mystery keeps us honest.
Honesty keeps us humble.
Humility keeps us curious.

And curiosity keeps us moving forward, into the trees, into the fog, into the dark.

Why We Still Need the Dark Places

There is a reason humans have always feared the forest — and it's not because the forest is dangerous.

It's because the forest is *unknown*.

Unknown places remind us of:

- our limits

- our vulnerability

- our imagination

- our hunger for answers

- our dependence on something bigger than us

When you remove the unknown from the natural world, you remove the soul from it.

Mystery gives the wilderness depth.
Depth gives it power.
Power keeps it alive.

We don't protect the wild because it is beautiful.
We protect it because it is **beyond us**.

Appalachia as a Living Mystery

After exploring all these stories — guardians, watchers, phantom travelers, vanishing structures, territorial spirits, voices, lights, footsteps, hollers that reject you, ridges that feel alive — one truth rises above the rest:

The Appalachians are a living mystery.

Not haunted.
Not cursed.
Not evil.
Not supernatural in the Hollywood sense.

Alive.

The mountains hold memory like water holds depth.
The land listens.
The forest chooses.
The ridges observe.
Some places welcome you.
Others push you out.

Some protect.
Some warn.
Some simply watch.

And that is exactly how it should be.

A wilderness without mystery is nothing more than a backdrop.

A wilderness with mystery is a world.

We Need Places That Keep Their Secrets

Human beings aren't built for certainty.
We aren't meant to understand everything.

Some truths are too big.
Some places too ancient.
Some forces too quiet to detect.

The Appalachians don't just hide their secrets — they guard them.
Not out of malice.
Out of purpose.

The unknown sustains the soul of the wilderness.

And the wilderness sustains the soul of the people who walk through it.

We need mystery.
We crave it.
We fear it.
We hope for it.

Because it reminds us of everything that still lies beyond the edge of the firelight.

Conclusion: Keep the Mystery Wild

If these mountains ever give up all their secrets, they will stop being the Appalachians.

If the watchers become obvious, if the guardians step forward, if the hollers explain themselves, if the voices announce their origins, if the land reveals its intelligence…

…the forest will lose something sacred.

Wilderness needs the unknown.
And people need wilderness that remains unknown.

The Appalachians teach us that some answers are meant to stay hidden.
Some stories are meant to unfold slowly.
Some places are meant to be felt, not understood.

In the end, mystery is not a problem to solve.
It is a landscape to protect.

These mountains don't need us.
But we need them — in all their darkness, beauty, silence, and secret.

The wilderness remains wild because mystery remains alive.
And mystery remains alive because the mountains keep their secrets.

Author's Note — The Pattern That Connects All Wilderness, and Why Appalachia Still Stands Apart

Every corner of North America holds its own wilderness mysteries.
You learn that the longer you explore them.

In the forests of British Columbia, people report tall figures moving silently between cedar trunks.
In the deep north of Ontario, there are stories of watchers standing at tree lines just before dusk.
In the Yukon and Alaska, strange lights drift across frozen lakes and disappear into treeless valleys.
In the Nahanni, entire prospecting camps vanished without explanation.
Even the Midwestern plains have their share of night voices and shadow-walkers.

Once you start comparing stories from region to region, a strange truth emerges:

**The details change,
but the patterns don't.**

People describe:

- footsteps following them

- companions they never see

- flashes of pale figures

- vanishing structures

- voices calling their names

- ridges that feel alive

- fog that moves with purpose

- lights that hover or drift

- silence that falls too quickly

- the sense of being watched

And these reports appear everywhere — from Arizona desert canyons to northern boreal forests to Pacific Northwest rainforests.

It doesn't matter what latitude you're standing in.
It doesn't matter what kind of trees are around you.
If the wilderness is old enough, untouched enough, and deep enough...

you will find the same phenomena repeating.

It's as if the land itself speaks a shared language across distances.
As if the wilderness across the continent holds a common thread that humans occasionally brush against — a thread older than cultures, borders, and names.

But even after recognizing that pattern, even after collecting reports from every major region, I can say with certainty:

Nowhere gathers these mysteries quite like the Appalachian Mountains.

There's something about this place — something deeper, older, heavier. Something that doesn't just hold mystery, but radiates it.

Other regions have hotspots.
Appalachia is a continuous band of strangeness stretching for two thousand miles.

Other regions have isolated tales.
Appalachia has a living, breathing ecosystem of phenomena.

Other regions have occasional unexplained encounters.
Appalachia has generations of them — stories from settlers, rangers, miners, hunters, Indigenous nations, modern hikers, and people simply passing through at the right (or wrong) moment.

Nowhere else in North America does the unknown feel so interwoven with the land itself.

Why Appalachia Stands Apart

After researching British Columbia, Alaska, Ontario, the Rockies, the Great Plains, the desert southwest, and the Pacific Northwest, a single conclusion kept appearing:

Appalachia carries the oldest stories.
And the land still remembers them.

These mountains are ancient — far older than the Rockies, the Sierra Nevada, or the Cascades. They have been rising and eroding and rising again for hundreds of millions of years. Everything else on the continent is new by comparison.

And within that deep age lies something rare:
continuity.

These forests have held humans, spirits, animals, guardians, and watchers for thousands of years without interruption.

The land has never been empty.
It has never been quiet.
It has never been young.

In the Appalachian range, the mysteries don't feel like isolated events —
they feel like expressions of an old consciousness, a memory-system
rooted in the ridges and hollers themselves.

It's not that the creatures or beings here are more dramatic or more
aggressive or more visible.

It's that they are **ever-present**.

Constant.
Subtle.
Enduring.
Patient.

You don't stumble into an anomaly here.
You walk through an entire world built on them.

A Shared Wilderness Intelligence

After years of speaking with researchers, rangers, hikers, and locals from
across North America, I've come to believe that the continent shares a
kind of wilderness intelligence — a presence distributed across forests,
mountains, lakes, and canyons.

Not a creature.
Not a spirit.
Not a ghost.

Something older.
Something that watches from the edges of our understanding.

In the Pacific Northwest, it steps lightly.
In the boreal north, it whispers along treelines.
In Alaska, it moves through fog and distance.
In the Great Plains, it touches the wind and sky.
In the Rockies, it hides behind altitude and stone.

But in Appalachia?

It walks closer.
It breathes down your neck.
It stands behind the next tree.
It moves between the ridges like a memory you haven't fully recalled.

Here, the wilderness intelligence doesn't feel distant or abstract.
It feels personal.

Not hostile.
Not kind.
Just **aware**.

Why People Keep Finding the Same Things

When you gather hundreds of reports — from BC, Ontario, Alaska, Appalachia, the Ozarks, the Great Lakes, the Yukon — you start seeing the repeating lines:

- tall watchers

- crawling figures

- mimic voices

- lights that wander

- beings in fog

- structures that vanish

- footsteps that match yours

- presences that escort rather than stalk

- things that live in silence

- things that move through water

- things that stand perfectly still

- things that walk the ridges

You can't help but wonder whether these are different species…
or the same presence manifesting differently in different lands.

Maybe the wilderness expresses itself in forms humans can interpret.
Maybe we give shape to something that has no shape.
Maybe the land is communicating in the only way it can.

Or maybe — as Indigenous nations have always said — there are **many watchers**, many guardians, many beings who inhabit the spaces humans don't belong to.

We don't know.
And maybe we aren't supposed to.

Some answers belong to the mountains.

Why Appalachia Is the Perfect Mirror

In the end, I believe the Appalachian Mountains aren't the strangest place in North America because they have the most creatures, or the most anomalous lights, or the most vanishings.

They're the strangest because **they reflect everything**.

Every mystery found somewhere else in North America can be found here, concentrated, layered, folded back over itself:

- beings like those reported in the Pacific Northwest

- lights like those seen in Alaska

- guardians like those known in Cherokee country

- pale roadwalkers like those in northern Ontario

- fog figures like those in Maine

- vanishing cabins like those in the Yukon

- watchers like those in British Columbia

- mimic voices like those in the empty plains

- disappearing hikers like those in remote canyons

All of it — every category of the unknown — exists here in one ancient spine of mountains.

The Appalachians are a crossroads of mystery.

But more than that, they are a **reservoir**.

A place where the land has held its stories, its beings, its guardians, and its warnings long enough that everything else feels like a reflection of this range rather than the other way around.

When you stand in a dark Appalachian hollow, you don't feel like you're in danger.

You feel like you're in someone else's territory.

Someone older.
Someone patient.
Someone who has seen the rise and fall of everything we call history.

In Closing

Every region in North America has its mysteries.
Every wilderness has its shadows, its watchers, its strange lights, its footsteps, its voices.

But Appalachia has something more:
a sense of presence that permeates the land itself.

Whatever lives in these mountains — whatever intelligence shapes the fog, the ridges, the silence, the echoes — it is not new. And it is not random.

It's woven into the roots.
It's folded into the rock.
It's older than the stories we tell about it.

And it's still here.

Watching.
Listening.
Waiting.
Choosing when to reveal itself.

The rest of North America has wilderness.
But the Appalachians?

They have **memory**.
They have **presence**.
They have **the oldest stories still walking among the trees**.

And that, more than anything, is why this region remains one of the greatest — and eeriest — wildernesses left on the continent.

APPENDIX A — Ranger & Warden Unexplained Incident Index
Unofficial Cases, Unsubmitted Reports & Off-Record Accounts From Across the Appalachian Mountains

The files in this appendix do not exist officially.
Most were never written down.
Some were drafted and later destroyed.
Others survived only through verbal accounts shared among rangers, wardens, and seasoned locals—people who've spent decades on the trails, hollers, ridges, and backcountry corridors where the public rarely sets foot.

These entries are condensed, anonymized, and stripped down to essentials. They represent patterns, not isolated events. Patterns that recur year after year, across state lines, across ranger districts, across generations.

Each case includes:
Year (approximate), general location, summary of event, and how the personnel involved described it afterward.

What follows is not legend.
It's the wilderness speaking in its own language.

Case 001: The Moving Screams

Year: ~2011
Location: Western North Carolina, deep backcountry zone
Summary: Multiple hikers reported screams echoing across ridgelines. SAR team dispatched. As the team approached the origin point, the screams shifted to another ridge. Each time they closed distance, the source moved again—always remaining ahead of them. After three hours, the sound ceased completely.
Ranger Comment: "Not animal. Not human distress. Sound moved with intention."

Case 002: The Fire Tower Footsteps

Year: 1998
Location: Eastern Tennessee
Summary: Fire lookout on overnight duty heard heavy footsteps circling the tower legs from midnight to dawn. Shined light repeatedly; no visual confirmation. Steps continued until sunrise.
Ranger Comment: "No prints. No wildlife. Felt observed the rest of the shift."

Case 003: The Empty Campsite

Year: 2014
Location: Shenandoah National Park, remote spur trail
Summary: Hiker's pack, boots, food, and water located beside a cold fire ring. No sign of struggle. No tracks leading away. Missing person never found.
Warden Comment: "Forest felt wrong. Heavy air. Like something was pushed back into place after he vanished."

Case 004: The Hollow That Shuts Down

Year: 2006
Location: Daniel Boone National Forest, Kentucky
Summary: Ranger patrolling old logging road entered a hollow where all sound ceased instantly. No wind, no insects, no ambient noise. Experienced vertigo and overwhelming feeling of being watched.
Ranger Comment: "Stepped out and sound came back like someone unmuted the world."

Case 005: The Lights With No Source

Year: 2019
Location: Northern Georgia
Summary: Solo ranger observed three white lights moving between trees on a ridge at 3 a.m. Lights moved slowly, without the beam signature of headlamps. Disappeared when ranger attempted approach.

Dispatcher Note: "No campers registered in area. Weather clear. No lightning."

Case 006: The Unclipped Leashes

Year: 2017
Location: Great Smoky Mountains
Summary: SAR dog team tracking missing hiker stopped abruptly. Both dogs' leashes unclipped simultaneously despite reinforced locking clips. Dogs refused to proceed forward.
Handler Comment: "Not fear. Alert. Like something else stepped onto the trail."

Case 007: The Shelter Knocks

Year: 2003
Location: Tennessee–North Carolina border
Summary: Two thru-hikers reported three slow knocks on shelter wall at 2 a.m., repeated twice. No one present upon inspection. No animal tracks.
Ranger Comment: "Too deliberate to be wildlife."

Case 008: The Singing at Dawn

Year: 1991–present
Location: Great Smoky Mountains (specific trail removed)
Summary: Recurring reports of a woman's voice singing or humming just before sunrise. Never located. No other campers present.
Dispatcher Comment: "Always same stretch of trail. Always around 4–5 a.m."

Case 009: The Rooftop Walker

Year: 2008
Location: Nantahala National Forest, NC
Summary: Camp host in ranger outpost heard slow, heavy footsteps

crossing metal cabin roof at midnight. Verified outside—no person or animal visible.
Ranger Note: "Steep angle of roof makes animal unlikely."

Case 010: The Ridge Shadow

Year: 2016
Location: Southern Virginia
Summary: Ranger observed a tall, dark silhouette standing motionless at edge of ridge before sunset. When he looked back after five seconds, figure was gone—no movement, no retreat path.
Ranger Comment: "Not a tree. Not a person. Too tall. Too still."

Case 011: The Vanishing Child Voice

Year: 2020
Location: Northern West Virginia
Summary: SAR volunteers searching for a lost 7-year-old heard faint crying ahead on ridge. Team approached — voice moved steadily uphill, maintaining distance. Missing child later found in opposite direction from where voice had led searchers.
Post-Incident Reflection: "Voice wasn't hers."

Case 012: The Fog Corridor Distortion

Year: 2015
Location: North Carolina high elevation zone
Summary: Ranger entered sudden dense fog along ridge. Radio static and compass malfunction occurred simultaneously. Heard footsteps behind him though trail was narrow and muddy (no second set of prints found).
Ranger Comment: "Didn't feel alone for one second inside that fog."

Case 013: The Blue Light on the Lake

Year: ~1984
Location: Western Pennsylvania
Summary: Anglers reported bright blue orb hovering 2–3 feet above still lake surface at dusk. Ranger arrived but saw only faint glow before it extinguished.
Community Notes: "Blue means keep your distance."

Case 014: The Crawling Figure

Year: 2012
Location: Shenandoah National Park
Summary: Backpacker encountered a human-shaped figure crawling rapidly across trail at dawn in heavy mist. No tracks located.
Ranger Note: "Witness adamant it wasn't wildlife."

Case 015: The Ghost Step Trail

Year: 1999
Location: Monongahela National Forest, WV
Summary: Ranger heard footsteps matching his pace exactly behind him along narrow ridgeline. Each time he stopped, steps continued for two additional beats.
Ranger Comment: "Felt like I was being escorted. Or measured."

Case 016: The Abandoned House That Isn't Empty

Year: 2007
Location: Eastern Kentucky
Summary: Warden checking old mining homestead heard coughing inside structure despite collapsed roof and rotted floors. Interior checked — empty.
Warden Comment: "Sound came from the center of the house. No way inside."

Case 017: The Whispered Name

Year: 2021
Location: Central Virginia, AT-adjacent
Summary: Solo hiker reported hearing his own name whispered beside his tent at 3 a.m. No other hikers nearby.
Ranger Note: "Witness refused to camp alone afterward."

Case 018: The Invisible Walker in Laurel Tunnel

Year: 1995
Location: North Carolina
Summary: Ranger moving through rhododendron tunnel heard someone walking behind him. Steps stopped when he turned; resumed the moment he stepped forward.
Ranger Reflection: "Felt inches away."

Case 019: The Returner

Year: 1982
Location: Eastern Tennessee
Summary: Missing hunter reappeared three miles from search zone with no memory of previous 36 hours. Reported "woods went quiet, then wrong."
Warden Comment: "He wasn't confused. He was terrified."

Case 020: The Silent Pond

Year: 2010
Location: Western Virginia
Summary: Ranger surveyed remote pond with mirror-flat water despite steady wind. Heard splash near center but saw no disturbance.
Ranger Comment: "Water swallowed sound."

Case 021: The Disappearing Lantern Light

Year: 2001
Location: Great Smoky Mountains
Summary: Ranger saw warm orange light moving through treeline as if carried. Disappeared instantly when approached.
Internal Note: "No campers registered. No fires allowed."

Case 022: The Pressure Drop

Year: 2018
Location: West Virginia
Summary: Two wardens tracking illegal campsite entered hollow where atmospheric pressure dropped sharply — ears popped, both felt nauseous.
Warden Comment: "Felt like something pressing down on us."

Case 023: The Child in the Trees

Year: ~1977
Location: Northern Georgia
Summary: Camper reported seeing small figure watching from tree branch at dusk. Ranger checked area — no tracks, branch too thin for human weight.
Ranger Note: "Witness sober and competent."

Case 024: The Footsteps Inside the Fog

Year: 2023
Location: Blue Ridge Parkway region
Summary: Ranger encountered fog patch where footsteps circled him at distance of 20–30 feet. No visual contact.
Comment: "Sound moved like it was thinking."

Case 025: The Echo That Isn't an Echo

Year: 2005
Location: Tennessee River Gorge
Summary: Ranger shouted to colleague; heard his own voice respond with different tone and pitch.
Ranger Comment: "Not echo. It was replying."

Closing Note on This Appendix

The cases here do not align neatly with folklore, known animals, or typical search-and-rescue anomalies. They reflect a persistent, cross-regional pattern of **intelligent, unseen presence** in the Appalachian wilderness.

Not malevolent.
Not benevolent.
Just aware.

And ever-watching.

APPENDIX B — Local Oral Warnings & Trail Lore
Traditional Sayings, Cautions, and Unwritten Rules of the Appalachian Backcountry

In every mountain town across the Appalachians — from eastern Kentucky to western North Carolina, from the Virginia ridges to the deep hollers of Tennessee — the same patterns appear in local speech. The language changes from place to place, but the warnings do not.

Some of these sayings come from Cherokee or Shawnee oral traditions, passed quietly across generations. Others come from miners, farmers, hunters, bootleggers, and backwoods wanderers who lived in these mountains long before the Appalachians became a hiking destination.

These phrases survive because they are *useful*.
They are not superstition to the people who speak them.
They are lived experience distilled into a sentence.

What follows is a curated set of warnings, proverbs, and whispered rules I collected while researching this book — things mountain people say only once, and only when they feel you understand what they're trying to tell you.

They don't explain these sayings.
They don't need to.

You'll understand them if you spend enough time in these woods.

SECTION I — Warnings About Sound

"If the woods go quiet, you leave."

This is the most universal Appalachian rule.
Silence is not natural.
Silence is presence.

A hunter in West Virginia put it plainly:
"The forest only stops breathing when something bigger than you has arrived."

"If you hear your name in the woods, it ain't your friend."

Reports of mimic voices stretch back generations.
Locals treat them the same way:
Ignore them.
Do not look toward the sound.
Do not answer.

"Whatever calls your name already knows where you are," one woman told me.

"Don't whistle after dark."

Some say whistling draws attention from things that follow sound.
Others say it calls spirits.
But when everyone in a place agrees on a rule, you follow it — even if the reason is unknown.

"If the footsteps stop when you stop, you turn around."

A Tennessee backwoodsman gave this advice without blinking.

"It's fine if something's following. Plenty of things follow.
But if it matches your steps... that's not wildlife."

"If the night sings, walk the other way."

This refers to reports of humming, distant chanting, or melodic voices.
You never go toward the sound.

One old farmer said:
"Songs ain't for you. They're for something else."

SECTION II — Warnings About Light

"Don't trust lights that wander."

Locals distinguish between:

- lantern lights

- campfire glows

- orb-like lights

- fast, unnatural lights

If a light moves through the woods with purpose, you do not follow it.

"Lights that look like they want to be followed are the ones you avoid," a ranger said.

"White light is safe. Yellow is a warning. Blue means leave."

Not superstition — just consistent local talk.

Blue lights in particular show up often in mountain folklore, especially around lakes, hollers, and abandoned mining roads.

"Blue's not for people," one retired logger told me.

"If you see a light where no campsite should be, don't take a second look."

A recurring theme:
It's not the first look that gets you in trouble.
It's the curiosity that follows.

"Light ain't meant to be studied," said a woman from north Georgia.
"It's meant to be noted."

SECTION III — Warnings About Places

"Don't sleep in a dead-silent holler."

If a hollow goes quiet at night, locals move uphill or leave entirely.
Silence in a valley is treated like a territorial sign.

"The holler owns the night," one Kentucky elder said.

"Avoid the old churchyards after dusk."

Even when the church is long gone, the ground remembers.
Mountain locals never linger in old graveyards.

"They're not empty," a coal miner told me.

"If the trees lean inward, that's not your place."

This warning is about certain sections of forest where trees seem to bend
toward a central point — the same areas hikers describe as oppressive or
heavy.

"You'll feel it," said a ranger. "Forest tells you no."

"Don't cross three logging roads at once."

Old three-way and four-way logging road intersections are widely
considered dangerous.

"They collect things," a hunter in Virginia said.

People pass through.
They don't stop.

"Avoid the ridges when the wind stops."

Windless ridges at height are treated as warnings.
Not weather-related — spiritual.

"If the wind won't touch a ridge, neither should you," said a woman in
North Carolina.

"Never camp where water is too still."

Refers to still ponds and lakes where wind fails to produce ripples.

"Water that doesn't move means something else is," said a fisherman.

SECTION IV — Warnings About Beings & Presences

"Walkers walk. Standers stand."

This is an old mountain saying referring to sightings of tall dark shapes
or human-like figures.

"You see something standing still in the trees? Leave.
You see something walking, you leave faster."

The meaning is never explained.
Everyone seems to understand it anyway.

"Guardians don't bother you unless you forget your manners."

A Cherokee elder said this with a wry smile.

Respect the land:
stay quiet, stay clean, stay humble.

"Guardians," in this context, do not refer to spirits benevolent or
malevolent — just old beings tied to place.

"If something crawls across the trail, you didn't see it."

This refers to the pale, human-shaped crawling figures described by hikers across several states.

Locals refuse to validate details.
They simply change the subject.

"That's trail business," one man said.

"If the forest steps with you, don't stop walking."

Essentially:
don't freeze if you're being shadowed.

Movement keeps things at a distance.

Stopping lets them close in.

"Some things follow. Some things escort."

This distinction is important.

Escort = protective.
Follow = curious or territorial.

Locals don't elaborate further.

SECTION V — Warnings About Time, Memory & Direction

"If the trail feels longer than it should be, turn around."

This is not about difficulty — it's about perception.
Certain trails distort a hiker's sense of time and distance.

"It'll feel like you're walking through someone else's years," a ranger said.

"If the forest looks different when you look back, don't keep going."

Hikers sometimes report subtle shifts in terrain after turning around.

The rule is simple:
Don't push forward into distortion.

"When the fog comes fast, don't stand still."

Fog that appears too quickly is treated as intentional.
Stillness invites confusion.
Movement keeps your mind anchored.

"Never step into a circle of stones."

Stone circles deep in the forest are widely considered thresholds.

"You step in, you're on their land," one local said.

Who "they" are is never clarified.

SECTION VI — Rules for Staying Safe

These are not superstitions.
These are survival rules repeated across the region.

Rule 1: Always tell the forest why you're there.

A simple spoken intention.
A courtesy, nothing more.

Rule 2: Don't camp at trail intersections."

Especially old logging intersections.

Rule 3: Don't whistle, call names, or shout after dark.

Sound travels strangely at night.

Rule 4: If your dog refuses the trail, trust the dog.

Locals say animals see what we don't.

Rule 5: If you feel unwelcome, leave without hesitation.

Do not debate.
Do not reason it out.
Just leave.

"The land gives you one warning," a ranger said.
"Only one."

Rule 6: Never approach a cabin you don't remember seeing before."

Especially if the windows are dark.

Rule 7: Trust silence more than noise."

Because noise has explanations.
Silence does not.

SECTION VII — Closing Thoughts

These sayings do not form a religion.
They are not folklore in the decorative sense.
They are survival tools, shaped through generations of experience in a wilderness that operates by its own rules.

You can ignore them.
Many do.

But the people who live in these mountains—who hunt here, farm here, wander here, and bury their dead here—follow these sayings for a reason:

Mystery is part of the land.
And the land warns you when it chooses to.

Appendix B exists to document those warnings, so the next traveler through these mountains knows what to listen for when the woods begin to whisper.

APPENDIX C — High-Strangeness Zones of the Appalachian Mountains

A Narrative Map of Regions Known for Silence, Sightings, Phenomena, and Unexplained Encounters

The Appalachian Mountains cover more than 2,000 miles of ancient ridgelines, deep hollers, fog-choked valleys, and backcountry corridors. But within that vast expanse, certain areas stand out — places where stories cluster, where rangers tread carefully, where hikers move faster, and where locals speak with lowered voices.

These are not exact coordinates.
Not places you'll find listed on a map or tourism brochure.

This appendix provides **general regions**, each described through the patterns, sightings, and historical reports associated with them. Some are only a few square miles. Others span entire counties. But every zone listed below carries its own personality — its own quiet intelligence.

What follows is a field researcher's guide to **Appalachia's most mysterious regions**.

1. The Black Hollow Corridor (Eastern Kentucky)

Phenomena:

- complete nighttime silence

- cold pockets

- false footsteps

- "moving scream" reports

- unexplained air pressure drops

This narrow valley cuts between two steep ridges and is accessible only by an overgrown former logging road. Locals avoid it after dusk.

Rangers describe the hollow as "unnaturally heavy," with wildlife refusing to enter during certain seasons.

In the 1970s, two different survey crews quit the job rather than finish marking boundary lines here. Both groups cited the same reason:

"The forest didn't want us there."

Long-term residents say the hollow has been this way "long before my granddaddy's time."

2. The Ridge-Crawler Zone (Western North Carolina)

Phenomena:

- human-sized crawling figures

- strange fog

- sudden winds

- tree knocks

- heavy pacing

- roof-walker encounters near shelters

Situated in Pisgah and Nantahala regions, the ridge-crawler zone includes several long, narrow ridges that run parallel like the ribs of an ancient creature.

Hikers describe seeing *shapes* move low across the trail at dawn — fast, deliberate, almost humanoid. No one follows. No one investigates. The few who speak about it say the same thing:

"It moved like it knew exactly where it was going."

Rangers acknowledge multiple reports but classify them as "misidentified wildlife."

The locals do not agree.

3. The Silent Wetlands of Monongahela (West Virginia)

Phenomena:

- swamp silence

- reflective eyes seen low to the ground

- moaning wind patterns

- lights that move across shallow water

- vanishing footpaths

The bogs and wetlands in the Monongahela highlands have a reputation among hunters and trappers: **things stay quiet not because nothing is there… but because something is.**

People report:

- watching lights skip across the surface

- hearing soft splashes with no movement

- walking into patches of cold mist

- feeling watched from the cattails

A biologist once described these peatlands as "ecosystems with memory."

Locals describe them as something else entirely.

4. The "Thin Ridge" Triangle (Eastern Tennessee)

Phenomena:

- dizziness

- phantom hands-on-back sensation

- sudden numbness

- full-spectrum silence

- dark silhouettes on distant ridge edges

This triangular region sits between three peaks whose names I intentionally omit here. The ridges between them are narrow — some as thin as a hiking boot's width — and create natural wind tunnels.

But wind isn't the issue.

Hikers crossing these ridges report overwhelming sensations of exposure, vulnerability, and the eerie sense of being inches from an unseen presence.

One ranger described it like this:

"It feels like you're walking across the top of something alive."

People don't linger here.
Some won't cross it at all.

5. The Vanishing Cabin Belt (Virginia–West Virginia Border)

Phenomena:

- old cabin structures appearing then vanishing

- impossible architectural angles

- windows with no inside

- dark interiors that absorb light

- lost-time sensations

This band stretches across the border region like a scar in the forest. Hikers, hunters, and trail runners have reported discovering cabins or ruins that:

- weren't marked on maps

- weren't there before

- cannot be found again

- sometimes vanish between one look and the next

These are not ghosts or illusions.
They are *structures* that behave like memory fragments.

Rangers rarely speak about them, except to say:

"If you see a cabin you weren't expecting, don't go inside."

Good advice.

6. The Blue Light Lakes (Northern Georgia)

Phenomena:

- hovering blue orbs

- still water in wind

- splashes with no surface disturbance

- nighttime humming patterns

The remote lakes hidden in the folds of northern Georgia's mountains are strange enough by day — perfectly still surfaces that reflect like polished metal.

At night, a different personality emerges.

Multiple long-term residents claim to have seen glowing blue spheres drift a few feet above the water before dissolving silently. These are not lanterns. They don't cast beams or diffuse light. They glow from within.

Fishermen say:

"Blue means keep your distance."

These lakes feel like mirrors for something deeper than water.

7. The Laurel Tunnels (North Carolina–Georgia Line)

Phenomena:

- shadow pacing

- branch snapping

- mimic footsteps

- sudden directional confusion

- pressure drops

These thick, interwoven tunnels of rhododendron and mountain laurel form natural corridors — claustrophobic, twisting passageways that trap sound.

Hikers report:

- footsteps following too close

- multiple footsteps for one person

- sudden vertigo

- wind that seems to reverse direction

- unseen presences "brushing" past them

A common phrase among locals:

"Don't stop inside a laurel tunnel."
"Don't *rest* there."

Whatever moves inside is not interested in having you stay.

8. The Fog Corridors of Southwest Virginia

Phenomena:

- instant whiteouts
- vanishing companions
- circling footsteps
- compass disruptions
- radio static

Rangers here speak very cautiously about fog. They know normal mountain fog; they grew up in it. But this is something else — fog that rises too fast and behaves too deliberately.

People caught in these corridors report:

- losing sense of direction
- hearing someone whisper ahead
- hearing someone breathe beside them
- feeling like time is slowing down

A SAR volunteer told me:

"The fog closes in like it's trying to get you alone."

No one moves slowly inside this zone.
Everyone walks fast.

9. The Guardian Ridges (Western North Carolina)

Phenomena:

- protective feelings

- footsteps that escort

- rustlings parallel to hikers

- unseen watchers

- cold/warm alternating pockets

Not every zone is hostile. Some seem to guide hikers safely along dangerous routes, especially near cliffs, deep ravines, and old logging cuts.

Reports include:

- feeling "accompanied"

- hearing pacing off to the side

- footsteps ahead navigating

- subtle pushes (non-threatening)

- sudden urge to turn around just before danger

Cherokee oral tradition speaks of **ridge walkers** — not ghosts, not spirits, not creatures, but guardians tied to place.

Rangers quietly acknowledge these accounts.
They don't mock them.

10. The Three-Road Crossroads (Multiple States)

Phenomena:

- multiple shadows

- directional illusions

- mimic voices

- sudden fear

- lights drifting at chest height

The Appalachian logging boom left behind thousands of abandoned roadbeds, many of which now intersect in forgotten places.

Crossroads in the deep woods have a reputation:
They collect echoes.
They gather movement.
They store energy.

Hunters and locals refuse to camp anywhere near one.

A ranger in Virginia told me:

"You stand in the center and feel like you're being watched from every direction."

Crossroads amplify the unknown.

11. The No-Wind Balds (Tennessee–North Carolina High Elevations)

Phenomena:

- dead-still air

- strange temperature inversions

- silhouettes at far distances

- distorted sound

- faint chanting in certain winds

Balds are open meadows at high elevation, offering breathtaking views. But a few are unsettling for a simple reason:

The wind doesn't touch them.

On most balds, wind cuts harshly across open grass. On the "no-wind" balds, air stands still — even during storms.

Hikers report:

- dread

- disorientation

- blurred vision

- seeing figures watching from tree lines below

Cherokee elders consider these places thresholds — openings between stories, between times, between worlds.

12. The Stillwater Ponds of Western Virginia

Phenomena:

- absolute stillness

- underwater shapes

- breath-like ripples

- absence of wildlife

- metallic echo to sound

These small, isolated ponds lie deep in remote backcountry. Their stillness is unnatural — even in strong wind. Wildlife avoids them.

Campers have heard splashes deep within, but the water never moves. Echoes return distorted, as if the pond reflects sound differently than it should.

One ranger noted:

"It's like the water listens."

Closing Interpretation of the High-Strangeness Zones

These zones share several common traits:

- **Silence where there should be sound**

- **Sound where there should be silence**

- **Light where there should be darkness**

- **Movement where nothing should be moving**

- **Stillness where everything else moves**

- **Seen shapes that disappear**

- **Unseen presences that guide or warn**

They form an invisible web across the mountains — a network of places where the veil between the natural and the unknown is thinner, sharper, more alert.

These regions do not mark danger in the traditional sense.
They mark **territory** — areas where the land expresses presence.

Some zones watch you.
Some protect you.
Some push you out.
Some simply observe.

But all of them remind you:

The Appalachian wilderness is not empty space.
It is inhabited — not necessarily by creatures, but by intelligence embedded in the land itself.

A map can show trails and rivers and boundaries.
This appendix shows something deeper:

Where the mountains breathe.
Where the forest watches.
And where the unknown steps closest to the surface.

APPENDIX D — Cherokee & Shawnee Spirit Lore

A Respectful Overview of Pre-Settlement Beings, Warnings, and Land Beliefs Across the Appalachian Mountains

Long before European settlers arrived, the Appalachian Mountains were home to rich, complex cultures whose understanding of this land far exceeded modern interpretations. The Cherokee, Shawnee, Catawba, Creek, and other Indigenous nations recognized the Appalachians as **a living world**, populated by beings, guardians, forces, and boundaries that shaped daily life.

To them, the forest was not empty.
It was inhabited — not by "monsters," but by **persons of the land**: ancient presences, intelligences, and spiritual beings tied to ridges, rivers, caves, mountains, and thresholds.

This appendix presents a careful, respectful summary of the most prominent beings and concepts relevant to Appalachia. These are not folklore details created for storytelling. They are cultural understandings passed down through generations.

The purpose here is not to explain the mysteries of the mountains, but to show that **those who lived closest to the land already knew the truths we are rediscovering today.**

1. The Nunnehi — The Immortals, The Ever-Present People

Nation: Cherokee
Region: Smoky Mountains, Blue Ridge, Western NC & TN

The Nunnehi are among the most important spiritual beings in Cherokee culture — often translated as *the people who live anywhere*, *the unseen people*, or *the spirit race that dwells within the mountains*.

They are described as:

• human-like

• peaceful

- protective

- powerful

- capable of appearing or disappearing at will

The Nunnehi live in places that align perfectly with modern Appalachian high-strangeness zones:

- ridge tunnels

- fog corridors

- sacred mounds

- waterfalls

- deep hollers

- rocky summit balds

- mountain thresholds

They are guardians, not threats.

Cherokee oral tradition says the Nunnehi guide lost travelers, protect those who show respect, and intervene when something dangerous lurks nearby.

One elder described them simply:

"Not ghosts. Not spirits. People.
Just not our kind of people."

This has striking parallels to modern accounts of:

- unseen footsteps alongside hikers

- protective presences

- escorting footsteps

- warnings to turn back

- strange music or singing in the distance

Modern hikers interpret these moments as strange or paranormal. Indigenous cultures understood them as **contact**, not coincidence.

2. The Uktena — The Great Horned Serpent

Nation: Cherokee
Region: Tennessee, Georgia, Virginia, Kentucky

The Uktena is one of the oldest beings in Cherokee tradition — a powerful horned serpent associated with rivers, creeks, caves, and deep mountain lakes.

It represents:

- primal danger

- hidden power

- forbidden knowledge

- places humans should avoid

Descriptions include:

- enormous size

- a horn or crest

- reflective, glowing scales

- thunderous movement

Although obviously not considered a literal creature in a modern biological sense, the Uktena is often described in connection with:

- dangerous water crossings

- drowning zones

- places where the river "pulls people under"

- lakes with still water

- ponds where the surface reflects unnaturally

These match modern accounts of:

- "stillwater ponds"

- blue light lakes

- underwater movements

- cold pockets near creeks

- sudden fear at water's edge

Indigenous voices treat these places with caution because **they belong to someone else** — a presence tied to water, not human beings.

3. The Tsul 'Kalu — The Great Forest Guardian (Long Man)

Nation: Cherokee
Region: North Carolina, Western Appalachian highlands

Tsul 'Kalu is sometimes compared to the concept of a Bigfoot-like being, but this is an oversimplification. In Cherokee tradition, he is far more than a creature:

He is **a land-being** — a guardian spirit of the mountains.

Descriptions include:

- immense size

- powerful presence

- sometimes visible, often not

- protective toward the Cherokee

- tied to hunting, survival, and forest law

Tsul 'Kalu is associated with:

- ridge lines

- deep hollows

- high-altitude balds

- rock faces

- ancient trails

He is not feared — he is respected.

Modern parallels include:

- large silent watchers

- tall dark silhouettes on ridges

- protective "escorting" footsteps

- sudden feelings of being observed

- animal tracks that end abruptly

The important takeaway:
He is not a "monster."
He represents the mountain's protective authority.

4. Little People / "Yunwi Tsunsdi"

Nation: Cherokee, Shawnee, multiple Appalachian tribes
Region: Widespread

Unlike popular culture depictions, the Little People of Appalachian tradition are not mischievous fairies. They are **serious beings** tied to the land's spiritual structure.

Common traits:

- small, human-like

- shy, elusive

- unpredictable

- sometimes helpful

- sometimes dangerous

- swift, silent, aware of boundaries

Long before modern hikers reported crawling, childlike shapes in trees or glimpses of figures perched silently on branches, Indigenous accounts described beings who:

- watched from trees

- guarded sacred places

- punished disrespect

- intervened when travelers were lost

Local sayings like:

"The child in the trees isn't a child."

…have clear parallels to these older traditions.

5. Kelandria / Keelut & Ghost-Dog Lore

Nation: Inuit (but adopted into Appalachian frontier lore), Shawnee variants
Region: Northern Appalachians, Pennsylvania highlands

While primarily an Arctic tradition, certain versions of ghost-dog and spirit-dog lore migrated into early Appalachian settlement culture. Shawnee scouts and early mountain men both described **silent dogs**, often white or pale, appearing before danger.

These are not negative beings — they are warnings.

Modern parallels:

- hikers reporting pale figures at a distance

- "escorting" shapes during fog

- silent animal-like watchers

They appear in multiple Native stories as **boundary guardians**.

6. The Manitou / Land Spirits

Nation: Shawnee, Lenape, Iroquoian groups
Region: Pennsylvania, West Virginia, Northern Appalachians

Manitou is a broad term meaning *spirit*, *presence*, or *power* — not a ghost, not a deity, but an **animating force** within the world.

The important idea is this:

Land has spirit.
Places have personality.
Some areas hold memory.
Some reject travelers.

This aligns perfectly with modern Appalachian experiences:

- dead-silent hollers

- oppressive valleys

- protective ridges

- hostile zones

- eerie churchyards

- crossroads that "collect movement"

Indigenous cultures did not see these as supernatural — they saw them as **expressions of place**.

7. The Moon-Eyed People

Nation: Cherokee (with older Southeastern origins)
Region: Georgia, Tennessee, North Carolina

The Moon-Eyed People are said to be:

- pale

- nocturnal

- small or slight

- sensitive to sunlight

- dwelling in caves or under ridges

These beings appear in Cherokee oral history as an ancient race who either:

- lived alongside humans,

- avoided humans,

- or left the region before recorded history.

Their presence is felt most strongly in:

- cave systems

- cliff-shelter zones

- underground passages

- ridge bases

- abandoned mining tunnels

Modern experiences described as:

- pale figures

- fast-moving silhouettes

- crawling shapes

- "something watching from the tree roots"

…echo the same pattern.

8. The Concept of "Forbidden Places"

Nearly every Indigenous nation in the Appalachian region acknowledges areas that should not be entered, including:

- deep hollers

- sinkholes

- steep ravines

- abandoned burial sites

- cave mouths

- bald mountaintops

- stone circles

Reasons vary:

- sacred

- dangerous

- inhabited

- dimensional thresholds

- resting places of spirits

- entrances to other realms

- territory of particular beings

Cherokee phrase:
"The place that remembers itself."

Shawnee phrase:
"Where the world bends."

This directly aligns with modern ranger wisdom and hiker instincts:

"If the place feels wrong, it is wrong."

9. The Voices That Call From the Forest

Cherokee and Shawnee both describe entities capable of **mimicking human speech**, especially names. The warnings are universal:

- never respond

- never follow

- never acknowledge

- do not search for the source

Modern hikers who hear someone whisper their name from the treeline are experiencing something long understood:

An intelligence testing boundaries.

10. The Land as a Living Being

Perhaps the most important concept shared across Indigenous Appalachian cultures:

The mountains are alive.
The wilderness is aware.
And certain presences are woven into the land itself.

These presences are not supernatural intruders — they *belong* to the mountains.

This explains why:

- some hikers feel protected

- some feel pushed away

- some experience dread

- some encounter silence

- some feel watched

- some lose time

- some see things that don't behave like animals

These phenomena are not random.
They are part of the land's ancient personality.

Closing Thoughts: Indigenous Insight Into Modern Mystery

Every strange encounter in these mountains — the watchers, the fog corridors, the mimic voices, the stillwater ponds, the crawling shapes, the silent hollers — fits into a framework Indigenous people already understood:

The land is shared.
The unseen people are real.

Some places belong to them, not us.
Some beings guard.
Some warn.
Some test.
Some protect.
Some reject.

Modern hikers see these encounters as paranormal.
Indigenous cultures saw them as part of living in a world filled with
more than humans.

This appendix is not meant to explain the mysteries of Appalachia —
only to show that the oldest residents of these mountains knew what we
are only beginning to rediscover:

The wilderness has inhabitants older than memory.
And if you walk the mountains with respect,
the mountains may let you pass.

APPENDIX E — Unofficial Appalachian Trail Reports

Anonymized Accounts Shared Quietly Among Thru-Hikers, Section Hikers, Trail Angels & Long-Distance Backpackers

The Appalachian Trail is one of the world's most extraordinary long-distance footpaths, stretching more than 2,190 miles from Georgia to Maine. Tens of thousands attempt it every year.

Only a few speak about the strange things they see, hear, or feel in the deep backcountry.

What follows are unofficial reports — the stories hikers don't tell online, don't post in vlogs, and don't include in trail journals. These are whispered accounts shared over wet gear, late dinners, or long quiet nights in three-walled shelters.

Each entry is anonymized and condensed but presented as the hikers originally described them.

These stories aren't folklore.
They're the unrecorded moments that linger in a hiker's mind long after Katahdin or Springer Mountain.

1. The Whisper in the Trail Tunnel

Location: Georgia
Year: 2019
A thru-hiker walking through a dense rhododendron tunnel heard a whisper directly behind his right ear. He turned instantly — no one there. The whisper wasn't a word. More like:
"...pshhhhh..."
Soft. Deliberate.
He sprinted the final 40 yards of the tunnel. Never camped alone again.

2. The Night Visitor at Blood Mountain Shelter

Location: Northern Georgia
Year: 2013

Two hikers shared the shelter. Around midnight, someone — or something — walked slowly past the opening. They saw a silhouette.
Tall.
Human-shaped.
Not wearing a pack.
When they shone their lights, the clearing was empty.
Footsteps continued in the leaves for almost a minute after it vanished.

3. The Footsteps on the Roof in North Carolina

Location: Near Standing Indian
Year: 2020
A woman hiking solo reported footsteps pacing across the tin roof of her shelter around 3 a.m.
No trees over the shelter.
No animals visible.
The pacing was heavy, slow, human-like.
When she shouted, it stopped.
Five minutes later, it started again.

4. The Crawl-Shape in the Mist

Location: Smoky Mountains
Year: 2011
Fog rolled in at dawn. A hiker saw a pale shape crawl across the trail ahead — fast, low, human-sized. He thought it was an ill person until it vanished behind a boulder.
He waited.
Nothing emerged.
No tracks.
No movement.
He left the area without investigating.

5. The "Second Hiker" That Didn't Exist

Location: Tennessee
Year: 2016

Two hikers kept hearing a third set of footsteps behind them.
When they stopped, the footsteps stopped.
When they walked, the third set matched their pace exactly.
They finally camped early due to fear.
At dawn, they checked the trail behind them.
No prints.

6. The Singing Before Sunrise

Location: Great Smoky Mountains National Park
Year: Ongoing reports
Several hikers have independently reported hearing a woman humming
or singing in the early dawn hours, usually between 4 and 5 a.m.
The singing is described as:

- soft

- melodic

- distant

- "beautiful, but wrong"
  Searches never locate the source.

7. The Invisible Campfire Companion

Location: North Carolina
Year: 2012
A section hiker camping alone heard someone walking in the leaves
around his campsite. The footsteps circled twice.
He spoke aloud.
Footsteps stopped.
Then began again on the opposite side.
He slept with his knife in his hand.
At morning: no prints.

8. The Lake Reflection That Wasn't a Reflection

Location: Virginia
Year: 2015
A hiker filling water at a still pond saw a reflection of someone standing behind him.
He turned — no one there.
Looked again — reflection still present.
He backed away slowly, without looking away a third time.

9. The Vanishing Headlamp Partner

Location: Shenandoah National Park
Year: 2022
A hiker night-walking saw a headlamp in the distance down-trail. The beam moved as if worn.
He tried to catch up for almost 40 minutes.
The light was always the same distance ahead.
Then it blinked out mid-step.
No hikers were camped ahead.

10. The Voice That Called His Trail Name

Location: Pennsylvania
Year: 2017
A man heard his own trail name whispered outside his tent at 1:30 a.m.
Whisper repeated twice.
He unzipped the flap — nothing.
Later found out another hiker had experienced the same phenomenon one year earlier in the same region.

11. The Frozen Clearing

Location: Maryland
Year: 2014
A hiker walked into a clearing where the temperature dropped at least fifteen degrees instantly.

His breath fogged in front of him.
Birds fell silent.
He backed out slowly and the temperature rose behind him like a curtain lifting.

12. The Shadow That Followed for Miles

Location: New Jersey
Year: 2021
A thru-hiker noticed a tall shadow moving parallel to him along a ridge.
Always the same distance.
Always just out of clear view.
He tried speeding up → shadow sped up.
Slowing down → it slowed.
Stopped → shadow froze.
When he reached a road crossing, it vanished instantly.

13. The Blue Glow in the Woods

Location: New York
Year: 2009
Two hikers reported a glowing blue sphere moving silently between the trees for several minutes.
It rose about six feet off the ground, then drifted into a ravine and faded.
No sound.
No flicker.
Nothing left behind.

14. The Shelter That Felt Occupied

Location: Connecticut
Year: 2018
A solo hiker arrived at a shelter at dusk.
He felt watched the entire evening — not threatened, but *studied*.
Every time he stepped outside the shelter, he sensed movement behind the tree line.

No animals visible.
He left before sunrise.

15. The Two Voices Arguing in the Dark

Location: Massachusetts
Year: 2010
Hiker heard two voices arguing in the woods behind his tent.
Human voices — angry, low, muffled.
He shouted asking if anyone needed help.
Voices stopped instantly.
Silence for the next six hours.

16. The Footsteps in the Snow — with No Prints

Location: Vermont
Year: 2020
Hiker traveling through early-season snow reported heavy footsteps pacing outside his tent.
He waited until daylight.
Snow was untouched around his campsite — no tracks of any kind.

17. The Crawling Silence

Location: New Hampshire
Year: 2014
A hiker felt a wave of silence hit him on the trail — sudden, total, unnatural.
As silence deepened, he saw something low and dark move between trees in a way that was neither animal nor human.
He left the trail early that day.

18. The Figure on the Summit

Location: White Mountains, New Hampshire
Year: 2003

A man summiting a peak at dusk saw a silhouette standing at the crest.
Human-shaped. Motionless.
When he took his last few steps to the top, no one was there.
No sound of movement.
No cover for retreat.

19. The Hiker Who Lost an Hour

Location: Maine
Year: 2010
A woman checked her watch at a stream crossing.
Next memory: reaching a shelter five miles further, her watch one hour ahead.
She had no recollection of the missing time.
No injuries.
No exhaustion.
Just a gap.

20. The "Accompanied" Feeling

Location: Multiple States
Years: Ongoing
Many hikers describe the same sensation:
Not followed.
Not stalked.
Not threatened.
Accompanied.

A presence that walks beside them — not close, not far — for miles at a time.
Never spoken.
Never seen.
Unmistakable.

"It felt like something old," one thru-hiker said.
"Something that had walked these mountains longer than humans ever have."

Closing Notes on Appendix E

The Appalachian Trail crosses some of the oldest land in North America — mountains older than bones, older than language, older than memory. What hikers encounter along its length is not fantasy or folklore.

It is *pattern*.
It is *presence*.
It is the wilderness speaking in the only ways it knows.

These reports, whispered without exaggeration, reveal something simple:

Hikers see more than footprints.
They are heard.
They are watched.
They are walked with.
And sometimes... they are warned.

www.ingramcontent.com/pod-product-compliance
Lightning Source LLC
Chambersburg PA
CBHW050448270326
41927CB00009B/1658